Edward Clodd

Jesus of Nazareth

Embracing a Sketch of Jewish History to the Time of His Birth

Edward Clodd

Jesus of Nazareth
Embracing a Sketch of Jewish History to the Time of His Birth

ISBN/EAN: 9783337031268

Printed in Europe, USA, Canada, Australia, Japan

Cover: Foto ©Lupo / pixelio.de

More available books at **www.hansebooks.com**

JESUS OF NAZARETH:

EMBRACING A

SKETCH OF JEWISH HISTORY TO THE TIME OF HIS BIRTH.

BY

EDWARD CLODD,

AUTHOR OF "THE CHILDHOOD OF THE WORLD," ETC.

" *Thou seemest human and divine,*
The highest, holiest manhood, thou."
In Memoriam.

LONDON :

C. KEGAN PAUL & CO., 1, PATERNOSTER SQUARE.

1880.

PREFACE.

THE object of this book is to present in com-
pendious form a sketch of the life and teaching
of Jesus of Nazareth, viewed from a purely
historical standpoint.

As such a treatment of the matter requires
that some explanation of the conditions out of
which he arose should be substituted for the
pre-natal legends concerning him, the story of
his race is traced from the dawn of history to
the time of his birth. In ordinary manuals
on this subject, which are seldom other than
summaries of the Scripture record, no account
is taken of the foreign influences which from

very early periods so deeply affected the religious development of the Jews, and in according
the needful space to these, the first part of this
work has run to greater length than was intended. I hope, however, that the abiding
interest which attaches to all that can be
learned concerning that remarkable people will
suffice as excuse for this.

The book, which is neither a simple history
for children nor an exhaustive treatise, will probably be found of service to those who, unable
to follow in detail the methods of modern
criticism, are eager to know what it has to
offer as a consistent and adequate explanation
of the career of Jesus. Moreover, the present
work is *constructive* in its aim, being a serious
endeavour to show that reverence for his character and sympathy with his teaching are
unaffected by the rejection of the mythical

and speculative elements which have mingled with the narratives of his life, and from which supernatural theories about him have been deduced.

Its preparation has involved the reading and consulting of books too numerous and varied to catalogue, but the foot-notes indicate generally the authorities to whom I am under obligation. My indebtedness should, however, be specially acknowledged to Kuenen's great work on the *Religion of Israel*, and, despite its prolixity, to Keim's *Jesus of Nazara*, while the material gathered in Hausrath's *New Testament Times* has been of service in the account given of the circumstances surrounding Jesus. I take advantage of this opportunity to commend to persons interested in the subject Knappert's excellent summary of Kuenen's volumes, and also the more important and often suggestive series entitled *The Bible for Young People*, which the competent pen of Mr. Philip Wicksteed has translated from the Dutch.

Certain matters, the fuller discussion of which would have encumbered the text, but of which some enlargement was desirable, are referred to an Appendix.

E. C.

Rosemont, Tufnell Park, London,
October, 1879.

CONTENTS.

BOOK I.

A SKETCH OF JEWISH HISTORY TO THE BIRTH OF JESUS.

SECTION		PAGE
I.	INTRODUCTORY	3
II.	THE ISRAELITES IN EGYPT	27
III.	THE CONQUEST OF CANAAN	53
IV.	THE EXILE IN BABYLON, AND THE RETURN	129
V.	THE WAR OF INDEPENDENCE	167

BOOK II.

JESUS OF NAZARETH.

		PAGE
I.	INTRODUCTORY	187
II.	SOURCES OF KNOWLEDGE ABOUT JESUS ...	223
III.	THE PUBLIC MINISTRY OF JESUS	231
IV.	HIS MODE OF TEACHING	239

SECTION		PAGE
V.	His Religion	243
VI.	Jesus and the Parties of his Time ...	261
VII.	Miracles	286
VIII.	Jesus asserts his Messiahship ...	296
IX.	Jesus in Jerusalem	311
X.	His Arrest, Trial, and Crucifixion ...	330

APPENDIX.

Note A.	The Semitic Family	363
,, B.	The Name Jehovah	365
,. C.	The Talmud	367
., D.	The Books of the Old Testament	368
,, E.	The Gospels	375
Index	... ...	379

MAPS.

The Distribution of the Semitic Races	*To face* 1
Palestine in the Time of Jesus	*At end*

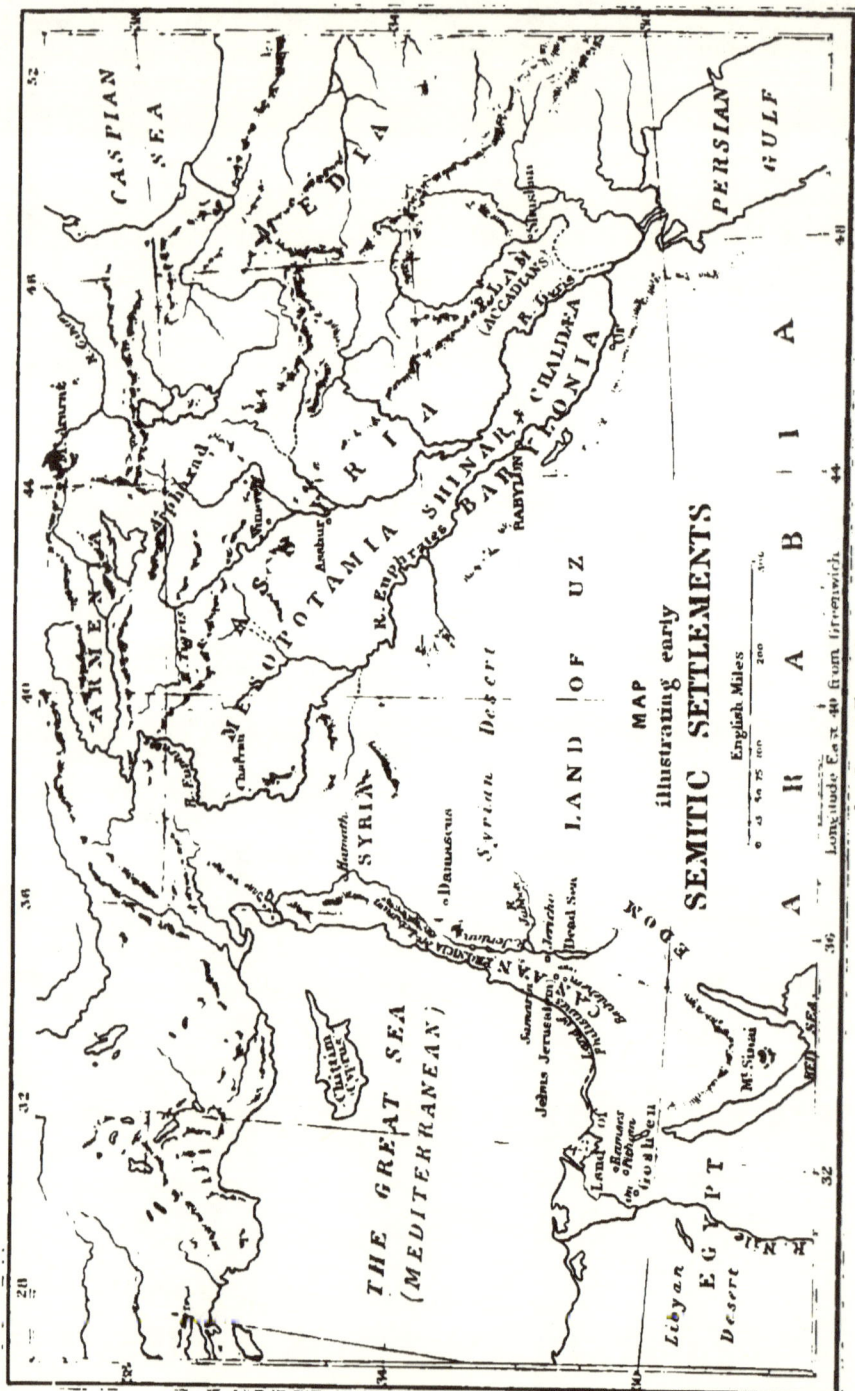

MAP
illustrating early
SEMITIC SETTLEMENTS

English Miles

Longitude East 40 from Greenwich

London; C. Kegan Paul & Co.

Edw.ᵈ Weller

CASPIAN SEA

ARMENIA

MEDIA

ASSYRIA

MESOPOTAMIA

SYRIA

SHINAR

BABYLONIA

CHALDEA

ELAM
(ACCADES)

LAND OF UZ

ARABIA

PERSIAN GULF

THE GREAT SEA
(MEDITERRANEAN)

PHŒNICIA

EGYPT

Libyan Desert

Syrian Desert

RED SEA

Mt Sinai

Dead Sea

Damascus

Jebus Jerusalem

Samaria

Jericho

R. Euphrates

R. Tigris

BOOK I.

A SKETCH OF JEWISH HISTORY TO THE BIRTH OF JESUS.

B

"Considering the infinite number and the difficulty which they find that desire to look into the narrations of the story, for the variety of the matter, we have been careful, that they that will read may have delight, and that they that are desirous to commit to memory might have ease, and that all into whose hands it comes might have profit.

"Therefore to us, that have taken upon us this painful labour of abridging, it was not easy, but a matter of sweat and watching; even as it is no ease unto him that prepareth a banquet, and seeketh the benefit of others. . . .

"To stand upon every point and go over things at large, and to be curious in all particulars, belongeth to the first author of the story: but to use brevity, and avoid much labouring of the work, is to be granted to him that will make an abridgement.

"Here then will we begin the story; only adding thus much to that which hath been said, that it is a foolish thing to make a long prologue, and to be short in the story itself."—2 Maccabees ii. 24–32.

I.

Introductory.

ABOUT the middle of the sixteenth century before Jesus was born, the forefathers B.C. of the Jewish people had, after many 1550? wanderings, pitched their tents in the rich pasture lands of Goshen, on the north-eastern borders of Egypt.

Like every other race of mankind which has advanced, they had risen by slow steps from a savage state; but as yet had reached no very high level, being shepherd tribes, rude and warlike in their habits and coarse in their beliefs and customs. They were under no fixed form of government, each tribe being ruled in loose fashion by the head of the oldest family, from whom the rest traced their descent. These sheikhs, or, as we call them, patriarchs (from a Greek word meaning " father-chief "), met together, however, for common counsel and action when danger from without threatened the clans, and maintained peace and settled quarrels among them as they best could in those lawless times. For strife would frequently arise over coveted green spots whereon to pasture flocks and herds, and snap the slender ties that held such roving folk together.

In common with other roaming hordes of kindred race and speech then scattered over the desert plains stretching from Syria towards Persia, they were known as "Hebrews," or "men from beyond," as we name other nations "foreigners," meaning "men from abroad;" but they called themselves "children" or "sons of Israel," after one of their most renowned forefathers, about whom they had a legend telling of his victorious struggle with one of their chief gods.[1] Since the time when they were freed from their captivity in Babylon they have been

---

[1] Gen. xxxii. 24· 28.

known as "Jews,"[1] a corruption of the word "Yehudim," or descendants of Judah.

The legend just spoken of is one among many proofs that, like other barbarous people, the Israelites, as we will for the present call them, had myths about the past, some of which we find common to races to whom they were related, the Hebrew legends excelling all the rest in the simple yet stately language in which their later forms are cast. As I have tried to show elsewhere, myths are the outcome of the wonder aroused in man by all that he sees and feels ; the answers, very real to him, which in his childlike bewilderment and utter lack of knowledge he frames to the questions, "Whence came all these things ? Whence came we ? What took place before us ? How did we come by our name ?"

We who have left this myth-making stage far behind have learnt, or should learn, as answer to the last of these questions—for the story is no dull or dry one—that the names of countries or of people, who, as making up tribes and nations

[1] Josephus, *Antiquities,* book xi. ch. v. 7.

are commonly called after the place where they live, were not given haphazard, but often hold within them some story of the dim and dateless past of which no other record remains, or describe some vanished or abiding feature of the land that most struck its first beholders. But men in bygone days had neither the skill to look for nor the aids to find such meanings in the names which they bore, and, often led astray by false likenesses between words, framed strange stories to explain them. For example, the well-known legend of the wicked Bishop Hatto, whose great stores of corn, which he would not part with in time of famine, were eaten by rats, and who, fleeing to his tower in the Rhine, was pursued and eaten by those vermin, arises from confusing "maut-thurm," or " customs-tower," with " mäuse-thurm," or "rat-tower." And in a still more famous legend[1] which grew around the Tower of Babel, the Hebrew narrator mistook that name, which signifies "gate of god," for the verb " balbel," meaning

[1] See p. 131 ; also Gen. xi. 9.

"to confound." One chief source of myths
about names springs from the confusion which
races at a low level make between them and
persons or things. For example, the savage,
who shrinks from having his likeness taken, in
the fear that a part of himself is being carried
away thereby, regards his name as something
through which he may be harmed or bewitched.
So he will use all sorts of roundabout phrases
to avoid saying it, will fear that any one seeking
to know it may steal it or gain power over him,
will give his children horrid names to frighten
demons away, will change his own name,
thinking thereby to elude his foes and puzzle or
cheat even death when he comes to look for
him, and will shrink from uttering the name of
a dead man lest it call up the ghost. The Bible
supplies examples of relics of such savage notions lingering among the Jews in the importance which they accorded to names, finding in
them omens of events and even in their sounds
mystic meanings, while they were not only
careful what they called their children, but

believed that a man's fate might be changed by
changing his name.   Their use, too, of another
word instead of "Jehovah" for their chief god,[1]
like the Mohammadan use of "Allah," which is
only a title for the "great name," may be traced
to the dislike which causes savages to shrink
from uttering the names of superhuman beings.
Names never being treated by barbarous people
merely as signs by which things are known, we
see how a tribe, in accounting for its name, could
not think of it apart from a *person*, and so invented its tales of a great ancestor, father and
founder of his people.   Fathers and founders of
course every people had;   but so remote are
man's beginnings, that it was not possible for
him to know aught as to whence or from whom
he sprang; hence the play of fancy about these
matters and the birth of myths.

Among rude races, as the North American
Indians, whom we find named after some animal,
as Bear, Beaver, Wolf, the tribes claim the very
creatures themselves as ancestors!   The nations

[1] See p. 163.

of Europe had, during the Middle Ages, quite a craze for tracing their origin to heroes of the Trojan war, as France from Francus, Paris from the son of Priam, Britain from Brutus, and the Greeks, the ancient name of whose country was Hellene, guessed that Hellen was their fore-father. In like manner we British, who are sometimes called in poetry "sons of Albion," might have made a similar blunder had we not learned that Albion was the name given to our island, more than two thousand years ago, as a "hilly land."

Now the oldest parts of the written history of the Israelites have preserved traces of a like confusion in their minds as to the source of their tribal and other names, some of which, as the tenth chapter of Genesis shows, are names of countries,[1] and, here and there, of the powers of nature transformed into patriarchs and heroes. But passing by the details concerning these, it suffices to say that they derived their origin and that of kindred peoples from

---

[1] *e.g.,* Cush, Asshur, Mizraim, Canaan, Arphaxad, and of cities, as Sidon.

forefathers who dwelt in the land of Shinar, or, using the Greek name given to it from its lying "between rivers," Mesopotamia. Their common ancestor was said to be Terah, who lived at Ur, and whose three sons were Abraham, Nahor, and Haran. Terah removed from Ur to Charran, and thence his sons and their families spread southward. The Israelites were in direct line from Abraham, the father of Isaac and grandfather of Jacob, afterwards called Israel, and the twelve tribes, into which they were said to be divided, traced their descent from Israel's twelve sons.

Let us now see what groundwork of fact underlies these legends.

The Israelites belonged to the Shemitic, or, to use its Latin form, Semitic race,[1] so called after Shem, whose name occurs as a son of the patriarch Noah in the Bible legend of a deluge. Such a term does not correctly describe them, but its meaning is now so fixed that its use cannot mislead us. It includes the Babylonians,

[1] Note A.

Assyrians, Phœnicians, Syrians, Hebrews, Arabs, and some lesser peoples, the kinship between all of whom is now well proven ; while history is ever yielding witness to the mighty part which the leading members have played in the world, how rich and varied their influence on the life and thought of men has been to this day, notably in religion, for from them have sprung the Jewish, Christian, and Mohammadan faiths, with their sacred books, the Bible and the Korân.

The earliest traces that we have of the Semites show them scattered over the deserts of Arabia and Syria, and from the uplands of Armenia to the countries watered by the Tigris and Euphrates.[1] Ages before this they had swarmed from their common home, and as they poured into the country lying near the Persian Gulf, found, as did the Aryan tribes when they crossed into Europe, an older and alien population, known as the "Accadians,"[2] or "highlanders," as coming from the mountains of Elam, settled in the land. These Accadians, whom it is not

---

[1] See Map. [2] And see Gen. x. 10.

easy to classify, but who appear to have been allied to the race from whence such peoples as the Mongols and Finns have sprung, had made their home in those fertile parts long before the Semites had separated, long before even Egypt had reached her prime; had founded kingdoms, built cities, among which was Ur, sacred to their moon-god, and reached no mean state of culture. They were the fathers of astronomy, for the clear air and unbroken expanse of their boundless plains invited to the study of the heavens; we owe to them both the signs of the Zodiac and the days of the week, which last were named after the sun, moon, and five planets; while, following the phases of the moon, whom they called the "lord of rest," every seventh and some intervening days were sabbaths, on which certain works were forbidden, mainly so as bringing ill-luck to the doer. "Every day of the year was under the protection of some deity or saint; the months were all named after the signs of the Zodiac,"[1] in the first of which the god Bel, so runs

[1] Sayces' *Babylonian Literature*, p. 55.

the legend, reminding us of that about Abraham
and Isaac, offered up his only son. The wedge-
shaped characters, called "cuneiform" (from
Latin "cuneus," a wedge), stamped on clay
tablets and cylinders, were their invention, and
among the precious relics of their vast libraries,
entombed for centuries, is a poem in twelve
books, answering to the months of the year,
the eleventh, or "rainy," having for its subject
the legend of a deluge from which a like legend
in the book of Genesis is derived.

Other fragments supply proof of their advance
from lower to higher stages of belief. They
point to a time when good and evil spirits were
thought to dwell in everything around, and
when the aid of sorcerers, with their charms
and magic arts, was sought to secure the favour
of the good spirits and avert the anger of the
evil spirits. In the course of time these beings
were arranged into classes, some being placed
above the rest and worshipped, often with
bloody sacrifices, as rulers over certain parts
of nature, as sun-gods, moon-gods, storm and

lightning gods. Among the first-named we read of Merodach, helper of mankind and bringer of the dead to life, akin to the Egyptian Osiris and other mythical mediators between earth and heaven, to whom man in his deep need has stretched forth hands and prayed.

Such creation of gods out of the lesser spirits of the older worship, which is quite in keeping with the mode of man's advance everywhere towards belief in one almighty being, was quickened by the blending of the religion of the Accadians with that of the Semites. This gave rise to numberless hymns of penitence and praise which breathe a spirit akin to some of the Hebrew psalms, as well as to mythical poems about the gods, from which many later legends are derived. And long after the Accadian language was dead, these hymns, venerated as sacred writings, were recited by Babylonian priests in that old tongue, as the Roman Catholic priests, use Latin in the services of their church ; while the ancient directions about spells and sorceries passed, through the Chaldæans, into

the common belief of the Semites, overran
Europe, and became the parent of the grim
beliefs which made life a terror for hundreds
of years, and which lurk in by-ways among the
unlearned yet.

Nor, happily, only these, for from Western
Asia, of which the old legends, ever holding
some truth worth the seeking, tell as the happy
home of the parents of mankind and the birthland
of culture, have come the germs of the arts,
sciences, and higher as well as lower religions
of both Jew and Gentile; while the customs and
traditions of the Accadians, borrowed by the
Semites, were carried by them westward, thus
becoming the possession of Greeks and Romans
and, through them, of the modern world.

Such is a brief outline of the rich knowledge
which has within the last few years come to light
about the foundation on which the civilization
of both Semite and Aryan rests. The wedge-
shaped characters on clay tablets, once mistaken
for ornamental figures or charms, have yielded
their secrets to the patience of man; the daily life

and manners of great empires of the East, of which classic historians speak only in vague hints, are before us in all their detail, and " we are brought face to face with men who have hitherto been but names on the pages of the Old Testament " and of Greek and Roman writers.

It would appear that at a very early date Semitic tribes from Arabia, to which present knowledge points as the common home of the race, crossed the Euphrates, and slowly forcing their way up the river valley, vexed the quiet of the Accadians. At last they gained the upper hand, and, mingling with the defeated race, founded the kingdom of Babylonia. Other Semites, pushing further northward, reached the banks of the Tigris, and, some centuries later, founded the kingdom of Assyria, while kindred tribes, forefathers of the Phœnicians and Canaanites, moving westward, settled among the hills and dales and along the coasts of Syria, subduing the more savage dwellers there. Whilst these earlier branches had thus secured for themselves rich districts, the regions around swarmed with less favoured tribes, tossed to and fro, and long remaining wild and lawless shepherd-warriors, their hand against every man and every man's hand against them.

Among these were the forefathers of the Hebrews, whose northernmost pasture-ground had been the slopes of Armenian hills in the district round Arphaxad. Thence they came into the rolling plains of Syria, once the bed of a great inland sea, but at the time of our story strewn, as now, after the winter rains, with grass and bright flowers, and still the home of Bedouins and their flocks, in mode of life scarce altered during thousands of years. Their manners and customs witness to the truth of the charming pictures of patriarchal times that enrich the Old Testament; revelling in their unpolluted air and boundless plains and jealous of their freedom, they despise the cramped life of towns, and it is among them that we may look for such stray relics as survive of the religion of the Semites while they were yet one people.

From these plains, as the herbage grew

C

scantier and the waterbrooks dried, the Hebrews still passed southward, some to Arabia, others to the uplands of the Jordan, and the rest, among whom were the " sons of Israel," to the borders of Egypt.

Here, then, we reach again the point from whence we started ; but we must tarry yet awhile in sight of pyramids and temples to learn what we can about the religion of the Israelites at this time.

A barbarous people cannot have other than a gross religion, and we may argue from the state of the Israelites what stage of belief they had reached ; but, apart from this, religions, like manners and customs and languages, always preserve some of their older features,[1] and from these we learn that the Israelites, when in Goshen, were worshippers of the powers of nature, as the sun, moon, and stars, and of lower things, such as trees and stones, which were either looked upon as superhuman or as the dwelling-place of such beings. No worship has prevailed more

[1] Kuenen, *Religion of Israel*, vol. i. pp. 270, 390.

widely throughout the world at one time or another than that of stones ; hundreds of years after the Israelites had left Goshen we find their yielding to it a cause of reproach and scorn from men of loftier belief.[1] The famous Black Stone at Mecca, adored by the ancient Arabs, is still dear and sacred to Mohammadans, while in England as late as the eleventh century laws were issued forbidding the worship of upright stones.[2]

But the idolatry which has had so early and lasting a place among desert tribes, is that of the host of heaven. The scenery amidst which a people lives gives its impress to their religion ; and while dwellers among mountains and forests hear the voices of spirits in the rustling of the leaves and the echoes from the hill-sides, and see their fleeting forms in the shadows, the eye of man in the flat and changeless desert is drawn upwards to the stars, on whose rising and setting his own life appears to depend, and on whose

---

[1] Isa. lvii. 6; Jer. ii. 27; Hosea iv. 12.
[2] Lubbock's *Origin of Civilization*, third edition, p. 299.

place in the sky his own fate to be fixed. While worship of the sun, brightest of them all, has been so widespread, leaving its traces among our own and other great religions in strange and un-dreamed-of ways, it is interesting to note that the moon seems to have had earlier homage paid her among desert tribes.[1] The reason of this is that as the well-being of such folk depends on their cattle, the sun-god was to them an evil power, because he dried up the streams and withered the grass and herb. Not so the moon, ruling at night, when the cool breezes blew, the kindly dew fell, and the welcome shade was overhead, so that the wanderers might travel un-blinded by the noonday glare, unwearied by its heat. Her waning saddened and alarmed them, while the new moon was greeted with feasting, and the moment of her birth flashed, centuries after the Israelites had settled in Canaan, by fire-signal from hill to hill. Such friends, too, were the star-gods, guiding the travellers aright, making known the coming of the rains and the changes

[1] Goldziher's *Mythology among the Hebrews*, ch. iv. *passim*.

of the seasons; but when the wanderer became
a tiller of the soil and needed the heat to ripen
his corn and fruits, the powers of the night-sky
fell into the second place. As an example of
this, the Israelites who settled as husbandmen
in Canaan adopted the worship of the sun-gods
as givers of plenty, while those who remained
nomads clung to the older belief.

Before the Semitic tribes left their common
home the names of their chief gods, as El, Baal,
Molech and others, had been fixed, and although
different ideas about them arose as the tribes
reached different states of culture, the general
features remained, one being that such names
are adjectives, expressing qualities, as the Strong,
the Bright, and another being the twofold way in
which the same power was regarded. That is
to say, the sun would be worshipped at one
time as giver of fruitfulness, and at another time
feared and appeased as a destroying power, the
one aspect or the other holding, as the feelings
of the worshipper might prompt, the chief place
in feast and frantic dance or bloody sacrifice

under groves or, more often, on "high places."
For there the fancy of man has fixed the earthly
dwelling of the heaven-gods, as on Sinai among
the Hebrews, Asgard among the Norsemen,
Alborz among the Persians, Meru among the
Hindus, and Olympos among the Greeks.

While the Israelites were in Goshen, we find
chief place given to one of the oldest Semitic
deities, El-Shaddai, the Strong or Mighty one,
a god not beaming with the sunny grace and
gladness of some of the Aryan deities, but a
fierce and withering desert-god, awakening awe,
but never love, in his worshippers. When afterwards his name gave place to Yahweh (commonly spelt Jehovah), loftier ideas had arisen
about him, but he remained the same stern and
dreadful one whom none could look on and
live,[1] who rode on the clouds, announced his
approach in the thunderclap and appeared
amidst fires and lightnings,[2] to whom was
dedicated and often slain the firstborn of every-

---

[1] Exod. xix. 21, xxxiii. 20.
[2] Exod. xix. 16–18, xxiv. 17; Psalm xviii. 8.

thing—in short, a sun-god. Long after the Israelites had left Goshen they continued to appease him with horrid rites, and to ascertain his will by lot and soothsaying ; the old notions about him enter into the latest form in which their sacred books are cast ; he is there spoken of as acting like a man, walking in a garden,[1] coming down from the sky to spy out what people are doing,[2] writing with his finger,[3] repenting that he had made man ;[4] acting, too, as a *bad* man, approving cunning and deceit,[5] commanding the slaughter of women and children,[6] and praised as a "man of war"[7] at whose bidding the revolting cruelties of the Israelites under their chieftains and early kings were committed. For since the god in whom a man believes stands in his mind for what seems to him the highest and the best, he strives to copy him in the things which he does, thereby both obeying and honouring him. In the sacri-

[1] Gen. iii. 8. [2] Gen. xi. 5-7, xviii. 20, 21.
[3] Exod. xxxi. 18. . [4] Gen. vi. 6.
[5] Gen. xxvii., xxviii.; I Kings xxii. 21-23.
[6] Deut. vii. 2, 10 ; I Sam. xv. 2, 3.
[7] Exod. xv. 3 ; Numb. xxi. 14.

fices with which he has everywhere sought, as
with gifts, to win the favour of his gods or
avert their anger, we find the notion widespread that they partake of the essence of the
offering. The solid part is seen to remain
untouched ; it is the incense of fragrant spices,
the "sweet savour "[1] of burning sacrifices, the
blood, which is "the life," that the gods are
thought to enjoy. Among the hot-blooded
Semites, children of the desert sun, we find the
sacrifice of life, of human life too, its choicest
form, prevailing. In Canaan children were
offered to Molech in the belief that the yielding of one's dearest was well pleasing to the
god and needful to ward off trouble from the
land. Indeed, at the heart of this ghastly custom there lies the truth that the thing most
precious to us must be yielded ; only until
long years had passed did men learn that this
is not in blood and death, but in the surrender
of self-love and self-will for the good of our
kind. In Phœnicia and its famous colony

[1] Gen. viii. 21.

Carthage, the fairest and bestborn were offered in time of distress, and long after the Israelites had left Goshen, their worship of Jehovah was stained with the blood of man. In one touching story we read of a father who, going forth to war, vowed, in accordance with the old custom of promising the god a present if an undertaking succeeded,[1] to offer to Jehovah whatever should first greet him on his return, if he gained the victory. As he came back from the battle which he had won, who should come forth to meet him in gladness but his dear and only daughter! Yet would not the sad father break his oath, but after giving his child leave to withdraw for a while to weep and pray, "did with her according to his vow which he had vowed."[2]

Before leaving this somewhat dim and misty part of Israel's history for surer ground, let me gather into a few words the sum of what has been said.

The Israelites were of Semitic race, the

---

[1] Gen. xxviii. 20–22. [2] Judges xi. 30–39.

common home of which is unknown, but believed to have been in Arabia. From thence
certain tribes marched to the land around the
Persian Gulf, where they found a settled population, from whom they borrowed much in science,
art, and religion, and whom they at last conquered, founding in their stead the empires
of Babylonia and Assyria. Tribe after tribe of
Semites followed till the whole country from
Syria to the Armenian mountains was covered
with them. Such of them as found no settled
abode or cared to find none, wandered to and
fro as shepherd-tribes, among whom were the
forefathers of the Israelites who, in their search
after "green pastures beside still waters,"
trended southward until they reached the rich
corn-growing flats stretching between Egypt
and Syria. They were at that time divided
into clans, rough and warlike in their habits,
and in their religion worshippers of both sun
and stones, paying, however, chief honour among
their nature gods to El, the Strong, whose worship was attended with bloody sacrifices. Among

their sacred seasons were those of the new moon and the seventh day of each week, but no uniform customs or ideas prevailed among such loosely united folk, whose roaming life tended to bring about unlikeness in their manners and notions.

II.

The Israelites in Egypt.

EGYPT is a long, ribbon-like strip of fertile land in the north-east corner of Africa, bordered on either side by low and barren hills, which on the west protect it from the blinding sandstorms of the Libyan desert, and on the east separate it from the narrow waters of the Red Sea.

It is in truth the bed of the Nile, " the gift," as an old writer calls it, of that mighty river which, supplied by the outpour of great lakes in Central Africa, flows through an expanse of rock and desert, and, broken here and there into splendid cataracts, at last enters the fissure along which it has spread a layer of fruitful soil.

In the autumn of every year, its waters, swollen by melting snows and tropical rains, flood the valley, leaving as they recede a rich mud, into which the peasants, a down-trodden race to this day, cast their seeds. This valley, the like of which is found nowhere else in the world, is but a few miles wide until it nears the coast, where the many-mouthed river has spread its deposits into a fan-shaped plain called the delta, from its resemblance in form to the Greek letter Δ.

The land was altogether happily placed for the growth of a great empire, and from a remote time had been peopled by a race which probably came from Asia. The Egyptians shared the weakness which causes nations and families to exalt themselves by proof of ancient or noble descent, for we find that like the Chaldæans, Chinese, Hindus, and other people, they had piled up fabled accounts of royal gods whose reigns stretched over tens of thousands of years; but when these are cast aside there is abundant proof left that their kingdom was a mighty one centuries before the Israelites arrived in Goshen.

Some of the huge tombs called pyramids, the building of which was begun by each king when he came to the throne and carried on till his death, so that the longer his reign the bigger became his tomb, were full a thousand years old when those shepherd tribes first saw them, and the priests of Sais when Solon came to visit their temple said to him with truth, "You Greeks are but children." For the knowledge and skill and control of men which are needed for vast structures come not ready to hand, and long ages pass before from roughly piling stones into cairns and circles, men are able to upraise shapely tombs and stately temples.

The king, or " Pharaoh,"[1] that being his common title, was worshipped as one of the gods, and ranked among them after his death. The whole of the land was treated as his, one-third of it, according to one account, being taxed for the support of the priests, who, to make the more

---

[1] Not from "P-ra," "the sun," as is often said, but from " Pir'ao," "the great house ; " as in Turkey the " Porte," meaning "gate," is applied to the supreme power ; as, too, in England we say "the court " for " the judge."

sure of so large a share, pretended, with the cunning of their craft, that it had been so decreed by the goddess Isis when she dwelt among men.

The picture-writings and paintings on tombs and temple walls, which the rainless climate has kept from decay, tell us the thoughts and set before us in minutest detail the daily life of men in the valley of the Nile five or perchance six thousand years ago. But the old and the new so mingled in their religion that much remains to be put in order before we may hope to get clear ideas both of its secret and open features, and any account of it is at best but patchwork. We know that each nome or province had its gods, who were grouped in series of threes or fours, the most famous "triad" being Osiris, Isis, and Horus. Around Osiris touching legends gathered of his mission to earth to bless men, of his death for their sakes at the hands of the god of darkness, of his resurrection and office as judge of the dead. He was one of many names for the sun; indeed, speaking broadly, the Egyptian religion was a worship of that orb

under the many aspects which he wore from
rising to setting, and in his yearly course through
the heavens. In the life-giving powers battling
with the powers of darkness, the river god with
the sand-blinding Typhon, the day with the
night, the same story meets us which attends
the nature-worshipping stage of every people.
The scenery of their solemn landscape lent
its impress to the fixed, awful majesty of the
Egyptian gods, among the crowd of whom we
seem to catch sight now and again of one loftier
than the rest, but all is vague. These deities
were not only carved in stone, but worshipped
through living animals in whom their spirits were
believed to dwell, doubtless a survival in higher
form of ancient animal-worship. Chief among
these were sacred bulls, which with other creatures had honour paid them while living, their
bodies, like those of the Egyptians themselves,
being embalmed after death to preserve them
from decay.

The Egyptians had an exalted code of morals,
in which honour to parents, kindness to the

needy, and the love of truth were enjoined. They were a gay and cheerful folk, but sobered their pleasures with thoughts of an after life and judgment, of which very full accounts survive in their writings. According to the " Ritual of the Dead," the soul when it descended with the setting sun to Amenti, the hidden land beyond the western hills, had to recite, before it was weighed in the hall of justice, the sins into which it had not fallen and the good deeds it had wrought, declaring in words which remind us of those said to have been used by Jesus in his account of a last judgment, " I have fed the hungry, clothed the naked," etc., and if thus justified was clad in a white robe and admitted to the heavenly places.

Below the soldiers, who ranked next to the priests, and below the lower classes of freemen, there were vast numbers of slaves, comprising in the reign of Ramses II. fully one-third of the entire population. From earlier times men had learnt that it was more gainful to set captives to work than to kill them, and hence

out of war arose slavery. But the ease with which
strong nations could thus get supplies of labour
was one, among other causes, which led them to
think lightly of human life, and to treat their
bondsmen more harshly than cattle, which it
was harder to replace. Whenever the numbers
fell off, the Egyptian soldiers went negro-hunting
or made raids upon the border tribes, and it was
by forced labour alone that the canals were cut,
lakes dug, tombs and temples and cities raised;
and on some of the wall paintings, in colours
still fresh and bright, the slaves are seen at their
grinding tasks, while overseers, whom no sight of
suffering moved to pity, stand armed with long
whips, ready to lash the toilers who slackened
in their work or sank fainting beneath it.

Now, although the word "Hebrew" has not
yet been found among the Egyptian records, the
fact of such oppression overtaking the Israelites
is undoubted. It appears to have begun   B. C.
during the later years of their sojourn,   1388
in the reign of Ramses II., one of the   —1322.
greatest of the Pharaohs, of whom it is said that

D

he "made Egypt anew." During a long and
brilliant reign he carried on many wars against
the Hittites and other Syrian tribes, his victories
over whom were the theme of prize poems,
while, as bringing so remote a name somewhat
nearer to us, his titles may be read on the
so-called "Cleopatra's Needle," recently brought
from Egypt and erected on the left or northern
bank of the Thames. The precise causes which
led to the bondage of the Israelites are not clear,
but we know that the Pharaoh would have little
scruple in forcing them to taskwork, and, moreover, would view their increase with disfavour,
remembering how in bygone centuries such
restless folk had invaded the land, and ruled
it as the famous "Shepherd-kings" for long
years. Be the causes what they may, the lives
of the "sons of Israel" were "made bitter in
all manner of service in the field," and in the
building or enlarging of the great temple cities,
Ramses and Pithom.

Such loss of freedom was the more galling to
a people who had lived the untethered life of

the desert, and at last the burdens laid upon
them so increased that they plotted to escape.
The common trouble drew the tribes together;
the times favoured them, for Ramses was dead
and Meneptah his son was busy quelling out-
breaks among his people; friendly tribes were
around; while, chiefest of all, the very leader
whom such a daring movement needed to insure
its success appeared in Moses, one of the noblest
men that ever lived. By the time that the account
of his life was set down in Jewish history, many
legends akin to those of other heroes had been
interwoven with it, but when these are cast aside
there abides for the love and reverence of men
the story of one who put away thought and care
for self, one full of tender pity for his stricken
race, of iron will to help them, and, what nerved
him most for the struggle against the chariots
and horsemen of the Pharaoh, of strong faith that
the god in whom he believed, Jehovah,   B. C.
perhaps the god of his tribe, would   1320
deliver them. And that deliverance they   (about).
had, although beyond the simple fact that the

Exodus, as it is called (from Greek words meaning "going out"), took place under the leadership of Moses, probably in the reign of Meneptah, all is clouded with legend. As years rolled away and the great event which coloured and shaped Israel's wonderful career loomed from the distance, everything about it was lifted into the marvellous; the details of the stirring story grew as fathers told it to their children, and as minstrels made it the burden of their songs. It was said that the god of Israel sent plague after plague, ten in all, upon Egypt; swarms of frogs, flies, locusts, lice, the river turned into blood, hail and lightning, darkness, grievous sores on man and cattle, and at last death in every home, because the stubborn Pharaoh would not let the Israelites go; and that when, repenting of the consent to their departure which the plagues wrung from him, he pursued them, the waters through which they had to pass divided and "were a wall unto them on their right hand and on their left," so that they crossed in safety, but returned on the Egyptians and "covered the chariots and horsemen and all the host of Pharaoh that came into the sea after them."

These tales of the wonderful are as a veil which covers and yet does not conceal the features of the story, which stand out when looked at in the light of knowledge of the ills to which Egypt is now and again subject. The Nile is sometimes red and unpleasant to smell, swarms of frogs cover the swampy fields after its rising, tormenting gnats and flies breed in its slime, locusts fill the valley, and the sand blown from the desert blots out the sunshine as with dark clouds. Such disasters, if happening together about the time of the Exodus, would not fail to be regarded then and long after as the judgments of the god of Israel on the tyrant who would not set the oppressed people free.

A like explanation applies to the passage of the Red, or more correctly, " reed " sea. Long ages back this was joined to the Mediterranean, but the channel then connecting them has been slowly silted up with sand, and at the date of our story was a place of swamps and

inland lakes larger in their extent than at this
day.   Over these the harassed and hunted
Israelites passed in safety, while the Egyptians,
delayed by their cumbrous chariots, were caught
in the darkness by the advancing tide or by a
sudden inrush of waters, and perished; and at
daybreak " Israel saw them dead upon the seashore."   This defeat, to Moses and the freed
people the crowning proof of the protection of
the god whom he served, called forth this noble
song of victory, from which, in quoting, I omit
certain lines added at a later time :

" I will sing of Jehovah, for he is glorious :
The horses and chariots he whelms in the sea ;
Jehovah, the God of my father, will I praise.
Jehovah is a man of war :
Thy right hand, O Jehovah, shatters the enemy.
The chariots of Pharaoh and his might he threw into the
    sea :
His chosen charioteers were drowned in the Red Sea.
The floods covered them ;
They sank to the bottom as a stone.
At the breath of thy nostrils the waters rose in a heap ;
The floods stood like a bank ; the floods ran in the midst
    of the sea.
The enemy said, I will pursue, I will overtake ;
I will divide the spoil ; I will satisfy my lust upon them ;

I will draw my sword and destroy them with my hand.
Thou didst blow with thy mouth, O Jehovah ;
The floods covered them ;
They sank like lead in the mighty waters.
Who among the gods is like unto thee, Jehovah ?"[1]

According to the story in the book of Exodus above two million persons must have left Egypt. This is a great overstatement ; and I refer to it simply to caution you when reading the Bible against placing faith in the numbers given, because Eastern writers used them in no very exact way, but often with a notion of their sacredness and to give the idea of completeness. This will explain why the same numbers occur over and over again, as 3, 4, 7, 10 and their multiples ; seven being most sacred as based on the moon's phases. An amusing proof of the veneration once paid to this number is given in the reply made by a Jesuit named Sizzi to Galileo, when the latter announced his discovery of the moons of the planet Jupiter. Sizzi told him that he must be mistaken, because the Jews and other nations had divided the week into

[1] Exod. xv. I-II.

seven days after the seven planets, and that if the number of planets was increased, the division of time into weeks would have to be given up!

The "sons of Israel" and the "mixed multitude" that went forth with them took a southward path,[1] their aim being to avoid any route which might bring them near the grip of Egypt, whose strong hand had long held Syria and lands beyond under tribute. This track brought them to the valleys and plains around Sinai, a range of granite rocks bare of any green thing, and broken into peaks and waterless ravines, but with green pasture lands about its base. The mountain takes its name from the moon-god Sin, for it was a sacred "high place" to the Semites; and to Jew and Christian hallowed memories gather round it still as the place where in common belief Jehovah came down in fire,[2] calling Moses to its top, where he stayed "forty" days and "forty" nights, receiving laws written on two stone tables by the god's finger.

[1] The arguments of Dr. Brugsch in support of a route by Lake Serbonis, given in the Appendix to his *History of Egypt*, are, to my mind, inconclusive.   [2] Exod. xix. 18.

We find like legends of laws given from heaven direct to man among the Egyptians, Persians, Greeks, and other nations, and in the days when men were rough and untamed, their passions unchecked by regard for others' needs, it was well that such notions concerning the origin of laws prevailed. For had they looked on the rules which curbed their fierceness as merely the work of fellow-men, they might have overturned them, whereas they feared to disobey commands which they believed the gods had given, and which seemed, like religion, heaven-born. As society, however, advanced, such notions became hurtful because they hindered the riddance or alteration of laws which had become unsuited to a better state of things. As an example of this, so long as men believed that every word in the Bible was inspired by God, they quoted texts from it in defence of many evil things, as slavery, " Cursed is Canaan, a servant of servants shall he be ; "[1] as witchcraft, " thou shalt not suffer a witch to live ; "[2] as war in its most cruel form,

[1] Gen. ix. 25.   [2] Exod. xxii. 18 ; Deut. xviii. 10.

"thou shalt consume all the people which Jehovah shall deliver thee; thine eye shall have no pity upon them;"[1] as the divine right of kings, "for who can stretch forth his hands against Jehovah's anointed?"[2] while we all know how its verses have been vainly cited in disproof of one fact after another which science has re vealed. We have, happily for man's progress and release from false fears, since come to see that laws rest on quite other ground, which does not make them the less but the more binding. They were not given by gods in human form and with human voice to men of old, but framed by man for man, and are the slow outgrowth of many ages, being at the outset shaped and carried out in rough fashion as a defence against brute force, and afterwards tempered with mercy born of human needs and man's sense of duty to his fellows.

It is worth our while to turn aside from the work of Moses for a moment, and inquire how the laws on which man's conduct is based arose,

---

[1] Deut. vii. 16.   [2] 1 Sam. xxvi. 9.

for we may learn thereby what is the ground,
and what should be the motive, for our acts:
truly a serious thing.

Man, at his lowest, has a sense of right to
anything which he has been the first to secure ;
and if another wrests his gains from him, he feels
that he has been wronged, while contrariwise,
if he were the spoiler, he would know that like
feelings were aroused in his victim. Only by
allowing other men to hold in peace what they
had gained could he expect to retain his. Self-
interest, in which were the germs of *duty*,
prompted this. When he joins himself with
others to form a tribe, this feeling is extended
to them, and it becomes the duty of one towards
another to guard property held in common, as
land, cattle, etc. ; laws are framed for the general
weal, whatever sustains the tribe in its struggles
against other tribes is approved ; whatever
weakens it is condemned, out of which grow
the sense of rightness and wrongness. Thus
arises a "tone," or "public feeling," as we call
it ; love of self and of one's family extending

itself to care for the welfare of the tribe ; then, as
men grow from tribes into nations, to the nation
as a whole, making them brave and eager to defend it, and to brand as cowards those who would
evade that duty. And as the sense of one's own
rights led to respect for others' rights, out of
which duty was born, so the sense of one's own
need and dependence creates feeling for others'
needs, and awakens those feelings of pity which
are expressed in kindly deeds, till man crowns
his life by acts of self-sacrifice which have
enriched the world and subdued its brute forces.
So great are the changes which arise in the slow
growth of men into nations, that laws are ever
altering, so much so that ofttimes that which
one age acts upon as right, a later time rejects
as wrong. Laws, therefore, can never be fixed,
nor can they be perfect, because when man is
perfect, that is, does right because he cannot do
otherwise, he will cease to need them. Towards
this he is nearer to-day than of old ; and this
through slowly learning to rule thoughts, words,
and deeds, in accord with the demands which the

whole world, not merely his little corner of it, makes upon him ; and one day, yet afar off, when the tribal feeling expands into an all-including human feeling, he will be at one with all around him, and "shall not vex or destroy."

Thus the *ground* of duty rests on no ancient code, but solely on the experience of what, after long ages of sore testing, man has come to feel to be best for man. "This commandment which I command thee this day is not hidden, neither is it far off ; it is not in heaven that thou shouldest say, Who shall go up for us to heaven, and bring it unto us that we may hear it and do it ? neither is it beyond the sea that thou shouldest say, Who shall go over the sea for us, and bring it unto us, that we may hear it and do it ? but the word is very nigh unto thee, in thy mouth and in thy heart, that thou mayest do it,"[1] while the *motive* which should suffice to impel us to right-doing should not be hope of reward, or fear of punishment, but obedience to the voice, which, in telling us

[1] Deut. xxx. 11-14.

what we "ought" to do, tells us, as that little word once meant, what we "owe" to do, since doing not this is to make discord in the order towards which all things tend, it is to be as a jarring note in the "music of the spheres."

The fame of Moses as a lawgiver rests mainly on the code called the Ten Commandments, or, in Hebrew, the Ten Words. We may accept the statement that he was skilled in the wisdom and learning of the Egyptians, and he cannot but have known somewhat of their moral code ; but the wrongs endured at their hands had aroused a bitter feeling towards them which prevented much borrowing, and the more so in matters of religion, as the struggle for freedom was to Moses and the people a battle between the god of Israel and the gods of Egypt. For Moses had regarded himself simply as an instrument in the hands of Jehovah ; and when the victory was given him, well might he and the tribes, as they called to mind how they, a downtrodden mass of slaves, had humbled the power which was to them the mightiest in the world, see in it a proof that they were a "chosen" people, and gladly "fear Jehovah, and believe Jehovah."

According to the book of Exodus, it was to Moses that El-Shaddai announced himself as Yahweh, or Jehovah. The latter is a very incorrect, and by no means old, form of spelling the name of this god ; but it has fallen into such common use, that any alteration might confuse ; and moreover, as a chief reason for retaining it, I think it well for us to bear in mind that it is the name of a Semitic sun-god, in the worship of whom we cannot join "in spirit and in truth." How far the loftier ideas with which it was linked in the mind of Moses were imported from Egypt, our present knowledge suffices not to say ; indeed, the exact meaning of the word, which is wrongly translated " the LORD " in our Bibles, is uncertain, although this much is certain, that it is connected with the verb "to be."[1] Enough that he made it entirely his own by connecting the Ten Words with worship of Jehovah, de-

[1] Note B.

claring disobedience to them to be disobedience to him whom he set before them, not only as strong and fierce, but as *good*, and as demanding goodness, thus for ever lifting him far above the other gods of the Semites and the crowd of gods that lined the banks of the Nile.

The earliest form in which the Ten Words were given is lost, and the two versions which are found in the Old Testament differ slightly; but the substance is as follows :—

> I, Jehovah, am thy God.
> Thou shalt have none other gods before my face nor make any image of a god.
> Thou shalt take no false oath.
> Remember to keep holy the sabbath day.
> Honour thy father and thy mother.
> Thou shalt not kill.
> Thou shalt not commit adultery.
> Thou shalt not steal.
> Thou shalt not bear false witness.
> Thou shalt not covet.

This code Moses delivered to the " elders " or tribal chiefs, and heads of families, in solemn assembly, and received their promises to aid him in carrying it out. A goodly part of it was of a kind suited to curb the lawlessness of desert tribes,

and pointed to no lofty standard, its newer and
nobler features being those which forbade image-
worship, and enjoined obedience to both father
and mother. The sabbath, which, as we saw,
arose out of moon-worship, was not kept by the
Egyptians, and it was a welcome act which restored to the once unresting bondsmen, and con-
secrated to Jehovah, the repose of every seventh
day, although, in doing this, Moses little dreamed
how Jew and Christian in after time would make
it a weariness and burden to both young and old.
He also retained or revived sundry old rites and
customs, as the dedication of the firstborn, expressed in milder form by the rite of circum-
cision common to so many races; laws dealing
with family life; the rights of masters and
slaves; the settlement of quarrels and revenge
of wrong. This last has ever been a sacred duty
among barbarous peoples; the Arabs and other
nomads still make the vendetta, or "thar," as
they call it, binding on the nearest friend of
a slain man as the "avenger," and, indeed, in
such rough code is the germ of laws framed by

E

nations for self-defence. "Life for life, eye for eye," ran the oldest forms, afterwards redress in goods or money, as among our forefathers, with whom each tooth and finger-nail had its fixed price.

This comprises the sum of the work of Moses as a legislator, for the laws which make up the main portion of the second, third, and fourth books of the Old Testament and are recorded as delivered by him, were not framed till centuries afterward, when the Israelites had become a nation with a fixed centre of government and worship. Moses could not foresee what laws would be needed in future times, and even if he could, the giving forth of rules about keeping festivals of seedtime and harvest, about cities of refuge and cities of the Levites, and other features of a settled state, would have been meaningless to semi-barbarous desert tribes. Images, as we saw, were forbidden in the Ten Words; but we read of a very important sacred object called an "ark," or chest, which was believed to be the dwelling-place of Jehovah, and to possess magical

powers. It was placed under the care of Aaron,
brother of Moses, and of other priests, and kept
in a tent or "tabernacle," before which the chiefs
met for counsel and sacrifice. Arks not only
figured in the Egyptian religion in " processions
of the shrines," but were in use among the
Accadians, and were copied by the Babylonians and Phœnicians, although the Israelites
in all likelihood borrowed theirs from Egypt.
One marked feature of the Egyptian religion,
however, they clearly did not adopt, namely,
its teachings about a future life. They had
the confused notions common to all semi-savage
races, arising from dreams, shadows, and such-
like unreal things, of a second self, which at
death went to the under-world or " hades ; "
a land of darkness and forgetfulness, where " the
wicked cease from troubling, and the weary are
at rest ; " where lie " the small and great, and
the slave is free from his master ; " [1] where the
tired shade, like Samuel's in the legend, when
the wizard's art summons it to earth, asks,

[1] Job iii. 17–19.

" Why hast thou disquieted me to bring me up ?"[1]   Such was "sheol," wrongly translated " hell " in English Bibles, and for hundreds of years the Israelites had no other belief than this vague one in a life after death.   Their lawgivers and prophets, Moses, David, Isaiah, and others, made no appeal to men's fears or hopes by the doctrine of a heaven or a hell ; the only reward for which the Israelite cared was to live long in the land which Jehovah had given him ; to die young, " cut off from his people," was his direst dread ; he whitewashed his tombs, and shrank from touching a corpse ; in his legends of a happy past the patriarchs are represented as living hundreds of years on the earth,[2] as in the prophet's vision of a brighter future " the child shall die an hundred years old."[3]

[1] I Sam. xxviii. 15.   [2] Gen. v.   [3] Isa. lxv. 20.

III.

The Conquest of Canaan.

WHEN the tribes struck their tents in Sinai, they turned northwards, and after some years of wandering and warring, had so far gained the mastery over other desert nomads as to secure a firm footing on the rich uplands east of the river Jordan. From these they could see Canaan, a land of hills and dales, of tilled plains, fertile valleys, walled cities, and other signs of settled life. The goodly sight raised their greed, and, made hardy by their bracing wilderness life, the bravest of them resolved to invade the land and win for themselves a settled home among vine-yards which they had not dressed, and trees which they had not planted. But the task proved neither short nor easy; for the Canaanites, who were also of Semitic race, were well armed, inured to war by many struggles, and moreover defending their homes. Their weakness lay in the hilly nature of the country, which divided them into thirty or forty petty "kingdoms," and for long years was a barrier to the union of the Israelites.

Canaan, or the "lowlands," since known by other names, as the Land of Israel, Palestine, Holy Land, is a narrow strip of country, hemmed in between the Mediterranean Sea and the river Jordan. From the mountains of Lebanon, which form its northern boundary, a range of lofty limestone hills, pierced with caverns and broken by many valleys, runs the whole length of the land as far as the desert of Sinai. On their western side these hills incline gently to fertile plains and a sandy coast, and on their eastern side descend more sharply to the deep and winding valley of the Jordan. The country is dotted in some places with the sites of old volcanoes, and in other parts is strewn with loose rocks, witnessing to the play of forces of terrible might, which ages back cracked and crumpled the crust, heaved the mountains and rent open the crooked valley, one of the most wonderful clefts in the world, down which dashes the Jordan, called from its rapid fall, the "descender."

In the north the hills and dales are verdant and fruitful, and the landscape richly varied, but the bold outlines slope into barren ridges and stony valleys as the south is approached, until in the wilderness country around the Dead Sea the scenery is dreary and the region bare of any green thing. This very remarkable lake, into which the Jordan tamely creeps to its grave, "tarrying," as an old writer says,[1] "as if loth to approach the hateful sea that swallows it up and spoils its precious waters by union with its own reeking waves," fills a wide part of the valley some 1300 feet below the level of the Mediterranean, and is walled-in on both sides by stern mountains; pillar-shaped masses of salt being scattered about its shores. Its clear but bitter waters, in which only very low forms of life are found, contain one-fourth solid matter, whereas common sea-water contains but one-twentyfifth; and as they have no outlet, are drawn off by the

[1] Pliny, *Nat. Hist.* vi. 5, 2.

sun's rays only, causing a dim mist to hang over the lake and adding to its weird appearance.

A great deal of nonsense has been written about this Dead Sea, or Sea of Lot, as the Arabs call it. It was said that dark clouds always floated over it, that no winds ever ruffled it, that no birds flew across it, that no creature could live in it, and that the whole land around bore witness to the curse of God. Such foolish talk arose from the belief in an old legend that certain "cities of the plain,"[1] Sodom, Gomorrah, and other places, had been destroyed by fire from heaven, and that the Dead Sea covered their site. One of the salt columns, which was shaped somewhat like a woman, was said to have been Lot's wife, who was thus punished for casting a longing look upon Sodom as she was escaping from it! Myths of this class are found the world over; in Africa and India certain queer-shaped standing stones are said to have been giants; the long rows of stones at Karnak to be petrified soldiers; one of the stone-circles in

[1] Gen. xix. 24-29.

England to have been a party of girls who had
danced on a Sunday; and in the tale of "Zobeide"
in the "Arabian Nights" we read of a city in
which all the infidel people were turned into
stone !

Such legends, indeed all legends whatsoever
and wheresoever, are the outcome of man's
ignorance concerning the universe. Among
the lower races the earth is believed to be
the centre of all things, and each department
of nature ruled over by a deity. Every unto-
ward event that happens is regarded as the work
of such beings, and this easy explanation suffices
until man learns how unvarying is the order of
nature and what sure effects follow certain causes.
Therefore, as knowledge advances, the number
of events which are looked upon as miracles or
the wilful acts of superhuman beings lessens ;
but while earthquakes, eclipses, and comets are
no longer thus explained by educated persons,
the notion still lingers that hurricanes, famines,
and pestilences on man and beast are sent by
the Almighty to warn or punish mankind.

Only as the wholesome lessons of science teach us that nothing happens by chance or caprice, and that " if law be anywhere it is everywhere," do such harmful notions of a lawless world ruled by a fickle God depart and give place to trust based upon eternal order, to love that casts out fear.

Like Greece and other small countries of renown, the place which Canaan fills in history is not due to its size, for it is under two hundred miles in length, and nowhere more than fifty miles in breadth, but largely to its position between the great rival empires of the past. Not only must their armies cross it as they strove to reach the Nile or the Euphrates, but its coast roads were great highways of trade between east and west, creating intercourse between divers races. Its history is one of ceaseless turmoil from the time when Semitic tribes fought with nameless savages of the Stone Age to our own day ; but more than all the fame given it as the arena of struggles between mighty empires is the renown bestowed upon it by that remarkable people whose career I am now sketching—Israel, "the lifter-up of the banner of righteousness, as Greece was the lifter-up to the nations of the banner of art and science."[1]

It was, as near as can be reckoned, about the middle of the thirteenth century before our era that some of the tribes crossed the Jordan under the command of Joshua, who had become leader on the death of Moses. Their bravery was rewarded by the fall of Jericho, a walled town, and by the defeat of many Canaanites in their mountain strongholds, but as they fought only on foot, they had small success in the plains. "Jehovah," naively says the old chronicler, "was with Judah, and he took the mountain and possessed it, but could not drive out the inhabitants of the low ground because they had chariots of iron."[2] So varying were the fortunes of the invaders that while in some parts they maintained the upper hand, in others they were glad to come to terms with the Canaanites, even paying them tribute; and more

B. C. 1250?

---

[1] *Literature and Dogma*, p. 355.　　[2] Judges i. 19.

than two hundred years passed before all the
land was theirs. For wars in that day and
long after sometimes dragged on for centuries,
even years being spent in besieging a single city.
In the history of our island the Saxons were
thirty years winning a corner of it, and two
hundred years elapsed before they had driven
the Britons across fen and forest to the fast-
nesses of Wales.

One great drawback to the more rapid success
of the Israelites was their disunion, which increased on the death of Joshua. No able leader
arose to fill his place, a wild and lawless time
set in, each man did what was right in his own
eyes, the tribes quarrelled one with another and
stood in grave danger of losing what was already
won. For on the east of the Jordan border
clans harassed and plundered them; along the
coast the powerful Philistines (an alien people of
uncertain origin, and of whose name "Palestine"
is a corruption), cramped for space, were pushing
their way inland, while remnants of the Canaanites were ever on the watch to regain lost ground.

Besides suffering from foes without and disputes
within, the Israelites were further weakened by
falling into the worship of the Canaanitish gods,
whose names and features had much in common
with their own. The chief shrine of Jehovah
had been fixed at Shiloh, and thither the tribes
gathered in yearly festival, but elsewhere he was
worshipped side by side with Baal and other
nature-gods, in whose honour impure and bloody
rites were practised. But great as was the peril
of all that was special to Israel being effaced by
contact with other peoples, the tribes had for ever
turned their backs upon a wandering life, and
their growth into a nation was only a question
of time. Whenever sudden danger threatened
them, brave leaders failed them not, women as
well as men, upon whom " the spirit of Jehovah
had come," who united the tribes and sustained
what faith and hope of unity was left. The
stories of these "judges," as they are called, of
their valour, not unmixed with the cruelty of
their age and race, form the heroic chapter in
Israel's confused history. With the famous

song of Deborah,[1] which chants their deeds, and
with the story of Gideon's craft and victory, there
mingles the legend of "Samson,"[2] telling how he
killed a thousand Philistines with an ass's jaw-
bone;[3] carried away the huge gates of a city;
pulled down a temple, crushing thousands of his
foes in the ruins, and, in a later fable, crumbled
two mountains to powder by rubbing them together!

But despite all the efforts of the "judges,"
the Philistines became masters of the land west
of the Jordan, reducing the Israelites so
completely as to strip them of their
weapons and compel them to come to their conquerors when they wanted their ploughshares
and billhooks sharpened. To fill their cup of
misery, the ark itself, which had been carried
into battle to ensure success, fell into the hands
of the foes,[4] although, so runs the legend,[5] it
brought such troubles upon its captors that they
were glad to be quit of it, and putting it on a

B. C.
1070?

---

[1] Judges v.   [2] Goldziher's *Heb. Myth.* App. ii.
[3] Judges xv. 15.   [4] I Sam. iv. 11.
          [5] I Sam. v. vi.

waggon drawn by cows, left the animals free to drag it whither they would, whereby the Israelites recovered it. About this time there arose the greatest man in Israel since Moses had died— Samuel, priest, nazirite, and seer. From his boyhood he had served at the shrine in Shiloh ; as a nazirite, or "one set apart," he drank no wine, thus opposing the drunken feasts in honour of Baal ; while as a judge he won the highest respect by the justice of his decrees. But it is as a seer that he is chiefly renowned. Under various names, as soothsayers, sorcerers, shamans, medicine-men, such a class is found among all barbarous people, and, concealed under more or less polish of high-sounding names, among civilized people also. It has its rise in the world-wide notion that the deity makes known his will to men by sign or "oracle," given through " seers," or through certain things, the meaning of which such as they can alone interpret ; being divined, among other ways, by the flight or cry of birds, the entrails of animals, the pointing of rods, the casting of lots. Among the

Israelites, the will of Jehovah was often looked for in dreams and visions, and we find all classes employing the priests and soothsayers to cast lots, as the "Urim and Thummim," before the sacred ark or images, and also calling in the aid of seers, who were believed "to see" into what was hidden, and foretell things to come.

The Hebrew words for this class are "rôeh" and "chôzeh," both meaning "one who sees." At a later time the word "nabi," meaning to "bubble forth," as does a fountain, was applied to men who in the days of Samuel were noted for the excitement, akin to frenzy, into which they worked themselves, often with the aid of music and dancing, after the manner of such all the world over to this day, both in savage and civilized countries. History abounds with examples of the harmful waste to which feeling runs unless wisely directed, and the great and serious work done by Samuel, who, himself once a soothsayer, had made a knowledge of the will of Jehovah his study, was to gather these seers into companies known as "schools of the prophets," and control them so that they "were changed into other men."[1] They praised Jehovah, whose "word" they poured forth, with harp and lute, devoted themselves to study of the past and of such traditions of the laws and teaching of Moses as had been preserved, kindling thereby an intense faith in Israel's distinct place and mission, and in unwavering service of Jehovah as the only hope of progress. Such men, by their teaching and their promotion of gentler manners in that rude time, were the humble forerunners of that "goodly fellowship of the prophets" so bold to reprove sin, so quick to comfort, so strong to endure, and so keen-eyed to see into the meaning of events.

Samuel, who was no warrior, felt that the only cure for the ills of his people was in putting away Baal, Ashtaroth, and other gods, as well as the teraphim or household gods which were worshipped in the home, and in serving Jehovah, who had brought them out of Egypt, given the law to Moses, whose was the land in which

---

[1] I Sam. x. 5, 6.

F

they dwelt, and who alone was Israel's king.
But there was a second party which with the
same aim in view as Samuel and his followers—
the union of the tribes—saw no hope of reaching it save by copying the nations around, and
having a king who could lead them to battle,
and impose his strong will upon their wilfulness.
Feeling ran high on both sides, and it is pleasant
to turn from the angrier features of the struggle
to read this old fable in ridicule of the kingly
office which is given in the book of Judges.[1]

Once upon a time the trees went forth to
choose a king ; and they said to the olive tree,
Reign thou over us. But the olive answered,
Shall I leave the oil for which gods and men
honour me, and wave my branches over the trees ?
Then they went to the fig tree, but he said, Shall
I leave my sweetness and my good fruit that I
may wave my branches over the trees ? Then
they asked the vine, but he would not leave his
wine which cheereth the gods and men. At
last, the trees turned to the bramble, and he

[1] Ch. ix. 8–15.

consented, for the noble and useful trees had no desire to be kings, only the fruitless bramble which, fit for naught else, took the crown!

The knotty question was cut by the sword. There had uprisen among the brave ones a man of noble presence, named Saul, whose valour in delivering a city had turned all eyes upon him as a born ruler of men. The high place to which he had earned a title, not by birth or fraud, but by gallant deed, was accorded him, and he became king of Israel. He B.C. 1055?[1] delivered his people from the Philistines, and laid the foundation of Israel's short-lived greatness as a kingdom. His zeal for Jehovah had secured him Samuel's support, but while the seer desired to have unity under one religion, stamping out Baal-worship, the king sought by permitting freedom in these matters to win all under one rule; and so they quarrelled, Saul at last persecuting the priests, and backsliding

---

[1] The dates from the Exodus to the destruction of the Temple are approximate only; those given are adopted from Max Duncker, no the bases laid down in his excellent *History of Antiquity*, ii. 112–115.

into belief in wizards. His power dwindled, the Philistines regained strength to attack him, and after seeing three of his sons fall in battle against them, he put an end to his troubled life. But the simple, manly way in which he had worn his honours, and the memory of his bravery, endeared him to his people, and the grief which his death called forth is shown in this ancient song,[1] which tradition ascribed to David :[2]

" O Israel, the beauty of the forest lies slain on thy hills !
How are the mighty fallen ?
Tell it not in Gath.
Publish it not in the streets of Askalon,
Lest the daughters of the Philistines rejoice ;
Lest the daughters of the uncircumcised dance for joy.
O mountains of Gilboa, let there be no dew upon you,
Ye fields and hills of death !
For there was the warrior's shield cast away ;
The shield of Saul, bespattered, all unanointed with oil.
From the blood of the slain, from the fat of the warriors,

---

[1] 2 Sam. i. 17–27.

[2] It was known among the archers of Judah, to whom David taught it, as the "song of the bow." The words "beauty of the forest" in the first line refer to Saul's son Jonathan, David's dear friend, and mean "Gazelle"—a name by which the slain man was known among his comrades.

The bow of Jonathan turned not back ;
The sword of Saul returned not empty.
Saul and Jonathan were lovely and pleasant in their lives,
And in their death they were not divided.
They were swifter than eagles, they were stronger than
  lions.
Ye daughters of Israel, weep for Saul,
Who clothed you in purple and splendour,
And threw jewels of gold round your necks.

  *   *   *   *   *

I am grieved by thy loss, Jonathan, my brother,
Thou wast very dear to me ;
More precious to me was thy love than the love of women.
How are the mighty fallen,
And the weapons of war perished."

The rapid rise of men of humble station to
high place in the state is not rare in the East,
and David, the next great ruler of Israel, was of
mean rank. His valour, or, according to another
account, his skill upon the harp, had brought
him under Saul's notice and favour, who gave
him a daughter in marriage, but later on,
thinking that he had an eye to the throne
itself, sought to kill him, whereupon David
fled, and was at last forced to take refuge among
the Philistines. On the death of Saul, one
of his sons became king; but the renown of

David and his zeal for Jehovah was such that
B.C. 1025? the tribe of Judah voted for him, the
priests and seers supported him, and
on the murder of Ishbosheth, he became ruler
over all Israel. His reign was warlike and
brilliant, and, with the aid of able commanders,
he extended his kingdom as far as the Euphrates,
but one of the greatest triumphs of his arms
was the capture of Jerusalem, then called
Jebus, the stronghold of the Jebusites. This
city, which was to acquire such immortal
renown, stands amidst barren scenery, "the
saddest in the world,"[1] on a rocky ridge broken
into deep valleys, which rendered its conquest
no easy task ; indeed, it was the boast of the
people that the blind and the lame sufficed to
defend it.[2] David chose it as his capital ; and,
aided by workmen from Phœnicia, with whose
king he was on friendly terms, built a palace
there. But he did a far more important and
prudent thing withal, securing thereby the sup-

[1] "Le plus triste pays du monde."—*Vie de Jésus*, p. 35.
[2] 2 Sam. v. 6.

port of the priests, in making the city the chief
seat of worship of Jehovah. Thither 　 B.C.
he brought the ark, "whose name is 　 1020?
Jehovah,"[1] in solemn procession, headed by
himself as king-priest, clad, like the Egyptian
priests, in white linen robe, and dancing like the
"nabim" to his harp, while, as the choir approached the gates, they sang—

> " Lift up your heads, O ye gates ;
> Be ye lift up, ye doors of old,
> That the King of Glory may come in ! "

the warders asking—

> " Who, then, is the King of Glory ? "

and the priests replying—

> " It is Jehovah, strong and mighty ;
> Jehovah, the mighty in battle."

Thus Jerusalem became the " city of David,"
the dwelling-place of Jehovah, and round the
tabernacle on Mount Zion the priesthood
gathered, causing the many shrines that had
been raised to that god all over the land to fall
one by one into neglect and disuse.

[1] 2 Sam. vi. 2.

The career of David had been an eventful one. As a youth, the task of guarding his father's sheep in the wilderness from robbers and wild beasts had inured him to hardship, and called into play his courage. He had cheered the loneliness of his shepherd life with music and song, for which he had great natural gifts, and fed his soul with thoughts about the god whose voice he heard in the thunder and the shaking trees, whose glory shone around him by night as well as by day. Called in the fitful fortunes of that rough age to serve near his king, he at last became king himself, although his path to the throne had lain through craft and murder. Even after making allowance for the times in which he lived, he was cruel and treacherous, slaughtering conquered foes with horrible torture, and when dying, ordering the murder of a man whom he had vowed to spare. Yet he could be a generous foe, and was a faithful friend; according to his light, a devout man, seeking to know and striving to do the will of his god. His later years were saddened by dis-

content and rebellion ; but, as he summed up
the events of his varied and romantic life, he
believed that Jehovah had guided him all
through, and thus he praised him in song—

" Jehovah, my rock, my fortress, my shield.
  With praise I called upon him,
  And was delivered from my enemies.
  He heard my voice out of his palace,
  My cry came into his ears.
  Then the earth quaked and trembled,
  The foundations of the earth trembled, for he was wroth.
  There went up a smoke from his nostrils,
  A consuming fire went from his mouth,
  A blast of burning coals.
  He bowed the heavens and did ride upon the cherubim,
  He rode on the wings of the wind.
  He made darkness his veil,
  The tempest and dark clouds his tabernacle.
  Jehovah thundered in the heavens,
  The Highest gave forth his voice—hailstones and coals
    of fire—
  He sent forth his arrows and scattered the enemy,
  The lightning fell and discomfited them.
  Jehovah girded me with power ;
  He made my feet like harts' feet,
  He taught my hand to war,
  So that my arm bent even a bow of iron.
  I followed my enemies and overtook them ;

I turned not back till they were destroyed ;
I scattered them like dust before the wind,
I cast them out like dung into the streets.
Thou, Jehovah, savest me from the strivings of the
　　nations,
And makest me their head ;
People whom I knew not serve me.
At the hearing of the ear they obey me ;
The sons of strangers do me homage ;
They come trembling from their strongholds.
Long live Jehovah ! blessed be my rock,
And praised be the God of my salvation." [1]

Long after David's time, when the glory of
the kingdom had departed, the Jews looked
back with fond regret to his reign as the
Golden Age of their country's history, and the
traditions of his gift of song caused them to
ascribe very many of the psalms to his pen.

He may be fairly called the father of Hebrew
psalmody, but the larger number of compositions
which comprise the "Book of Psalms" are far
too sublime and varied to have been the work of
one man in that day, still less of a rough soldier
such as he, the burden of whose songs was of

[1] Psalm xviii.

war and valiant deeds. Neither could they
have been the work of one age, for the phases
of life with which they deal are far too
changeful to have been passed through in a
few years. Indeed, we know that the collection
stretches from the reign of David to the time
of the Maccabees, that is, between 800 and 900
years; but only in a few cases do the contents
of a psalm enable us to fix its date, and even
after stripping away the misleading titles which
were added in a later age, any attempt at arrangement in order of time is hopeless. They have
been fitly called "the hymn-book of the second
temple," for onwards from the writing of the noble
psalm, probably the 68th, sung at the dedication
of that building, was the period when Hebrew
poetry reached its fullest perfectness.

We may take it that most of the psalms
which praise the works of Jehovah, which chant
his might as a "man of war," and which breathe
a fierce and revengeful spirit are among the
earliest; that the later are those rich and
mellowed songs, whose theme is the joy of the

people in the temple and the law, and still later the plaintive cries wrung from them when exiled from fatherland or suffering grievous persecution at the hands of the tyrant. Much of their vividness and depth of feeling is lost in translating them from the Hebrew, and their beauty is further obscured through their being printed as prose writings in our Bibles instead of as poems cast in lyric form. For this latter reason it is better, after acquainting yourself with their general history, to read them in a "paragraph" version, or a book like the "Golden Treasury Psalter," where they are set down with some regard both to order and to "rhythm," or measure.

Instead of quoting from songs whose strains have been repeated by the uplifted and castdown through many ages since, and which will always rank among the world's noblest poems, I will cite one which is not found in the Psalter;[1] and which was ascribed to David.

[1] It is given in some psalters of the Septuagint (see p. 166); here it is quoted from Baring Gould's *Old Testament Legends*, ii. 175.

Its subject is his slaying of a giant named Goliath.

PSALM CLI.

" I was small among my brethren, and growing up in my father's house I kept my father's sheep.

" My hands made the organ and my fingers shaped the psaltery. And who declared unto my Lord? He, the Lord, he heard all things. He sent his angel and he took me from my father's sheep : he anointed me in mercy with his unction.

" Great and goodly are my brethren, but with them the Lord was not well pleased.

" I went to meet the stranger and he cursed by all his idols.

" But I smote off his head with his own drawn sword and I blotted out the reproach of Israel."

We have reached a point when something should be said about the sources of our knowledge concerning the early history of the Israelites, for although they were doubtless acquainted with the art of writing while in Egypt, they were in too great a state of turmoil from that time until their settlement as a nation under kingly rule to permit of much thought being given to the shaping of such records of the past as had been preserved among the several tribes.

And here, for the clearance of the matter, I would first say a little about the growth of history, taking an old Greek myth for my text.

It says that the goddess of Memory had nine daughters, called the Muses, who were the inspirers and patrons of music, song, and all learning among men, and the temple sacred to whom gave its name to the famous "Museum" at Alexandria, and to like buildings since in which treasures of science and art are gathered. Of these nine sister-goddesses Klio, the eldest, was the Muse of history and epic poetry, which latter treats of real or fabled events. Now this myth holds a great truth, for memory is the mother of history, since all history has its birth in the stored-up recollections of men about things which they have heard or seen or done, and the earliest form which it takes is song. The song itself is both old and young; old as having its birth long before the art of writing was invented, and

young as being the outcome of ages too vast to
be reckoned by years, throughout which man,
although he knew it not, was making history.
Far back as we can trace his presence we find,
as I have already explained in the " Childhood
of the World," the tools with which he worked,
and the weapons with which he fought, and
these tell us how wild and savage was his
earliest state, but it was not till he began to
think, *to know that he was*, that memory grew
strong to do its silent work of hoarding up what
eye and ear brought to it, and at last to give
forth of its store in song and "saga" (or thing
said), as the Norsemen called it. And the
earliest of them, like that fine song of triumph
on the shores of the Red Sea, or Lamech's
remarkable little poem in Genesis iv. 23, 24, told
of war and valiant deeds, and sounded the
praises of those who wrought them, such a scene
of fighting has this poor earth ever been. With
these were preserved legends of the kind named
in the beginning of this book, and thus piece-
meal grew the traditions "handed down" (as

that word means) from one to another by
word of mouth, told round the camp fires, and
chanted by the minstrels, until they were fixed
in writing. While in floating form they were
coloured and altered by the art and fancy of
the story-teller, and yielded to the impress of the
scenes amidst which they had arisen; but they
never lacked the wonderful, for both they who
narrated and they who listened had no facts
wherewith to check the wild and unlikely tales,
nor did doubts ever cross their minds about
them. Nature had not yet become the scene
of order that fails not; earth, sea, and sky were
one vast wonderland, and every nook and cranny
the home of myth, and haunted by the goblins
and fairies with whom man in his ignorance
peopled them. Moreover, as the tradition became
older, so old that none could tell whence or how
it came, it was revered as the gift of heaven; they
of whose deeds it spake loomed large and grand,
and were lifted to the dwelling of the gods. And
thus the words themselves became sacred words;
their care fell in the course of time to a special

class, who committed them to memory and had great honour paid them as keepers of the treasured history. Wonderful as it may seem to us who have so many books to aid our memories, and have to crowd those memories with so much about so many things, the entire traditions of tribes, the ballads and stories which make up long epics like the Iliad, the Volsungs and other famous poems were preserved, word for word, during hundreds of years by the memory of man. In recent proof of this, the great epic of the Finns called the Kalevala,[1] which contains some twenty thousand lines, has within the last forty years been taken down from the mouths of peasants and fishermen, old women and young folks, by a learned man, who with untiring zeal wandered, year after year, from cabin to cabin through the length and breadth of Finland, and whose labours had

---

[1] It may not be out of place here to say that if the needful leisure can be secured, I hope, in conjunction with the accomplished translator of previous books of mine into Swedish, to make some tales from this beautiful epic known to young folk in England.

great reward, for when he came to piece together the fragments he had thus gathered, they formed one noble whole which scholars pore over with keenest interest and to which children listen with delight.   Again, there are Brahmans who make it the sole business of their lives to commit to memory the sacred hymns of the Veda, and this they do with such care that Prof. Max Müller says where any question arises as to the exact language of the verses, he would rather trust the memories of these men than any written or printed copy.

Such then, in brief outline, is the mode in which knowledge of the past has come down ; and as, owing to the very air in which they were born, the traditions are crowded with legend and miracle, the work of our time has been to seek for the facts within them, never forgetting that the legends themselves are of value as witnesses to the thoughts and beliefs of the people among whom they arose.   When we reflect how hard it is to get at the truth about any event near at hand, because every one will describe it in his own way, we shall the better understand how much more this applies to events which happened hundreds and thousands of years ago in other lands, for an account of which we have to trust to histories which have grown out of stories held in the memories of unlearned men, ready to believe whatever they were told. It should make us careful not to draw too hard and fast conclusions from records so uncertain; still more should it teach us the unwisdom of building systems of religion upon them, and of condemning those who seek a surer foundation. Now it was once commonly believed, and the notion still prevails among the unlearned, that whatever histories might have to be re-written in the light of new knowledge, that of the Jews would not, because it was written by men guided by the spirit of God, and therefore kept free from error. But we now know that it grew as all recorded history has grown, centuries passing before its various books were, after many alterations and additions, gathered into one collection; that the writers of the earliest portions lived

hundreds of years after the events which they
narrate and that they had to depend entirely on
tradition.   They knew nothing about the primitive state of their own and other races, neither had
they any idea of the close relation of their several
histories, or of the witness which these bear to
the commingling of one people with another;
while instead of taking pains to get at the facts,
and let them speak for themselves, they warped
them to support foregone conclusions.   The chief
among these were that Israel was Jehovah's
chosen people, to which the call of Abraham,
the Exodus, and the conquest of Canaan witnessed, and that whatever trouble had fallen
on the tribes was due to their faithlessness to
that god and to the law which he had given by
Moses.

Based upon these events, there had arisen
before the time of David the idea of a "covenant," which Jehovah was said to have made
with the Israelites through the patriarch Abraham, and by which they were to receive the
blessing and guidance of that god in return for

obeying his commandments and keeping his law.

The priests, who were the earliest compilers of Jewish history, therefore made it their first care to collect from the scattered records, the traditions, and old customs, all that related to this law, adding thereto such accounts of the early history of the tribes as had been preserved among them. It was claimed for the ritual, with a certain amount of truth, that it had formed part of the legislation of Moses, and this at least had the double effect of securing its acceptance by the people as binding upon them, and of upholding the importance of the priests, without whose aid none could observe the " covenant " aright.

Politics and religion being combined in the Israelitish commonwealth, and not things apart, as among other nations, its records are not like theirs, mere annals of events, but written to edify more than to inform ; Hebrew history was the Hebrew Bible—a fact to be always kept before us for the right understanding of the Old Testament, and in view of which we do not the less, but rather the more, carefully, sift and test its statements.

To gain knowledge in itself and for itself is profitless as the hoarding up of money; to be useful, it must be employed, and when the facts about things are reached the next course is to find out their relation to other facts and their meaning. Otherwise history, which is now our subject, fulfils no higher purpose than a novel to amuse us, for it is of use only as we are able through it to trace the causes which brought certain events to pass that have quickened or retarded man's progress in knowledge, goodness, and freedom. And one result of placing the histories of races side by side is to show how much each, although unlike in detail, has in common, and how the mind of man has everywhere worked in the same way, in language-making, myth-making, worship, etc., as everywhere he has at starting made shift with the same rude implements. Seeing this, it is not possible to look on the world's history, any

more than on the world itself, with the eyes of
our forefathers. To them it was the centre of
all things, even sun, moon, and stars being lesser
bodies, and made to give it light. To us it is a
tiny ball, member of one system among vaster
systems ; each bound to each as parts of a great
whole, a *uni*verse, as it has been called in full-
ness of meaning to which science is ever adding.
To them its history seemed centred in one race
chosen alone of God, favoured beyond all
others ; to us no race stands by itself, but is also
a part of a great whole, so interwoven with it
that, whether it will or no, it cannot live to itself,
Accadian, Semite, Aryan, all intermingling and
treading the same slow and slippery path, on the
same mother earth, from the base to the noble.
That is why, in this outline sketch of Jewish
history, we may not pass in silence over the
place of the Jews in the human family, and
the influences which went before them and surrounded them, taking us, as these do, into Egypt
and the lands about the Euphrates, to gather
from beneath mounds and tombs and on temple-

walls the long-hidden story of the debt which Jew, Greek, and Roman, and through these the world, owes to those ancient empires as teachers of science, art, law, and religion.

Now what is true of the race is true of each member of it; for no human life can be rightly understood apart from knowledge of the age and country in which it was spent, and of the race from whence it sprang; for which reason, before giving any sketch of Jesus, I am tracing the history of his people to the time when he lived—an account the more needful because, as will be seen, the facts about him are so scanty and uncertain.

To resume our story. David was succeeded by his favourite son Solomon, in whose reign B.C. the kingdom reached the height of its 993? glory. While he did not neglect to make its borders and capital secure, he formed friendships with neighbouring kings, and the peaceful state of the nation permitted the people to devote themselves to commerce and the arts.

Trade was carried on with Egypt; ships, manned by Phœnicians, for the Israelites were no sailors, voyaged to Arabia and the mouths of the Indus, returning laden with the rich products and strange creatures which, with their Sanskrit names, are recorded in the book of Kings. After the custom of the East, Solomon had many wives, the chief among these being a daughter of the Pharaoh for whom he built a splendid palace in Jerusalem. A more notable building than this was the small but magnificent temple which, by means of the treasure which his father had left, he erected to Jehovah on Mount Moriah. It was of stone, lined with the fragrant cedar-wood of Lebanon, and, since images of living things were forbidden by the second commandment, enriched with carvings of flowers, fruit, and various symbols of nature-worship, wrought by skilled workmen from Tyre, and doubtless borrowed from their religion. After the manner of Phœnician temples, it was divided into two parts, in one of which, the "holy," an altar and table for the shewbread was placed, and in the

B. C.
990?

other, the "holy of holies," into which the high
priest only could enter, the ark was kept, but
hidden even from his sight.   Like the innermost
place in Egyptian shrines, there was no image
of the god, but above the ark two human-headed
bulls with wings, called cherubim, were put as
guardians.   These were probably borrowed from
the Phœnicians, although figures somewhat re-
sembling them appear in pictures of the Egyptian
arks ; indeed, they all belong to the great class
of fabled beasts, dragons, harpies, and sphinxes,
which abound in classic myth ; the "cherub," or
Greek "gryps," surviving among us in the
"griffin," half eagle, half lion, often seen carved
on castle gates and painted on coats-of-arms.

We must not think of this temple of Solomon
as at all like Christian cathedrals or Mohammadan mosques, for its main purpose was as
a place of sacrifice, and its arrangements approached nearer to those of a slaughter-house
than a place of worship.   The carcases of
animals sacrificed were laid on an altar in the
outer court in front of the temple, and near this

altar was a great basin called "the brazen sea" for cleansing the priests, for whose use a number of rooms were built round the temple.

The erection of this beautiful building in place of the sacred tent added greatly to the power of the priesthood, who had already flocked to Jerusalem from local shrines. As priests of the ark, those who claimed to be of the "house" or family of Aaron had the chief place, and below them the other priests, singers, and temple servants, ranked according to the duties given them.

But Solomon also raised temples to the gods of his foreign wives, and the general tendency of his intercourse with other nations was to efface whatever made Israel unlike them. It is during his reign that a class of men appear who were neither priests nor prophets, who spake no lofty thoughts moving men to noble endeavour, yet whose words carried weight. They are called "sages," or the "wise," and were gifted with the power of treating questions that lay near men's "business and bosoms" in a telling way, putting maxims of worldly wisdom, good counsel, and manners, here and there dealing with the higher aims of life, in pointed, pithy sayings, in proverb, and in fable. All races, however barbarous, have their stock of proverbs, but the East is especially their home, and their crisp, short sentences catch the ear when wordy preachings pass unheeded. Like our own many "wise saws," like the maxims of the Egyptians, whose influence in Solomon's reign must be taken into account, they were caught up, and lived among the people until they were gathered into the book of Proverbs and like Hebrew writings both inside and outside the Bible. Tradition placed Solomon, the native power of whose mind is undoubted, as the first of the sages. It is said that "his songs were a thousand and five," that he spake three thousand proverbs; also that he had knowledge of all trees, from the stately cedar to the plant in the crannied wall, and of all beasts, birds, and fishes; his fame being so great that people, among them the queen of the Sabeans, flocked from every part to hear him.[1]

[1] 1 Kings iv. 32-24.

Although the book of Proverbs and other
books which bear his name were not compiled
till long after his time, they may preserve some
of his sayings, which, as coming from the lips
of a king, would be the more heeded and repeated from mouth to mouth.

Among the most famous of the stories of
Solomon's wisdom which survive in Arabian
and Jewish traditions, is the following from the
book of Kings,[1] concerning two women who once
came before him into the hall of justice :—

One said, " I and that woman lived in the same
house and each of us bore a male child. In the
night the son of this woman died. She rose,
laid her dead son at my breast, and took my
living child to her bosom. When I woke I had
a dead child in my arms, but in the morning I
saw that this child was not the son which I had
borne." The other woman said, " No, the living
boy is my son, and thine is the dead child."

Solomon then asked for a sword and said,.
" Cut the living child into two parts, and give

[1] I Kings iii. 16-28.

half to the one and half to the other." Then
tenderness for her child arose in the mother of
the living child and she said, "O my lord, give
her the living child and slay it not;" but the
other said, "Let it be neither mine nor thine,
but divide it." Then the king said, "Give her
who prays me to spare it the living child, she is
its mother."

Among the stories magnifying the wisdom
of kings and sages common in the East,[1] there
is one told of Gautama the Buddha, which so
strikingly resembles the foregoing, that I cannot
resist quoting it, the less so as it will be new to
many readers.

A woman came with her infant to a pool in
order to bathe, and, leaving him, on the bank,
went down into the water. As soon as she had
done so, a wicked woman seeing the child and
wishing to have it, said, "Friend, is this pretty
baby yours? May I nurse it?" The mother
replied, "Why not?" upon which the evil-
hearted woman took the infant, and after nursing

[1] Cf. Denny's *Folk Lore of China*, p. 139.

him a little while, ran off with him. The mother
pursued screaming for her child, while the false
woman boldly cried, "When didst thou own a
child? It is mine." Whilst the quarrel went
on, they came near the Buddha's hall, and he,
hearing the noise, asked what was the matter.
Being told this he said, "Will you abide by my
judgment?" to which they both agreed. He
then had a line drawn on the ground, and the
child laid upon it, and telling the false mother
to seize its arms, and the real mother its legs,
said, " He shall be son of her who pulls him
over the line." The wicked woman agreed, for
she was the stronger, but the mother seeing that
the child must suffer pain, said, weeping, " Let
her take the boy, I cannot bear to see him hurt."
Then the Buddha asked of those who stood
around, "Whose hearts are tender to the children?" They replied, " O Pandit, mothers' hearts
are tender!" Then he said, " Which think you
is the mother?" and all answered, "She who
let it go is its mother." He then restored the
child to her, and sent her glad-hearted away.

But with all his acuteness Solomon was not wise enough to study the well-being of his people. The barbaric splendour of his court far exceeded that of David's, and ill contrasted with the modest state of Saul ; moreover it was maintained, like all selfish ease, at the cost of suffering and undue toil on the part of the many. Great discontent arose at the burdens laid upon the people in heavy taxes and forced labour, and the feeling was stronger among the tribes of the north, who had no share in the glory they upheld, palace and temple being in Jerusalem. Indeed, the ties between north and south had never been strong. They had been drawn together under one king, but the tribal feeling remained, and when David, who was of the house of Judah, was elected, Ephraim was jealous, for the "judges" from Joshua to Saul had come from the house of Joseph.

The upshot was that when Solomon died, the kingdom which the able hands of Saul and David had upreared fell asunder, never to be joined again, the immediate cause

B. C. 953?

being that Rehoboam, his son, having refused the prayer of the people for lighter taxes, nearly all the tribes revolted, and choosing their leader Jeroboam as king, set up the kingdom of Ephraim, or Israel, which comprised the larger and richer portion of Canaan, while the remnant who remained faithful to Rehoboam, barely two tribes, formed the smaller but longer-lived kingdom of Judah.

The separation was followed by wars in which Judah was defeated, Jerusalem being pillaged by the Egyptians, who were friendly to Jeroboam, but now and again the two kingdoms were allied. B. C. 949?

The annals of Israel are stormy; there being no settled line of kings, one warrior after another snatched the crown by force, creating frequent turmoil and civil war. There were disputes, too, of another sort which concern us more, because they show the general state of the people, of whom far too little account has, until our own day, been taken in history-books. These disputes were about the gods, and they prove into

II

what widespread neglect the laws of Moses had
fallen. As a substitute for the sacred temple,
which remained to Judah, Jeroboam founded a
priesthood and set up golden bulls, old symbols
of Jehovah-worship, at Dan and Bethel; but
among the kings who followed him, doing "evil
in the sight of Jehovah," was Ahab, a
man of weak will, who at the counsel of
his wife Jezebel, a Tyrian princess, gave foremost place to the Phœnician god Baal. The
prophets, of whom, though not idle, we hear but
little since the days of Samuel, now came boldly
forward to denounce with untempered zeal the
faithlessness of the king, who, goaded by his
queen, had them hunted and slain, and the altars
of Jehovah thrown down. Chief among them was
Elijah, a fierce and fearless man, who rebuked
the king, and in the end won him back to service
of Jehovah. Vivid sketches of this powerful
prophet, of his courage and sufferings, of the
miracles he was believed to have worked, were
preserved in the traditions of the nation; like
many other heroes he disappears in a cloud of

B. C.
875 ?

legend, carried in fiery chariot by a whirlwind
to the skies, and when, many centuries after, a
preacher in the prophet's garb of sheepskin
mantle fastened by leathern girdle, and uttering
the prophet's message, appeared in Judæa, men
called to mind the old story and the words of
Malachi,[1] and said that Elijah had come to earth
again.

The prophets, as the life of this man and
others show, were not merely students and
writers, tracing the footsteps of Jehovah in their
nation's history, and recounting the story in
glowing words, but men of action, moving in
affairs of the state, making their voice heard in
its councils, in the choice of kings, in questions
of peace or war. And so we find them delivering their message, "the word of Jehovah," not
only in the open street, temple-court, and market-
place, but in the palace itself and the houses of
the great. The earlier among them were not
"monotheists," or believers in one god; Jehovah
was to them Israel's god, but they did not dis-

[1] Mal. iv. 5.

pute the claims which other nations made on behalf of gods of their own, and it is not until the time of the later prophets that we find a higher belief reached, that "all the gods of the nations are idols, but Jehovah made the heavens."

As a class, however, from the time that Samuel formed them into companies, they tower far above the priests. The two had little in common. The duty of the priests began and ended with fulfilment of the details of the law, and, so long as they were employed to perform the ceremonies, it mattered not much to them to what god they were performed. While they were busying themselves concerning the correct mode of carrying out rules about rites, as if the well-being of a man's life depended on sacrificing "the two kidneys and the fat upon them, which is by the flanks and caul above the liver,"[1] the prophet was insisting on conduct, on pure thoughts, words and deeds, pointing out to the heedless the meaning of things past

[1] Lev. iii. 10.

and present, and the significance of human life, asking in language that moves us as a solemn chant—

"Wherewithal shall I come before Jehovah? shall I come before him with burnt offerings, with calves of a year old? Will Jehovah be pleased with thousands of rams or with ten thousand rivers of oil?

"Shall I give my firstborn for my transgression, the fruit of my body for the sin of my soul?

"He hath shewed thee, O man, what is good ; and what doth Jehovah require of thee but to do justly, and to love mercy, and to walk humbly before thy god." [1]

"Bring no more vain oblations ; incense is an abomination to me ; the new moons and sabbaths, the calling of assemblies, I cannot away with ; . . . . they are a trouble unto me ; I am weary to hear them.

"Wash you, make you clean ; put away the evil of your doings from before mine eyes ; cease to do evil ; learn to do well." [2]

"Is it such a fast that I have chosen? a day for a man to afflict his soul? is it to bow down his head as a bulrush, and to spread sackcloth and ashes under him?

"Wilt thou call this a fast, and an acceptable day to Jehovah? Is not this the fast that I have chosen? to loose the bands of wickedness, to undo the heavy burdens, and to let the oppressed go free, that ye break every yoke?

"Is it not to deal thy bread to the hungry, and that

---

[1] Micah vi. 6-8.   [2] Isa. i. 13-16.

thou bring the poor that are cast out to thy house? when thou seest the naked, that thou cover him ; and that thou hide not thyself from thine own flesh ? " [1]

The prophets at last brought about the fall of the house of Ahab, seating upon the throne a king faithful to Jehovah, and from this time the chief place of that god was assured. The kingdom reached the height of its brief glory under Jeroboam II., during whose reign the great prophet-reformers, Amos, Hosea, and others, flourished. By this time, however, the " schools of the prophets " had sadly fallen off; unworthy, self-seeking men and those who caught at an excuse for shirking honest work had joined them, and the danger (fatal above all to the prophetic gift, the essence of which was its unfixed and fitful action,) of its professors becoming a caste and stiffening into a class, crept in and worked their ruin. Amos and his friends stood aloof from these companies, and were as one against the many ; their fervid appeals found slight response among a people whose glaring vices were fast sapping

[1] Isa. lviii. 5–7.

the strength needed to withstand the restless foes around, ever watchful to pounce upon the weak. Among the nations then making rapid advance was Assyria, rising a second time to power, and throwing its shadow over the land as its armies moved westward on their conquering march. Before them great kingdoms of the East had fallen; the Syrians, who stood in their path, had been mowed down; the outlying tribes of Israel subdued and, after the custom of the victors, the wealthier carried away captive. Samaria only now lay in the way of the Assyrian army, and the folly of king Hosea in breaking faith with Assyria and leaning towards Egypt, led to Israel's overthrow. Samaria, his capital, was besieged, and being strongly placed, held out for three years, when disease and hunger made its defenders yield. The king and the greater number of the people were carried to a remote part of Assyria, from whence they never returned, causing the hapless fate of the ten "lost tribes," who were scattered among stranger races, to give rise to the wildest guesses;

eccentric persons, ignorant of the commonest facts of history, appearing at intervals to this day to contend that now one race, now another, be it English[1] or Red Indian or Irish, are the descendants of the Israelites! The vacant places were filled by colonists from Assyria, who, mixing with the remnant left behind, formed the "Samaritans," still a distinct people in Palestine, but now dwindled to less than one hundred and fifty in number.

Thus the northern kingdom, after a troubled existence of about two hundred and fifty years, came to an end, and from that time Jewish history is centred in the southern kingdom.

For the first century and a half the annals of Judah are dry and scanty. There was less of turmoil than in Israel, owing to a settled line of kings and a fixed centre of unity and worship; but the story of the state of religion is well-nigh the same. All over the country there were

---

[1] A monthly magazine exists for the advocacy of this craze, and during the present year Exeter Hall has been the scene of public debates on the question "Are Englishmen Israelites?"

scattered remnants of the Canaanites who clung to the gods of their fathers, sacrificing "on every high hill, and under every green tree," and the result was that Jehovah was regarded only as one among these; images to Molech and other deities filled the streets and glittered from the housetops, and in the temple itself altars were raised to the sun and moon.

The kings leaned now to one party, now to another, the priests taught for hire, false prophets divined for money; the people loved to have it so, and the only bright spot is the faithful witness of the great prophets.

One of the chief among these, Isaiah, lived about the court and temple, and his writings, apart from the exceeding beauty in which their lofty thoughts are expressed, are of value for the insight which they afford into life and manners in Judæa above two thousand five hundred years ago.

His rare, deep sense of the purity and holiness of his god made him the more keenly awake to the evils around, and the more severe, yet

sorrowful, in his rebuke. In scornful words he
gives us graphic sketches of the vain triflers, of
the women who "walk with stretched-forth neck
and leering eyes, mincing as they go, and
tinkling with their anklets,"[1] the main thought
of whose trivial life is what they shall wear ; of
the men of purposeless life, or with bad purpose ;
of those who, regardless of the merciful laws of
old, seize the land, lay " field to field," grind the
poor, prey on the widow and the orphan ; of
the false guides who call evil good, and darkness
light ; of the soothsayers who gull the foolish
and overawe the timid in pretending to rule their
fate by charm and spell, or to read the future in
dreams and stars, and, in imitating the "squeak-
ing and gibbering" of ghosts, to call back the
spirits of the dead.

The watchful eye of Isaiah saw in the fall of
Israel a forecast of the fate that awaited Judah.
In the signs unheeded by the giddy crowd he
read the anger of Jehovah, and the approach
apace of punishment for sin ; yet his hope was

[1] Ch. iii. 16.

strong that the anger of God would not endure, and that the glory of old would return. Nor he alone, for among all the prophets, from the ninth century downwards, the same hope stirs their pens to bright pictures of the future. It is not easy to fix the exact meaning of words written so long ago, the more so as figures of speech enter largely into them, but much confusion is avoided by bearing in mind this ruling idea of both priest and prophet—that the reign of David was the golden period of Israel's history, which would return with the advent of a king descended from David, and born in Bethlehem, his native place.

As thus Micah :—

" From thee, O Bethlehem Ephratah, though thou be small among the thousands of Judah, out of thee shall come forth one who shall rule over Israel, one whose descent is from ancient times. He shall stand and feed in the strength of Jehovah, in the majesty of his name ; his greatness shall spread to the ends of the earth, and in his time shall be peace. When the Assyrians come into the land we shall send seven shepherds to meet them ; yea, we shall send eight princes, and they shall waste the land of Assyria with the sword. Then shall the remnant of Jacob be amongst the peoples like dew upon the herbs ;

amongst great nations as a lion among the beasts of the forest." [1]

Thus Isaiah :—

" There shall come forth a rod from the stock of Jesse (the father of David) and a branch shall grow out of his roots ; and the spirit of Jehovah shall rest upon him, a spirit of wisdom and understanding, a spirit of counsel and might, a spirit of knowledge and the fear of Jehovah . . . with justice shall he judge the helpless and give sentence to the meek of the land . . . and with the breath of his lips shall he slay the wicked ; justice shall be the girdle of his loins, and faithfulness the girdle of his reins. Then shall the wolf dwell with the lamb, and the leopard lie down with the kid, and the calf and the young lion and the fatling together, and a little child shall lead them. . . . They shall not hurt nor destroy in all my holy mountain, for the land shall be full of the knowledge of Jehovah as the waters cover the sea." [2]

Thus Jeremiah and others, picturing the union of the scattered tribes :—

" Behold the days come, saith Jehovah, that I will raise unto David a righteous branch and a king shall reign and prosper, and shall execute judgment and justice in the earth. In his days Judah shall be saved, and Israel shall dwell in safety, and this is his name whereby he shall be called, Jehovah is our righteousness." [3]

" In that day will I raise up the tabernacle of David

---

[1] Micah v. 2, ff.   [2] Isa. xi. 1-9.   [3] Jer. xxiii. 5, 6.

that is fallen, and close up the breaches thereof, and I will build it as in the days of old. That they may possess the remnant of Edom, and of all the heathen, which are called by my name, saith Jehovah who doeth this." [1]

"Afterward shall the sons of Israel return, and seek Jehovah their god, and David their king, and shall fear Jehovah and his goodness in the latter days." [2]

"Rejoice, O daughter of Zion ! Be glad, O daughter of Jerusalem ! Behold thy king comes to thee, righteous and victorious, a kindly man riding on an ass, a she ass's colt. Then shall the war-chariots be cast out of Ephraim and the horsemen from Jerusalem ; the weapons of war shall be broken, and he shall proclaim peace to the heathen. He shall rule from sea to sea, from the Euphrates to the end of the earth." [3]

And to quote Isaiah once more :—

"Thine eyes shall view the king in his beauty ; they shall see a land that reacheth afar off. . . . Thou shalt view Zion the city of our solemnities : thine eyes shall see Jerusalem an easy habitation, a tent that wandereth not, whose nails are never drawn out, neither are any of the cords thereof rent, but where Jehovah shall be for us a place of broad rivers and streams whereon shall go no galley with oars, neither shall stately ship pass thereby . . . and no inhabitant shall say, I am sick : the people that dwell therein shall be forgiven their sin." [4]

The hopes which the prophets thus express

---

[1] Amos ix. 11, 12.   [2] Hosea iii. 5.
[3] Zech. ix. 9, 10.   [4] Isa. xxxiii. 17–24.

concerning the future of their nation are known as the "Messianic," from the Hebrew word for "anointed," which was applied to kings and priests, on whom the holy oil was poured, and hence the king who was to spring from the house of David is sometimes spoken of, not only as "son of David," but as "Messiah," or the "anointed one." The form which such an expectation took varied at different times in different minds; in some it was tinged with sadness, yet loftier and wider than among the prophets quoted above; later still, as will be seen, it was wild and tawdry, but one feature is common to all—the belief in a better that lies ahead, not behind, as some have vainly thought; in a Golden Age, vision of the poets and seers of every land, for which holy and earnest men have longed and laboured, and which, in this world, where they have waged such splendid fight, has been the source of all patience, all noble doing. And though the dreams of Hebrew patriots and prophets never came to pass in the form in which their fancy had shaped them, they are being slowly

fulfilled in larger ways wherever gentle hands
are ministering and human voices are uplifted
against wrong.

> " The years are slow, the vision tarrieth long,
> And far the end may be ;
> But one by one the ancient fiends of wrong
> Go out and leave earth free ! "

Many piles of books have been written, many
millions of sermons preached, about this Messianic hope, but all that need be said at present
is comprised in these few words, to which a
remark or two should be added, as aid in
clearing away a crowd of false notions about
the meaning of the Jewish scriptures, and
chiefly of the prophets' writings.

People are apt to forget that for the understanding of the books which make up the Old
Testament, and indeed, the New Testament as
well, no slight knowledge of ancient history, of
Eastern customs and modes of speech is needful,
and the difficulty is increased by the changes
which they have undergone in translation out
of languages whose nice shades of expression

cannot well be reproduced. Yet these books, as to the meaning of which widely different opinions exist among the learned, are, with injury to themselves and confusion to their readers, scattered broadcast and placed in the hands of unlettered persons, both young and old, as if some charm or magical power attended them by which they could be made clear at a glance. And what might have been made clear with small effort on the reader's part is too often so ill-arranged and maltreated as to quite hinder this, for in their eagerness to support foregone conclusions, Christians in receiving the books comprising the Old Testament from the Jews, have so dealt with them as to entirely misrepresent their meaning. For example, the writings of the prophets, with which we are now dealing, have been sorted regardless of the time when they were penned; placed according to length, and not according to date or importance; the words of men who lived many years apart have been mixed together, and in cutting up the books into chapters, which often wrongly " divide

the word of truth," tables of contents have been
added which are utterly false, and which, allowed
to remain in Bibles issued to this day, betray
wilful ignorance. One glaring instance of this
occurs in the chapter-headings of a poem, called
the "Song of Solomon," the subject of which is
the virtue of pure and constant love. A beautiful young shepherdess who is betrothed to a
shepherd is taken from her village home in fair
Galilee, where the "vines flourish, the tender
grapes appear, and the pomegranates bud," to
the court of Solomon, where she resists temptation, and, pining ever for her home and true love,
is at last sent back by the king and marries him
to whom she had given her heart. The poem
would never have been admitted among the
Jewish scriptures, and indeed was tardily received, but that the caprice of the rabbis saw the
love of God for Israel set forth in its figures of
speech; and some of the early Christian writers,
who were slaves to the wildest fancies, "explained" it as designed to exhibit the love of
Jesus Christ for the Church which they believed

I

he founded, even interpreting the closing verse,
where the bride says, "Make haste, my beloved,
and be thou like to a roe or to a young hart
upon the mountains of spices," as "the Church
praying for Christ's coming!"

The same writers, in dealing with the prophetical books, were hampered by the old notion
that Jehovah made known future events through
seers; and assuming that the foretellings of these
men concerning a "Messiah" or "Christ" (from
Greek "Christos" = anointed) were fulfilled in
Jesus of Nazareth, forced a meaning disputed
by the Jews to this day, and altogether foreign
to the books themselves, into the whole of
the Old Testament. Passage after passage from
Genesis to Malachi was quoted as support-
ing that notion; whereas the simple truth is
that throughout those books there is not a
single verse which, taken in its plain meaning,
and not torn away from the writings to which it
belongs, can be shown to foretell the birth, life,
or death of Jesus, or indeed any other event
which took place long after each writer's time.

Such harmful and unfair use of these ancient writings will go on until they are re-arranged, issued with truthful notes and comments as to their origin and meaning, and read in the light of knowledge of the times when they were composed, and of the events either happening or which it needed only keen foresight to see must happen. Then will their real value and peerless beauty be seen, and the danger, which all devout minds desire to avert, namely, that people, angry at having been misled, will cast them aside as fables and vague talk of bewildered dreamers, pass away. Because it will be seen that the greatness of the prophets could never be in writing down word-puzzles in which lurk dates and mystic hints about the birth of men centuries hence, the fall of kingdoms and the end of the world ;[1] but in setting forth the certain doom of the people and nation that forget God, and the beauty of the steps of the

[1] "It is not in an arbitrary 'decree of God,' but in the nature of man, that a veil shuts down on the facts of to-morrow, for the soul will not have us read any other cipher than that of cause and effect."—Emerson, *The Over-Soul.*

preachers of righteousness as " heralds of good tidings."

Returning to Isaiah, we find him comforting king Ahaz, when dismayed at the approach of the armies of Syria and Israel, with the promise that Jehovah would give him a sign of their defeat in the birth of some child (perhaps one expected by the king or by the prophet himself), who should be named " Immanuel," meaning " God with us," and declaring that before such child was old enough to know good from evil, Judah should be free from danger.[1]

The piety and promise of the youth of Hezekiah, son of Ahaz, over whom Isaiah rejoiced, giving him after the manner of the East, long and high-sounding titles,[2] was fulfilled when he came to the throne, for he swept away the

---

[1] Isa. vii. 14, ff.

[2] " Unto us a child has been born, a son given us, government shall be laid upon his shoulders ; and men shall call him ' Wonderful-Counsellor, Mighty-God, Everlasting-Father, Prince of Peace,' for the increase of the government and for peace without end upon the throne of David and over his kingdom." Isa. ix. 6 7.

pillars and images of the gods, and the altars on
"high places." The chief event of that time
was the sudden destruction of a vast number of
the Assyrian army by one of the awful plagues
which at times desolate the East. The Syrian
nations had rebelled against Sennacherib   B. C.
and been worsted. Hezekiah had dared   701 ?
to resist him, and now, as he approached to
punish—

> "The might of the Gentiles, untouched by the sword,
> Had melted like snow at the blast of the Lord."

The event brought vividly before the Judæans
the deliverance of old, when their fathers saw
the Egyptians dead upon the seashore, and the
psalms of that time, as the forty-sixth and
seventy-sixth, witness to the impulse which it
gave to the worship of Jehovah, who, in smiting
the invader, had shown his care for the city in
whose holy place he dwelt "between the cherubim." So they sang—

> "In Judah is God known,
>   His name is great in Israel :
> For at Salem he made his tabernacle,

And his resting place in Zion.
There brake he the arrows of the bow,
The shield, the sword, and the battle !
The proud were stripped, they slept their sleep,
And the men of might found not their hands ;
At thy rebuke, O God of Jacob,
Both chariot and horse lie fallen."

But the danger over, the people backslided, and it was not until the reign of Josiah that a more lasting reform came about. It appears that while some repairs were going on in the temple, the chief priest, more likely by design than accident, found a roll, " the book of the law of Jehovah given to Moses."[1]   This was taken to the king, who, when he learnt what judgments were written in it against idol worship and neglect of the commandments, rent his clothes in token of grief, and ordered the heads of the people to be assembled that the book might be read to them.   This done, he made known his will that Jehovah only should be worshipped, and then began a course of relentless persecution. Images and altars were once more thrown down, the

[1] 2 Chron. xxxiv. 14.

priests who had served them, the wizards and
the soothsayers, slain, and a great feast called the
Passover kept in solemn splendour. Some writers
think that by the " book of the law " the first five
books of the Bible are meant, as the material
for these, which as we saw was collected by the
priests in the time of the early kings, had been
some century before the reign of Josiah worked
up by the prophets, who, beginning the history
with the days of the patriarchs, brought it down
to the conquest of Canaan. Others, with more
reason on their side, think that it meant the fifth
book only, Deuteronomy, the contents of which
apply so clearly to the evils which had long
prevailed.

It was at this time that the second of the
notable invasions of Judah occurred. Great
movements of races, cramped for room and eager
for plunder, were taking place, and among the
most warlike and lawless were stranger hordes
called the Scythians,[1] who greatly harassed
the land as they rode towards Egypt, but who

[1] Cf. *The Psalms*, by Four Friends, p. 125.

were at last beaten back or bought off. But
a more fruitful cause of sorrow arose through
the death of Josiah. Against the advice of the
prophet Jeremiah and that monarch himself, he
had opposed the passage of the king of Egypt
on his march to the Euphrates against the
Assyrians, whose power was on the wane, and,
wounded in battle, died before he could reach
Jerusalem. The nation mourned his loss, the
prophet "Jeremiah lamented for him, and all the
singing men and singing women to this day,"
wrote the chronicler. The faith of the faithful
was shaken ; in their despair and bewilderment
some of the people ascribed the trouble to neglect of the older gods, and the worship of these
was revived, while the reckless gave way to
excesses of sin, causing the prophet to pour forth
the sorrow of his soul ![1]

"Oh that my head were waters, and mine eyes a fountain of tears, that I might weep day and night for the
slain of the daughters of my people. . . . Oh that I had
in the wilderness a lodging place of wayfaring men ; that

---

[1] Jer. ix. 1, ff. ; viii. 20.

I might leave my people, and go from them ! for they go from evil to evil, and weary themselves to commit wickedness. . . . When I would comfort myself against grief my heart is faint within me. The harvest is past, the summer is ended, and we are not saved."

Jerusalem will become "a heap and den of dragons ; the cities of Judah desolate, without an inhabitant." Assyria received its death-blow at the hands of the Medes (an Aryan race) and the Babylonians, and in these rising powers Jeremiah saw the scourge wherewith Jehovah would punish the Judæans. They were enraged at his gloomy forebodings ; they mocked and persecuted him —as in every age its prophets are stoned—threw him into prison, and shrank from killing him only because he spoke in the "name of Jehovah." And yet while uttering the desponding truths which have made "jeremiad " a by-word, he told them that when the "seventy" years during which, speaking in round and sacred numbers, they were to be exiled from fatherland had passed, Jehovah would gather them again to Judæa.

"After those days I will put my law in their inward parts and write it in their hearts, and will be their god, and they shall be my people. And they shall teach no more every man his neighbour and every man his brother, saying, ' Know Jehovah,' for they shall all know me, from the least of them to the greatest."[1]

Not in what they have, but in what they are, is their life :—

" Let not the wise man glory in his wisdom, neither let the mighty man glory in his might, let not the rich man glory in his riches ; but let him that glorieth glory in this, that he understandeth and knoweth me, that I am Jehovah exercising lovingkindness, judgment, and righteousness in the earth, for in these things I delight, saith Jehovah."[2]

Among the Hebrew writings called forth at a time when men's hearts were failing them and the success of the wicked puzzled them, the book of Job may perhaps be placed. I say perhaps, because many learned men think it was not written till a later time, but its exact date and authorship can never be known. Neither do we know to what happy chance a work so unlike any of them was admitted into the Jewish scriptures, enough that it has preserved an ancient poem of wondrous beauty and majesty.

[1] Jer. xxxi. 33, 34.   [2] Jer. ix. 23, 24.

The riddle which it seeks to solve is that world-wide one which once so greatly perplexed man : why the good often suffer and why the wicked often prosper ; and the author, instead of writing a tedious treatise, puts the matter in the form of a story or " drama," *setting forth action*, as that word means.

There was a man named Job, who lived in the land of Uz. He was very rich, blessed with " seven" sons and " three" daughters; and there was none so upright as he in all the earth, or so kind to his fellows : "when the ear heard him, then it blest him . . . and he caused the widow's heart to sing for joy." One day when the angels of Jehovah appeared before him, Satan, whose duties were to act as a spy on men's doings, taunted him that Job did not serve him for naught, adding that if he were stripped of all that he had, " he would curse thee to thy face." So Jehovah, to test the truth of this, gave Satan full power over Job short of taking his life. Blow after blow then fell upon the accused man, robbers seized his cattle and killed his servants, death smote his children, and he himself was made loathsome with leprosy. Stripped of everything, his wife bade him curse Jehovah and die, but he said, " Shall we receive good at his hand, and not evil also ?" and would not "sin with his lips." Then three old friends, hearing of his troubles, came to him, and after sitting in silence "seven days and seven nights," Job, moved by a sympathy the more intense because unspoken, poured out his grief and cursed the day of his birth. His friends, taking the common view of the matter that if ill befalls a man he deserves it, saw in all Job's sufferings the just punishment of Jehovah for some sin, for said one, " Who ever perished being innocent, and when were the righteous cut off?" But Job, knowing that he had done no wrong, denied that his affliction was a proof of sin, and complaining that the power of Jehovah is used to crush him, upbraids his god : " Is it good unto thee that thou shouldst oppress and despise the work of thine own hands. . . . Thou knowest that I am not wicked," and in touching pathos appeals to the shortness of life :

"Cease then, let me alone, that I may take comfort a little, before I go whence I shall not return,
even to the land of darkness and the shadow of
death ; a land of darkness without any order and
where the light is as darkness." He takes comfort in the thought that one near to him as kin
will arise and avenge his wrongs [1] :—

> "I know that my Goel lives
> And that he shall arise, the last, upon the earth,"

a passage which, with those following it, has,
oddly enough, been quoted as referring to Jesus
of Nazareth, and as a proof of the resurrection of
the body !

A younger friend now appears, and urging that
suffering is sometimes sent for man's good, re-
proves Job for vindicating himself instead of
justifying "the ways of God to man."

So the debate runs on, Job adhering to what
he has said, his friends getting angrier with him,
even to charging him with wicked acts, till
Jehovah himself answers him "out of the whirlwind," and in words of unsurpassed grandeur

[1] See p. 49.

bids him look on the world around and learn the
folly of contending with its Maker. Then the
troubled man confesses his fault and is forgiven ;
twice as much as he had before is bestowed upon
him, and " in all the land were no women found so
fair as the daughters of Job." After all, the author
of the poem evades the question he has raised.
He failed to see that nobleness and goodness
have nothing whatever to do with what men
have ; not even with happiness, which thousands
of good men have died failing to possess ; that
" the only happiness a brave man ever troubled
himself with asking much about was, happiness
enough to get his work done,"[1] leaving the rest
to take care of itself, because " the well-being of
our souls depends only on what we are."

At last the storm broke. Egypt was crushed
at Carchemish by the Babylonians, or as they
should now be called, the Chaldæans, a name
which they took from the Chaldai, a conquering
race of uncertain origin, who appear in history

---

[1] *Past and Present*, p. 134.

during the ninth century B.C. The peoples subject to Egypt passed under their rule, the Judæans
submitting quietly; but four years afterwards a
rebellion brought the armies of Nebuchadnezzar,
the conqueror of Nineveh, to Jerusalem. The city
was taken, the temple treasures seized,   B. C.
and a large number of the wealthier   597.
classes carried across the Syrian desert to Babylon.
In less than ten years the stubborn people again
revolted, and the Chaldæan king once more
laid siege to the famous city. It was bravely
defended; as breaches were made in the walls
stones were taken from the palaces and houses
to stop them. Famine so raged that noble
ladies picked garbage from the dungheaps and
parents ate their own children; and   B. C.
at last, after a year and a half, the   586.
Chaldæans forced an entrance, this time to blend
no mercy with their vengeance. The ringleaders
were put to death; the king, after seeing his sons
killed, had his eyes plucked out and was carried
prisoner to Babylon with large numbers of his
subjects. The city was then given over to the

soldiers for plunder and afterwards set on fire ; the " holy and beautiful house where their fathers praised Jehovah," cherubim, altar, ark, all burnt.

So fell Jerusalem, in the sight of whose ruins from the heights around the vanquished poured out their lamentations, because " abroad the sword bereaveth and at home is death."

" Alas ! how doth the city sit solitary, that was full of
people !
How is she become as a widow ! she that was great among
the nations,
The princess among the provinces, how is she become
tributary !
Captive is Judah gone forth because of affliction and
because of great servitude :
She dwelleth among the heathen, she findeth no rest :
All her persecutors overtook her in the midst of her
straits.
Men ! unto you do I call, all ye that pass by ; behold, and
see
If there be any sorrow like unto my sorrow, which is done
unto me,
Wherewith Jehovah hath afflicted me in the day of his
fierce anger."[1]

The land was so desolated that scarcely a man of note was left in it, only " the poor to be vine-

---

[1] Lamentations i. 1-4, 12.

dressers and husbandmen," and a few faithful like Jeremiah, for he, though invited to Babylon by the king, preferred to remain. On the breaking out of a third tumult, in which the Chaldæan governor was killed, many fled to Egypt, forcing Jeremiah to go with them, while another batch being exiled, the land was well-nigh cleared of every Judæan.

IV.

The Exile in Babylon, and the Return.

THE vast desert which stretches across Africa and Western Asia is broken first by the hills that enclose the valley of the Nile, and then by the rising ground watered by the Tigris and Euphrates. Like the delta formed by the Nile, the low-lying country near the Persian Gulf has been laid down by those rivers. Its fertile and well-watered soil, the native home of the wheat-plant, invited the settlement and favoured the growth of great empires,

K

so that it became at a very remote time a
centre of civilization, equal to, if not greater
in importance than, Egypt, with which power
its people so long contended for the mastery
over Syria. It was here, as we have seen
already, that the Babylonian branch of the
Semites had settled, and become the ruling
population, fixing their capital at the city which,
translating its Accadian name into their own
tongue, they called Bab-el, or " gate of God."

During the brilliant reign of Nebuchadnezzar
the kingdom was extended from the Tigris to
the Mediterranean, and · Babylon became the
most splendid capital of ancient times. It stood
on both banks of the Euphrates, and was built in
the form of a square, each side of which is said
to have been fifteen miles long ; but of so vast a
walled province, as it might be called, the greater
part was park, field, and garden. Among the most
famous buildings was the king's palace, with its
mimic mountain-terraces of trees and flowers
called " hanging gardens," accounted among the
" seven wonders of the world." There was also

the lofty temple of Bel, raised by Nebuchadnezzar in seven tower-like stories, faced with the
colours of the sun, moon, and five planets, the
topmost story being crowned with a temple. It
was around this building that the legend had
grown how the god had baulked the efforts of
the workmen to raise it high as heaven to save
themselves against another deluge, by confusing
their speech. Babylon was not only a seat of
gaiety and worship, but of commerce, art, and
learning. There the ships called on their
voyages between Arabia and India, bringing
the rough products of those lands to be exchanged for its finely wrought goods; there the
far-famed Chaldæan astronomers watched the
stars, and strove to read in their movements
the fate of men and empires. Palm-groves
still relieve the tameness of the landscape, and in
early spring the plain is covered with grass and
flowers; but, save by Arabs and a few villagers,
the ancient sites are deserted, and the remains of
canals that once carried the surplus waters to
barren parts wind across swampy flats to which,

if well drained, the fruitfulness of old would
return. No piles of stately ruins, as at Athens,
Baalbek, or Thebes, mark where Babylon and
Nineveh once stood ; shapeless rubbish heaps,
happily undisturbed for centuries, are the graves
of palaces and temples yielding for our wonder-
ment and knowledge priceless treasures of
literature and art ; seals with tiny images of
gods and priests ; monster slabs depicting the
exploits of mighty men, or shaped into winged
human-headed bulls and lions ; book-cylinders
and tablets, whose strange arrow-like strokes
are not only complete annals of the empire, but
range from spelling-lessons to works on astronomy, from lists of charms to ward off evil
and tables of omens from dreams, to epics and
hymns to heaven-gods.

It was over this land that the Judæans were
scattered. Although " stripped bare," as the
word by which they spoke of the exile means,
they were on the whole mildly treated, living
under their own elders, unhindered in the practice of their religion, and permitted to settle

as farmers and traders, some among them even
rising to high office in the state. While the more
easy-going strove to make the best of their lot by
adopting the belief and customs of the Chaldæans, the firmness of others kept Israel from
becoming so merged among the conquerors as
to efface what had hitherto kept it apart from
races around. To these faithful ones the kindest
treatment could never have atoned for banish-
ment from fatherland, and for the destruction
of the holy shrine ; "by the river of Babylon,"
which, centuries before, their barbarous ancestors
crossed and recrossed in their wanderings, "they
had sat down and wept when they remembered
Zion." Their yearnings for lost home and
temple, expressed in psalms, were nourished by
hopes of freedom drawn from the words of dead
and living prophets, when "the ransomed of
Jehovah shall return, and enter Zion with
shouts," when "everlasting joy shall be upon
their heads and sorrow and sadness flee away."
The influences of the exile were very marked ;
the devout, drawn together by their common

needs, met from time to time, most likely every
Sabbath (of the keeping of which but slight
traces occur from the Exodus to the Captivity),
for the reading of the law and for prayer,
the value of which they learned when cut off
from temple and altar. And, although after the
return the rebuilt temple was the chief seat
of worship and only place of sacrifice, the "synagogues," so called from a Greek word, meaning
"assembly," which were founded in Palestine
and wherever else the Jews were scattered,
were the prime means of spreading a knowledge
of the law and maintaining the faith and unity
of the race. For they did what a temple and
priesthood confined to one place could not do ;
and, although the importance of the temple was
not lessened, the class who read and explained
the law rose by degrees above those who carried
it out. While in Babylon, the priests busied
themselves in drawing up new laws, grafting
them upon old ones, and re-casting the traditions,
and legends, adding to these, in the course of time,
those relating to the creation, as given in the first

chapter of Genesis ; to "paradise" (a Persian word meaning an "enclosed garden"), and man's fall, of which a like myth is found in the sacred books of the ancient Persian religion ; and to the deluge, which had its rise in Chaldæa, a land exposed to violent floods.

On the death of Nebuchadnezzar, after a reign of forty-three years, the power of B.C. Chaldæa declined, and the victories of 562. Cyrus, king of Persia, over the Medes and other peoples, set aglow the hopes of the exiles. It was about this time, when the rapid success of the Persians turned all eyes upon them, that one of the loftiest and richest minds among the exiles poured forth, in words of unsurpassed grandeur, the feelings which stirred in noble breasts. Since his name is unknown, he is commonly called the "second Isaiah," because his writings are found in the last twenty-seven chapters of the book of Isaiah. His theme is the advent of Cyrus, by whom Jehovah, declared to be the only true god, is to deliver Israel ; the sufferings of the pious and faithful servants of

Jehovah, which shall have their reward in the return of the ancient glory and the ancient faith, this in its fulness gathering into itself all mankind. He opens with words of good cheer, bidding the prophets comfort the people, because Jehovah is on his way to save them. He

" Will come like a valiant one, while his arm ruleth for him ; his reward is with him, and his recompense before him. He shall feed his flock like a shepherd : he shall gather the lambs with his arm and carry them in his bosom, and gently lead those that are with young." [1]

Compared to the tree stumps which men hew down, and burning part thereof in the fire wherewith to warm themselves, make of the rest a god, what an Almighty and wise God is Jehovah ! " To whom will ye liken him ? "

" Hath it not been told you from the beginning ? Have ye not understood it since the foundations of the earth ? It is he that sitteth upon the vault of the earth, so that the inhabitants thereof seem as locusts, that stretcheth out the heavens as gauze, and spreadeth them out as a tent to dwell in. . . . Who hath made yonder heavens ? It is he that bringeth out their host by number, that calleth them all by names, by whose infinite might and

---

[1] Isa. xl. 10, 11.

power not one is wanting. . . . Hast thou not seen? hast
thou not heard? Jehovah is the Everlasting, the maker
of the ends of the earth; he fainteth not, neither is
weary; there is no searching of his understanding.
Youths may faint and be weary, and the strongest men
may stumble; but they that wait upon Jehovah shall
renew their strength: they shall lift up their wings as
eagles; they shall run and not be weary, and they shall
walk and not faint." [1]

Wherefore the exiles need not fear,

" For I, Jehovah, thy God, the Holy One of Israel, thy
Saviour, have given Egypt for thy ransom, Ethiopia and
Seba for thee. . . . I am Jehovah, and beside me there is
no Saviour; I will work, and who shall hinder? Thus
saith Jehovah, your Redeemer, for your sake I have
sent to Babylon, and will drive them all away, even the
Chaldæans into their proud ships." [2]

Cyrus is spoken of as the "anointed," [3] not
as Messiah, but as the chosen instrument to free
Israel by smiting the Babylonians. For in the
second Isaiah we find the ideas about the
Messiah altogether changed. He is no longer
expected as a king of David's house, or indeed
a king at all; but portrayed as the righteous
"servant of Jehovah," who cries not, whose

[1] Isa. xl. 21-31.　　[2] Isa. xliii. 3-11.　　[3] Isa. xlv. 1.

voice is not heard in the street, who, as a son of
Israel, must bear its sorrows, be bruised for its
iniquities, and the measure of whose sufferings
shall be the measure of its after glory, because
for that servant's sake Jehovah, to whom in common belief atonement must be made, will be
merciful.   Now it is under such a figure of
speech, not uncommon to the Hebrew prophets,
that Isaiah, as he himself declares, speaks of the
pious section of Israel, not of any one man, and
it is these pious ones who, as a part of the
nation, must be " wounded for its sins," and thus
secure from its appeased god the reward of that
self-sacrifice in the good of the whole.   Thus
did the prophet dimly see a truth which is the
life of the world, and which to Jesus, with his
still more exalted views of God's relation to
man, came with such power that he not only
proclaimed it, but died for it.

At last the looked-for event occurred.   The
soldiers of Cyrus vainly tried to scale or batter
down the thick and lofty walls of Babylon, and

so had recourse to secret measures. They dug
a canal which diverted the waters of the Euphrates, and then, while the besieged, trusting
to their strong defences, were feasting, crossed
the river-bed under cover of the darkness, crept
under the unguarded water-gates and b. c.
took the city. 538.

" The under-world is stirred below, and comes forth to
    meet thee :
It stirreth up the shades for thee, even all the leaders of
    the earth :
With one mouth they cry to thee,
Thou, too, art an empty shadow as we : thou art become
    like unto us !
Thy pride is brought down to the under-world, and the
    melody of thy lutes,
How art thou fallen from heaven, O shining one, son of
    the morning !" [1]

Soon after this great victory, Cyrus gave the
Jews, as we may now call them, leave to return
to their native land and rebuild their temple,
the sacred vessels of which he restored. Whether

---

[1] Isa. xiv. 9–12. In the quotations from the Isaiahs I have
adopted the scholarly translation of Mr. Cheyne, the forthcoming issue of whose book in an expanded form one is glad
to note.

or not any service rendered to him by the exiles
had prompted this kindly act, it was a wise one,
because it secured him the gratitude of a brave
people who, thus placed on the western outposts
of the empire, would be its trusty defenders
against attacks from Egypt. In such psalms as
the 126th,

> " When Jehovah brought home the captivity of Zion,
> We were like them that dream,
> Then was our mouth filled with laughter,
> And our tongue with singing,"

we read what joy their release from bondage
gave the Jews. But while some thousands, and
these mainly the priestly and poorer classes—
" the chaff," as they were called—availed themselves of the leave to return, the larger number,
" the wheat," preferred to remain in the land
which had so long been their home. Indeed,
when we remember that nearly fifty years had
passed since the fall of Jerusalem, it is clear that
most of the earliest captives must have been
dead ; others then young had grown old, and to
those who had been born in Chaldæa, Judæa was
a strange land round which no memories of

childhood or regrets of manhood gathered. No
wonder, therefore, that these lacked zeal and
courage to pluck up roots firmly struck in their
rich foster-land and transplant them in barren
Judæa, and that they shrank from a long journey
across an unbroken desert, where supplies of food
and water were fitful, and which was infested with
robber-tribes. But they who braved these dangers
were buoyed up with the hope of seeing Jerusalem, and taking part in the glorious work of
raising the fallen temple. They cheered the
way with songs which they could not sing "in a
strange land," and at last, after months of toil
and hardship, reached their journey's end. They
found the land desolate, for what the mad havoc
of war had spared had been destroyed by the
wild tribes that swept over it ; but they set to
work with a will to " build up the old ruins, and
rear the places that had long lain waste." An
altar to Jehovah was raised at Jerusalem on the
temple site, and the foundation of another   B. C.
temple laid amidst songs of praise and   535.
sound of trumpets and cymbals ; but an un-

toward event hindered the completion of the
B. C. 516. building until the reign of Darius. The
Samaritans came forward with offers of
help, saying, "We likewise, as ye do, obey
Jehovah!"[1] but their aid was spurned because
they were not pure "sons of Israel"—a foolish
blunder, for the Jews had more or less inter-
married with other races from the Canaanites
downwards, and among the returned exiles were
members of the ten tribes, who had fewer scruples
than the Judæans. At any rate, the refusal so
angered the Samaritans that they laid false
charges against the Jews before Cyrus, who with-
drew his permission for the rebuilding, and thus
arose undying hate between the two races.

The arrival of the Persians in Babylon had
not only given freedom to the Jews, but, in the
course of time, wrought certain changes in their
customs and beliefs, influencing these the more
because the religion of the Persians, who were of
Aryan race, was far purer and loftier in kind

[1] Esdras v. 69.

than any other with which the Jews had come in contact. In their oldest hymns they praise one Creator of all things, of whom they had no image, and whom they worshipped on hill-top with symbol of fire. Beneath him they pictured hostile hosts of light and darkness, the head of the evil spirits being Ahriman, who sought to spoil the good work of God, tempted the first pair to sin, and brought death among mankind. But his triumph was for a time only, and one day the "hero of prophets," Saoshyas, a saviour, virgin-born, would renew the earth, and make even the wicked pure.

Now the Jews already believed in angels dwelling around Jehovah ; but from the time of their contact with the Persians we find this belief much enlarged, orders of angels, whose names are borrowed from the Persian, playing a very active part between heaven and earth, ruling the elements and seasons and placed as guardian angels over nations and persons.[1] Jehovah was said to create such spirits daily ;

[1] Cf. Matt. xviii. 10.

the good deeds and thoughts of a man are transformed into them, as in the beautiful story from the Persian sacred books which I have quoted in the "Childhood of the World," they await his soul with welcomes as it enters Paradise.

The Jews had regarded Jehovah as author of both good and evil ; but now their views changed, and they began to believe in crowds of demons, ruled over by an arch-fiend, the ideas about whom were transferred to Satan. These demons had their home in the middle air, and were invisible, because "the Holy One, blessed is he, had created their souls, and was about to create their bodies when the Sabbath set in ;" but "if power were given to the eye to see them, no creature could exist." Every one has 10,000 at his right hand, and 1000 at his left hand, and since they rule chiefly at night, no man should greet another lest he salute a demon. They haunt lonely spots, often assume the shape of beasts, and it is their presence in the bodies of men and women which is the cause of madness and other diseases.

The Persians believed in the resurrection of the dead, in a heaven called " paradise," and also " house of hymns," because the angels were said to sing hymns there ; in a hell, or "house of destruction," and in a bridge between the two places along which the souls of the pious alone passed in safety, while the wicked fell from it into hell. For awakening the dead, restoring life destroyed by death, and holding the last judgment, the great "prophet" Saoshyas will appear.[1] To what extent these ideas were borrowed by the Jews, or were worked out by themselves, is uncertain, as no traces of advance beyond their crude notions about " sheol " are found till long after the return from exile. We know that the influence of the Persians spread in divers forms through the Jews who remained in Babylon, and who had settled westward in Persia, for as late as the third century before Jesus the feast of Purim was introduced from thence, and the influence of Jewish schools in

---

[1] Haug's *Essays on the Parsis,* p. 313.

L.

Babylon long survived the destruction of the Jewish state.

For some sixty years after the second temple was finished the records of Jewish history are scanty. Enough, however, exists to show that the zeal of the exiles had died away and a lax state of things crept in, bringing with it the old danger that other gods would be worshipped by the side of Jehovah. But a great change came about on the arrival of a second batch of exiles under the lead of Ezra, a priest and scribe "who had prepared his heart to seek the law of Jehovah and to do it."

B. C. 458.

The scribes, a class who from this time take a leading place in Jewish history, were in bygone days clerks of the state, to whom, as skilled in writing, fell the duty of copying the records, making out lists of soldiers, etc., and afterwards of transcribing Israel's law and history, which, as has been said, became its sacred books.

Ezra was armed with full power to reform and uphold the religion of his fathers, and he set

about his work with ardour. As a strict Jew
one thing greatly shocked him, namely, to find
that the " chosen " of Jehovah had not kept themselves apart from other people, some among them,
priests as well, having married foreign women.
Bowed down with grief and wearing all its signs,
he besought Jehovah to forgive this sin, and gave
the offenders no peace until they had vowed
that these women and their dear children too
should be sent away! It was a terribly harsh
and cruel thing to do, for it was better that the
Jews as a *race* should perish utterly than that
the law of unselfishness and justice should be
set aside and the love of fathers for innocent
mothers and little ones crushed : but the history
of this tearful world is full of such examples of
misguided, loveless zeal, and the notions which
caused Ezra to act so heartlessly prevail with
far less excuse even to this day.

That larger views than these were taken by
some is shewn in the fresh and lovely story of
Ruth the Moabitess, which is thought to belong
to this time.

A Jew named Elimelech, with his wife Naomi, and their two sons, driven by famine from Judah, had settled in Moab. In the course of time the father and sons died, and Naomi, hearing that " Jehovah had visited his people in giving them bread," resolved to return to Judah. She begged the widows of her two sons to stay in their native land, and after hesitating a little, Orpah kissed her and returned " unto her people and gods," but Ruth refused to stay behind, saying, " Intreat me not to leave thee or to return from following after thee, for whither thou goest I will go, and where thou lodgest I will lodge : thy people shall be my people, and thy god my god. Where thou diest will I die, and there will I be buried ; Jehovah do so to me and more also (a form of oath to the god) if aught but death part thee and me."

So they came together to Bethlehem, Naomi's native place, and it being harvest time Ruth went out to glean, and " her hap was to light on a part of the field belonging to Boaz, a rich man and near kinsman of Elimelech," who, coming

among his reapers, asked who she was, and
learned the story of her devotion to the forlorn
Naomi. He approached her with kind words,
and bade her, when the resting-hour came, join
the reapers and eat with them, quietly saying to
them, "Let her glean even among the sheaves
and reproach her not, and let fall also some of
the handfuls of purpose for her, and leave them
that she may glean them, and rebuke her not."

When she returned well-laden to Naomi and
told her story, Naomi instructed Ruth to claim
her rights under the "levirate" law, by which
the near relative was required to marry the
widow of his brother or other kinsman, and the
end was that Boaz took her as his wife. Whatever other motives the writer of this exquisite
story may have had, it certainly tended to show
that love and duty were to prevail over laws
against intermarriage with the "stranger," and
he even makes Ruth to be mother of Obed, from
whom king David was descended.

We hear no more of Ezra for thirteen years, a
time which he probably spent, with other scribes,

known as "men of the Great Synagogue," in re-
shaping the records of his nation into one Book
of the Law, or the Pentateuch, nearly in the
same form in which it still exists. That is to
say, Ezra added to the older version of that work
the laws and legends drawn up and arranged by
Jewish priests in Babylon, and thus it received
its final touches at the hands of those who
regarded everything from a priestly standpoint.
The voices of the prophets were hushed, for
Ezekiel with his fantastic figures and tedious
details about the temple and its "courts for
boiling and baking"[1] has small title, despite
some high moral teaching, to foremost place
among them, while even Malachi, the last of
that goodly company, who asks, "Have we not
all one father?" fell below the lofty standard of
Amos and others and promoted the narrow ideas
of Ezra. So it came to pass that the simple
desert code of Moses, with such unwritten laws
as applied it to after times, the traces of nature-
worship and still lower idolatries, appeared,

[1] Ch. xlvi.

after excluding image-worship, human sacrifices, magic, etc., as a great body of rules dealing with the priests, the temple services and sacrifices, the feasts, chiefly those of Passover, Weeks, Tabernacles, and New Moon, the Sabbath, foods clean and unclean, trial by ordeal, and a crowd of details whose only interest and value now consist in the light which they throw upon the history of religious rites and ceremonies.

Thus arose the "Thorah" or "Law," which was made binding on every Jew as the law of Jehovah, and that no one might plead ignorance of it, Ezra appointed stated times for its reading in public. In this he was aided by the arrival of Nehemiah, a devout Jew, B. C. cupbearer to the Persian king. Moved 445. with pity for the forlorn state of his country, he was at his own prayer made governor of Judæa, and on arrival at once set about rebuilding the walls and gateways of Jerusalem, the ruined condition of which laid the city open to constant attack. So hindered were the workmen by the jealous tribes around that "the builders every

one had his sword girded by his side and so
builded ;"[1] but the bulwarks were at last com-
pleted, and the people were gathered in peaceful
assembly to hear the law read.   In the vivid
account given in the book of Nehemiah,[2] Ezra
is said to have paused from time to time in his
reading that the Levites or priests' assistants
might "give the sense and cause them to understand the reading."   This shows that the law
had to be translated or explained, the reason
being that the Hebrew language in which it was
written was then a dead language, for the exiles
had dropped its use during their captivity
and acquired the mixed tongue called Aramaic
or Syro-Chaldaic, which remained the written
and spoken language of Palestine till after the
time of Jesus ; indeed it is, with certain changes,
the speech of the peasants there to this day.
Then again, some parts of the law were so old
that their meaning and first purpose were forgotten or had no bearing on the state of things
which had arisen during the changing fortunes

[1] Nehemiah iv. 18.   [2] Ib. ch. viii., *passim.*

of the Jews; that which was adapted to Babylon
was not suited to Judæa, and hence arose not
only Aramaic versions of the sacred book, but
the famous body of oral or unwritten law as "a
hedge"[1] about the written law, to protect and
explain it, to find in its sentences and words,[2] or,
failing these, in the very shape of its letters,
meanings that could be converted into rules
applying to any and every case that might arise.

The veneration in which the "thorah" came
to be held knew no bounds and led to the
wildest ideas. It was said to be one of the
"seven" things which existed before the world,
and to have supplied the pattern by which
Jehovah made all things.[3] He himself, as Chief
Rabbi, wears phylacteries (slips of parchment
with passages from the "thorah" written on
them, bound as charms round the forehead and
arm), and spends three hours every day in reading

---

[1] "Be deliberate in judgment; raise up many disciples; and
make a fence (or hedge) to the Thorah." *Pirqe Aboth* (or
Sayings of the Fathers), ch. i. 1. Edit. Rev. C. Taylor.
Cambridge University Press.

[2] Cf. Deutsch's *Lit. Remains*, Art. "Talmud," p. 14.

[3] *P. Aboth*, p. 27.

the "thorah" and discussing it with his angels!
While the world and all therein was made in
six days, the law was not given till after forty
days, and then in every language, Israel alone
having the wisdom to accept it. "Turn it and
again turn it," said the scribes, "for the all is
therein and thy all is therein,"[1] and in this belief
they stretched its words and commands to cover
the life of every Jew in its smallest details. As
time rolled on the oral law became so revered as
to be regarded of equal value with the "thorah,"
and to have been given by Jehovah to Moses at
the same time. Such an extreme notion of
course raised the men who were its guardians
and expounders into high importance; "the
fear of the master" was to be as the "fear of
heaven;" and to dispute with a rabbi was to
argue with Jehovah himself. For centuries the
ever-growing mass of oral law was preserved in
the memories of these scribes, or masters, or
rabbis, and it was not till above a century after
the final overthrow of the Jewish state that the

[1] *P. Aboth*, v. 32.

huge body of laws and legends was gathered into the "Talmud."[1] This enormous book is known only to a learned few, and it is from their writings upon it that I have culled here and there a blossom of wise counsel, parable, or story which they have found growing in the tangled wilderness of its grotesque legends, trivial talk, and maunderings over superstitions dead or dying.

The humblest Jew might rise to a place among the "Masters of the Law," and it is to the credit of this class that they were not paid as teachers, but lived by some handicraft. Many of the greatest rabbis followed such trades as carpenters, tentmakers, weavers, and in the Talmud we find an exalted place given to work. Its union with piety is taught in the following story. "One day a sage walking through a crowded market-place met the prophet Elijah, and asked him who out of the multitude there would be saved. Elijah first pointed to a turnkey who was merciful to his prisoners, and next to two common-looking

[1] Note C.

working-men. The sage, meeting them, asked what were their saving works, and they, greatly puzzled, could only say, 'We are but poor workmen who live by our trade. When we meet anybody who seems sad we join him and we talk to him and cheer him so that he forgets his grief. And if we know of two people who have quarrelled we talk to them, and persuade them until we have made them friends again. This is our whole life.'" Among the parables, so favourite a mode of instruction in the East, we have these on " death " and " dependence on God."

" Man is born with his hands clenched, he dies with them wide open. Entering life he desires to grasp everything ; leaving the world, all that he possessed slips away. Even as a fox, is a man ; as a fox which seeing a fine vineyard lusted after its grapes. But he was too fat to creep between the narrow palings, and so after three days' fasting became thin enough to get through. Having then feasted on the grapes, he again grew fat, and could not get out until he had fasted three days more. So with man; poor and naked he enters the world, poor and naked does he leave it."

"The scholars of Rabbi Simon ben Jochai once asked him: 'Why did not Jehovah give to Israel enough manna to suffice them for a year at one time, instead of meting it out daily?' The rabbi replied, 'I will answer ye with a parable. There was once a king who had a son to whom he gave a certain sum once a year. It so happened that the day on which this allowance was due was the only day in the year when the father saw his son. So he changed his plan and gave his son each day his allowance for that day only, and then the son visited his father every morning. So was it with Israel: each father, being dependent upon the manna sent by Jehovah every day for the support of his family, had his mind thereby directed to the Great Giver.'"

The three pillars that sustain the world are "the law, worship, and the bestowal of kind-

nesses."[1] The law begins and ends in charity, as
it is written, "And the Lord God made unto
Adam and to his wife coats of skin and clothed
them,"[2] and in the account of the death of
Moses, "And he buried him."[3] Meekness we
learn from God himself, for "he chose Mount
Sinai from which to give his commandments,
because it is the lowliest of the mountains, to
show that his spirit rests only upon the meek
and lowly. He called to Moses not from a lofty
tree, but from a lowly bush. When he spoke
to Elijah, he came not in the wind or the lightning or the earthquake, but in the 'still small
voice.'" Six hundred and thirteen commandments were spoken to Moses—365, according to
the number of days in the solar year, and 248
answering to the parts of the human body.[4]
These David in the fifteenth Psalm, verses 2-5,
reduced to eleven; Isaiah (xxxiii. 15) rests them
on six; Micah (vi. 8) on three, and Habakkuk
on one (ii. 4), "The just shall live by his faith."

---

[1] *P. Aboth*, i. 2.   [2] Gen. iii. 21.   [3] Deut. xxxiv. 6.
[4] Edersheim's *Jewish Nation*, p. 380.

In another place the same idea occurs, "The law has grown to be a wide sea, but it will some day shrink into this one command, Walk before God and be holy."

Among the foolish comments on the Jewish scriptures, Adam is said to have been created with two faces, as it is written, "Thou hast beset me behind and before." When Esau embraced Jacob, the neck of the latter became marble; the haunchbone of Og was three miles in extent, and his teeth grew so long that they were entangled in the rocks, as the Psalmist says, "Thou hast broken the teeth of the ungodly;" gems fell from heaven with the manna; whatever a man wished for, that he had, as it is written, "Thou hast lacked nothing;"[1] good angels are created daily, as it says, "They are new every morning."[2] Of the twelve hours of the day, the Holy One, blessed be he, sits during the last three and amuses himself with Leviathan, as it is written, "the leviathan whom thou hast made to play therein."

[1] Deut. ii. 7.   [2] Lam. iii. 23.

Here are a few of the wise proverbs and counsels that glitter amidst pages of dulness:

" Say little and do much."

" Not learning but doing is the groundwork."

" Say not, when I have leisure I will study, perchance thou mayest not have leisure."

" The day is short, and the task is great, and the workmen are sluggish, though the reward be great, and the Master of the house is urgent. It is not incumbent on thee to complete the work, but thou must not therefore cease from it."

" Who is wise? He that learns from every man, for it is said, ' From all my teachers I get understanding.' "

" Who is mighty? He that subdues his nature ; for it is said, ' He that is slow to anger is better than the mighty, and he that ruleth his spirit than he that taketh a city.' "

" Who is rich? He that is contented with his lot, for it is said, ' When thou eatest the labour of thy hands, happy art thou, and it shall be well with thee.' "

" Despise not any man, and carp not at any thing, for thou wilt find that there is not a man that has not his hour, and not a thing that has not its place."

" He who learns as a lad, to what is he like? To ink written on fresh paper; and he who learns when old, to what is he like? To ink written on used paper."

" Regard not the flask, but what is therein."

" Rejoice not when thine enemy falleth, and let not thine heart be glad when he stumbleth."

" When the righteous dies it is the earth that loses."

" Repent one day before thy death."

" There are three crowns: of the law, the priesthood, the kingship, but the crown of a good name is greater than them all."

" Not the place honours the man, but the man the place."

" The reward of good works is like dates, sweet and ripening late."

" The best preacher is the heart ; the best teacher is time ; the best book is the world; the best friend is God."

To return to our story. Nehemiah left Jerusalem for a time, and on a second visit found that the reforms which he and Ezra had brought about with such fair promise had failed. The law was neglected, all manner of work was done on the sabbath, the gifts to the temple had fallen off, and the priests had ceased to perform their duties. The zeal and anger of Nehemiah were aroused ; he stopped the sabbath trading, levied a general tax for the temple service, and summoned the priests and Levites to return to the sanctuary. The people, as of old, had married foreign women, and among the offenders was a grandson of the high-priest, who, refusing to put away his wife, departed with her to her own country, Samaria. With the B. c. permission of the Persian king, he built 419. a temple on Mount Gerizim, founded a priesthood there, and claimed that it and not Mount

M

Moriah was the place where "men ought to worship." This act and the refusal of the Samaritans to acknowledge as sacred any other book than the "thorah," in which were the stories of the patriarchs, whose relics, the well of Jacob, the grave of Joseph, and the oaks under which Abraham sacrificed, were around them, widened still more the breach between them and the Jews.

For under the rule of Nehemiah a *second* batch of books, known under the common term of the "prophets," was added to the Hebrew scriptures. According to the book of Maccabees "he, founding a library, gathered together the acts of the kings, and the prophets, and of David, and the epistles of the kings concerning the holy gifts."[1]

This verse is commonly explained as follows: The letters from foreign kings related to the gifts which they had made to the temple; the things concerning the "kings" are the books of Joshua, Judges, Samuel, and Kings, these last

[1] 2 Macc. ii. 13.

two being treated as one by the Jews ; the
"prophets" are the books of Isaiah, Jeremiah,
Ezekiel, and the twelve minor prophets, these
last making-up one book in the Jewish scriptures.
" The acts of David " are certain psalms which
tradition ascribed to him, but these formed part
of later additions to those scriptures.

I spoke at page 8 of man's avoidance of
uttering the names of his deities, and it is about
this time that we find the practice spreading
among the Jews of using another word for
Jehovah, the most frequent being " Adonai,"
that is, " Lord " or " Master." They did this
in obedience to a supposed command in the
" thorah " (Leviticus xxiv. 16), rendering the
word translated in our version "blaspheme" by
the phrase "pronounce distinctly." Their traditions say that " Jehovah " was uttered but once
a year by the high-priest, on the Day of Atonement, when he entered the " holy of holies," and
that it was spoken for the last time by Simon
the Just. Henceforth, says the Talmud, he who
attempts to pronounce it shall have no part in
the world to come.

The law was now once more supreme, and although the scribes, as its guardians and expounders, were slowly superseding the priests, whose duty was limited to carrying out its decrees, both classes were one in the zeal with which they urged its commands on the people. And these responded with a glad obedience to that which, interwoven with their history, awakened their interest and formed a bond of unity, while the splendour of the temple service and the feasts which ever and anon brought them from far and near, kindled their love for the shrine where Jehovah was believed to dwell. Under the mild rule of Persia, which left them unmolested so long as their tribute was paid, they increased in wealth and content. The real power was in the hands of the high-priest, and the people, freed from the unrest which attended struggles for kingship, pursued their way in peace, and found in their religion a joy and strength which manifests itself in the psalms and other writings of that quiet time.

Their history ends in the Old Testament with the death of Nehemiah, and for upwards of two hundred and thirty years after that event our information is of the scantiest kind, although the little that is known is of much value for understanding how changes were wrought in the thought and life of the nation.

When in its turn the Persian empire, into whose grip Egypt had come, fell before the armies of Alexander the Great, the Jews, after a slight show of resistance, passed to the dominion of the Greeks. The change B. C. made at first small difference in their 332. condition, but it profoundly touched their beliefs despite all that the more strict among them could do to hinder it. The victories of Alexander had broken down the few remaining barriers between East and West; Greek towns fringed the coast of Palestine and were dotted around Judæa; the walls of Jerusalem were powerless to keep out Greek customs and ideas, which spread apace. Numbers of Jews were carried to the newly founded city called Alex-

andria, which, on the decline of art and culture
in Greece, became, under the mild and humane
Ptolemy, to whose share Egypt had fallen on
the death of Alexander, the chief seat of learning
and centre of its diffusion over the world.   The
Jewish settlers there numbered one-third of the
population, and enjoyed equal rights with the
Greeks and Egyptians.   It was not possible for
them to live unaffected by such surroundings; the
selfish dream of a race dwelling apart from other
races was never to be fulfilled, and we find them
willing disciples, learning the arts and sciences
of their neighbours, adopting even the Greek
language, and falling into ways of thinking
which were afterwards to greatly affect early
opinions about Jesus.   It was at Alexandria
that the "thorah," and afterwards the entire
Jewish scriptures, were translated, with certain alterations, into Greek, for the use of the
Egyptian Jews.   This version is known as the
"Septuagint;" and although the stricter Jews in
Palestine looked on such a work as profane, and
even observed the day of its completion as a day

of fasting, its use was so extended that nearly
all the quotations from the Old Testament which
are given in the writings making-up the New
Testament are taken from it.

V.

The War of Independence.

THE long years of quiet under the rule of the
Persians and the Greeks were followed by
stormy times which reached the height of their
fury in the reign of the Syrian king, B. C.
Antiochus Epiphanes, or "the Brilliant," 175.
surnamed from his freaks, both terrible and
comic, Epimanes, or "the Madman." On the
faith of a report that he was dead the B. C.
Jews revolted and imprisoned the high- 172.
priest, a creature who had bought the place which
he held. When Antiochus heard of the outbreak,
he was not sorry for the pretext which it gave
him to punish the Jews and enforce his designs
upon them. Twice was Jerusalem given over

to the fury of his soldiers, "who smote it very
sore and destroyed much people of Israel,"[1]
and in the end he issued a decree commanding
all his subjects to worship the gods of Greece
alone. Some complied ; the temple on Mount
Gerizim was, with the consent of the Samaritans, dedicated to Jupiter, but the opposition of
the faithful Jews brought on them a bitter persecution. The temple at Jerusalem was made a
shrine of Jupiter Olympius ; a sow was sacrificed
B. C.   on the altar, and broth prepared from its
167.   flesh sprinkled over the holy place and
on copies of the law. The synagogues were destroyed, the keeping of the sabbath forbidden,
and the Jews who refused to yield were put
to cruel torture and lingering deaths.

Had Antiochus left their religion alone, it
would, as in the past, have quietly imbibed the
ideas floating around it ; but his efforts to uproot
it gave rise to a movement which planted it the
more firmly, so that in after time it put forth the
fair native flower of the religion of Jesus. For

[1] I Macc. i. 30.

at this crisis an aged priest, named Mattathias,
who with his five sons had withdrawn to the
village of Modin, had, in slaying at the idol altar
an apostate Jew, kindled a spark which set the
whole land ablaze. He lived only a short while
after this ; but the number of gallant and faithful
men who flocked around him were already a
little army, and they found the needed leader in
his chosen son, Judas Maccabeus,[1] a brave
and withal gentle man, "so that he was
renowned unto the utmost parts of the earth
and received unto him such as were ready to
perish."[2] He won nearly every battle, and
at last retook Jerusalem, cleansed the temple,
cleared the courts, where " the shrubs grew as
in a forest,"[3] built a new altar, and " sacrificed
the sacrifice of deliverance and praise." He
died fighting against overwhelming numbers

B. C.
160.

---

[1] This name, commonly translated the "Hammerer," is of
uncertain meaning, but is believed to have been a title of Judas
himself, like "Martel," the surname of Charles of France. An
admirable life of him, by Lieutenant Conder, has been recently
published in the "New Plutarch" series.

[2] 1 Macc. iii. 9.   [3] 1 Macc. iv. 38.

of the Syrians, and was succeeded by his
brothers Jonathan and Simon, under whom
B. C. the complete freedom of the nation
135. was secured. John Hyrcanus, son of
Simon, greatly extended the kingdom ; Galilee,
Samaria, the lands of Edom and beyond
Jordan were subdued, and, crowning triumph for
the Jews, the rival temple on Gerizim, which
B. C. had been an offence to them for two
130. hundred years, was razed to the ground.

So for a brief space it seemed as if the
visions of the prophets had come to pass and
the former days returned ; for the Jews were
their own masters, subject only to the law of
Moses as expanded and expounded by the
scribes, paying no tribute, and, among other
tokens of independence and increase of wealth,
giving cheerfully the temple tax in coin bearing
the inscription of the high priest.

Although each had its rise at an earlier time,
it is during the Maccabean period that mention
is first made of two great schools or parties

among the Jews, namely, the Pharisees and Sadducees, of whom some account will more fitly
follow in speaking of the relations between them
and Jesus.

Save in a few misleading words from Tacitus,[1]
we look in vain for any remarks upon the
heroic struggle, with its brilliant but short-lived
success, in any Greek or Roman writer, and
indeed the most celebrated among these last
exhibit such ignorance about the Jews and such
contempt for them as to render valueless the
little that they say concerning them.

The history of the Maccabean time survives
in Jewish writings alone, and of these the most
important are not included in the Old Testament. In some of the psalms, as the 74th and
the 79th, we hear the cry of anguish wrung from
the tortured people, but it is in the "books of the
Maccabees" that the story is given in detail,
and this with a beauty and simple pathos which

---

[1] " Antiochus strove to free the Jews from their superstitions
and give them Greek manners, but was prevented by the
Parthian war from reforming this hateful people."—*History*,
v. 5, 9.

causes us to marvel at the unwisdom of the men
who, in admitting such writings as the "Book
of Esther" and the "Song of Solomon," accorded no place to these.   The "Book of Daniel"
(in which the author, following a not uncommon
practice of the past of speaking in the name
of some man of note, uses that of a Jewish
"seer" of rank, who lived in Babylon during
the Exile) gives us insight into the desires that
filled the faithful, and it seems to have been
a favourite study then as since, because it
appeared "not only to unfold the future, as
the other prophets, but to give the exact time
when events would occur."[1]   The sad state of the
nation, as forcibly described in the opening
chapter of the "First Book of Maccabees," had
rekindled in nobler minds not all-forgetful of the
past the Messianic hopes of old, and amidst
the legends and visions of the "Book of Daniel"
there are sober attempts to find in the events
of the time the signs of near fulfilment of old
foretellings.   Antiochus will be punished as

---

[1] Josephus, *Antiq.* x. 11, 7.

Nebuchadnezzar had been, the kingdom of the Greeks should fall as that of the Chaldees and others had fallen, and the pious who had died for the faith would rise again into everlasting life.[1] For it is now that the Jewish belief in an after state of the good and bad makes a distinct advance, impelled by men's efforts to find an answer to the perplexing question—What reward shall be theirs whose life here has been one of suffering and their death one of martyrdom for Israel's God and law?—an answer given thus in the book of Daniel: "and many of them that sleep in the dust of the earth shall awake, some to everlasting life;"[2] and in a later book of exceeding beauty, "The souls of the righteous are in the hands of God . . . in the sight of the unwise they seemed to die, but they are in peace . . . they shall judge the nations and have dominion over the people."[3]

The shades of the dead which reposed in "sheol" would, it was said, rise at a judgment

---

[1] 2 Macc. vii. 9, 29.   [2] Dan. xii. 2.
[3] Wisdom of Solomon iii. 1, 2, 3, 8.

day, to be ushered in by dreadful signs, when
God, the "Ancient of Days," seated on his
throne, would deliver power into the hands of
the "son of man," by whom, like the suffering
"servant of Jehovah," the pious in Israel are
meant. These should exercise lordship over
the earth, the chief city of which would be a
"new Jerusalem," while the wicked, awaking
to "shame and everlasting contempt," would
be hurled into hell, a place of punishment
figured by the valley of Hinnom or "Gehenna,"
near Jerusalem, where sacrifices were once
offered to Molech, and into which was since
cast the offal of the city and the bodies of
beasts and executed criminals, fires being kept
burning to prevent pestilence from the putrid
remains inbreeding preying worms.[1] How current these notions were in Palestine in after
times is shown both in the Talmud and the
New Testament, and in them is the source of
the forms in which are clothed the ideas still
so widely entertained by Christians about the
destiny of mankind in a hereafter.

[1] Isa. lxvi. 24 ; Mark ix. 44, 46.

The same chapter in the second book of Maccabees which speaks of Nehemiah's "library," tells us that "in like manner also Judas gathered together all those things that were lost by reason of the war,"[1] by which is understood the *third* portion of the Hebrew scriptures, namely, the Psalms, Proverbs, Job, the Song of Solomon, Ruth, Lamentations, Esther, Daniel, Ezra, Nehemiah, and Chronicles, known to the Jews under the common term of the "writings." Very different opinions, however, prevailed for some centuries as to which should be admitted in this division ; but at last all the books which now comprise the Old Testament were held to be of equal authority, and were accepted as divine alike by Jews and Christians.[2]

From the time of Ezra the work of the "men of the great synagogue" had been carried on by pious and learned Jews, the last of whom was the high-priest Simon the Just. Their work must in any case have come to a standstill during the dark days when Antiochus

B. C.
219?

---

[1] Ch. ii. 14.   [2] Note D.

ruled, and it is in the reign of John Hyrcanus that we find a " house of judgment " existing, to which the name " Sanhedrin " was given. This supreme court of the Jews, which was composed of priests, elders, and the more learned among the rabbis, about seventy-one members in all, dealt with matters of public worship—the fixing of sacred times and seasons, especially that of the new moon—as well as with all offences against the law, for which in very rare cases it passed sentence of death, although under the Roman rule it had no power to carry out that penalty.

As partly explaining the presence of the Romans in Palestine we are told in the first book of Maccabees that Judas Maccabeus had heard of their fame. " That they were mighty and valiant men, and as such would lovingly accept all that joined themselves unto them, and that they were men of great valour." It was told him also of their wars and noble acts . . . " that they had conquered kingdoms both far and nigh, insomuch as all that heard of their name

were afraid of them . . . yet for all this none
of them wore a crown or was clothed in purple.
Moreover how they had made for themselves a
senate-house wherein three hundred and twenty
men sat in council daily consulting alway for
the people, to the end they might be well
ordered, and that they committed their government to one man every year who ruled over all
their country, and that all were obedient to that
one, and that there was neither envy nor emula-
tion among them." [1]

With these Judas made an alliance, which,
however, was to prove fatal to the independence
of his people. For the price of Roman protection was submission, and a few years after
the death of John Hyrcanus the bloody contests
which arose between the Jewish princes for the
supreme power gave the Romans a pretext to
interpose.

When their famous general, Pompey, was
on his conquering march in Syria, each
of the two rivals sought his support,   B. C. 63.

---

[1] 1 Macc. viii. 1, 2, 12–16.

N

and one of them, Aristobulus, fearing an adverse judgment, prepared to fight. He fell back on Jerusalem, whose gates the followers of his opponent threw open at the approach of the Romans, but his supporters betook themselves to the temple-fortress, and there sustained a siege for three months, when the stronghold was taken, and

B. C. 63.
its capture followed by great slaughter. The priests were slain at the altar, the temple was profaned, Pompey, to the horror of the Jews, entered the sacred building, and even drew aside the veil that hung before the "holy of holies," finding, to his surprise, no image or symbol of the god of the Jews. Aristobulus, with a crowd of other captive princes, was made to grace the triumph of the victor on his entry into Rome, and the doom of the Jews as a subject people was sealed. Judas had courted the friendship of Rome and her grasp was as of iron. By her aid a hated stranger, Herod, surnamed "the Great," was, after varying fortunes,

B. C. 37.
made king of the Jews, and it was in the

B. C. 5.
latter part of his reign that Jesus of Nazareth was born.

Although very much of detail has been left out in this sketch of Jewish history, so that the more important events might appear in clearer outline, the picture may yet seem confused and overcrowded, and it will be helpful if, before passing to the next part of this book, I gather into a few words the substance of what has been said.

The forefathers of the Jews were rude, nature-worshipping shepherd tribes who, after many wanderings over Syria, settled in Egypt, where the Pharaohs enslaved them. On regaining their liberty, mainly by the skill of their brave and pious leader Moses, who gave them a code binding them to the service of Jehovah, the god whom he praised for their escape, they resumed their nomad life for some years, and then invaded the land of Canaan, which they gradually conquered, advancing in part to a settled state as tillers of the soil, and worshipping the gods of the country side by side with Jehovah. For a long time they were ruled by chieftains or "judges," the most noted of whom, as imbued

with the spirit of Moses and as the founder of
schools of the prophets, giving rise to a class
of men unique in history, was Samuel.   But the
influence of these "judges" was fitful and limited
over such half-barbarous tribes, harassed by foes
amongst and around them, and it was not until
the adoption of the kingly form of government
that unity was secured.   The advance then made
was rapid ; in the reign of David a capital and
chief seat of Jehovah-worship was founded and
the kingdom extended to the Euphrates ; in
that of Solomon the nation reached the height
of its outward glory.   But oppression and waste
bred discontent, and on his death a rebellion
broke out which rent the kingdom asunder ; ten
of the tribes forming the kingdom of Ephraim
or Israel, and the remaining two the kingdom
of Judah.

Contests for the throne and struggles between
the religion of the Canaanites and the Israelites
kept the larger kingdom in constant unquiet,
and the one bright spot in its overcast existence
is the witness of the prophet-reformers, who, in

ever-advancing loftiness of belief, insisted on
faithfulness to Jehovah and holiness of life as
the conditions of well-being. But the fate of
neighbouring nations at last befel the weakened
Israelites ; the Assyrians conquered them and
carried away captive the cream of the people,
leaving a remnant who, mingling with settlers
from their empire, formed the Samaritan race.

Judah had a longer and less troubled career,
but the same elements of strife about the gods
were present, shrines and images abounding,
and the rulers foolishly mixed in the wars
between the great rival empires on either side,
so that in the end the country was conquered by
the stronger power, the capital and shrine burnt,
and the upper classes carried to Babylon.

The great dividing line in Jewish history, which
from the fall of Israel centres in Judæa, is the
Exile ; for the changes, whatever their cause,
which were brought about by that event, were
marked and momentous in their bearing on the
future of the captives. Deprived of temple and
altar, thought was turned to the past ; the law of

Jehovah and the words of his prophets, of whom
well-nigh the last and noblest, proclaiming him
the only true god, had spoken, were deeply
studied ; the one took into itself new and abiding
elements[1] from Chaldæa, and the other fed hope
in deliverance and in a return of the ancient
glory.

On the fall of Babylon, the exiles received
permission from its captor, Cyrus, king of Persia,
to return to their fatherland, and a goodly number availed themselves of this kindly act, bestir-
ring themselves on their arrival to repeople the
waste cities and rebuild the temple.   Progress,
however, was slow, until a zealous scribe named
Ezra stirred the laggards to active obedience to
the law of Jehovah, which he recast and enlarged,
and the explanation of which gave rise to a huge
mass of oral rules and comments, the work of
scribes and rabbis, which ceased not for a thousand years.   The entire policy of Ezra and of
the governor Nehemiah was the erection of a

---

[1] "Many voices were blended there ; unknown voices, speaking out of the early dawn."—*God and the Bible*, p. 185.

priestly state, in which the law of Jehovah was supreme, the simple but more sublime teaching of the prophets falling more and more into the background.

Under the rule of Persia, and afterward of Greece, the Jews had peace, but the savage persecution of Antiochus Epiphanes, designed to stamp out their religion, led to a bloody war, in which the gallant resistance of the Maccabees was successful and the freedom of the nation secured. The influence of Greek thought on the Jewish religion was thus checked, and the distinctive features of the latter more strongly marked than ever; but the independence of the race was brief, for internal quarrels gave the Romans an excuse to interfere in its affairs, and they acquired a hated mastery over it by placing upon the throne the brave and able, but cruel Herod the Great.

BOOK II.

JESUS OF NAZARETH.

I.

Introductory.

THE land of Palestine, over which we have followed the tread of each great empire of the East in its turn, was divided, at the time of the Roman rule, into the provinces of Galilee, Samaria, and Judæa.

In the rough outline of its features given at page 54, I spoke of the more favoured parts as lying to the north, and the histories of the time we have reached witness to their fertility and beauty. The rabbis, in their fanciful way, said that in Galilee men " waded in oil," and that it was " easier to rear a forest of olive trees there than one child in Judæa." From the historic heights, crowned with Jewish villages and farmsteads, the eye rested on a garden-like land of dales and hills, on towns built both in the Greek and Roman style, on the gleaming sea dotted with the sails of the "ships of Tarshish," on the sandy coast along which ran one of the busy highways of trade, the "via maris" or "sea road ;" and, among other ports, on ancient Tyre, famous for its glass and dye works, while inland was the lake of Tiberias, covered with boats catching the fish with which it swarmed.

Galilee, from "galil," a "circle," was the name formerly given to a small part of Palestine occupied by strangers, but at the Roman period it was applied to the province I am now describing, for not only were there remnants of the older Canaanites (still, so M. Ganneau affirms,[1] surviving in the fellahîn or peasants) scattered among the Jews, but a large population of Phœnician, Syrian, Arab, Greek, and other settlers.

The intercourse which could not fail to arise between these and the "chosen" people enlarged the ideas of the latter and freed them from that narrowness which their traditions fostered. But

[1] Cf. *Palest. Explor. Fund Quarterly Report*, Sept. 1875. *Unknown Palestine*, pp. 9-12.

their separation from the sacred city and temple deepened rather than lessened devotion to their faith and eagerness to defend it unto death. " Cowardice was never their failing," Josephus tells us, and they who had given to Israel in the past many prophets and patriots, whose frontier land, bearing the brunt of attacks, had called forth their courage and made them brave defenders, were the more frequent rebels against the Romans, and the ringleaders in the tumults which arose at the great festivals in Jerusalem, which they failed not to attend. Their stricter brethren of the south, boastful of untainted descent and a purer creed, laughed and scoffed at their boorish manners and the rustic brogue by which they were at once known ;[1] but their ignorance of the nicer subtleties of the law was well atoned for by a wider knowledge of "the best book, the world," and their surroundings nourished a piety of more manly type.

Between Galilee and Judæa lay the country

---

[1] Matt. xxvi. 73.

of the detested Samaritans, or Cutheans, as the
Jews called them, from Cuthah, whence many of
them were brought by the Assyrian king.[1] The
causes which led to bitter hatred between the
two races have been stated, and the bad feeling
was increased under the Romans, whose conquest
the Samaritans welcomed for the gain it brought
them in trade, and for the revenge which it
seemed to them, as they looked on their ruined
temple, to inflict on the Jews. To these a
Samaritan was more hateful than a heathen, for
a Gentile might be a friend, and of such an one
there was hope, but of a Cuthean, never ; "he
who takes bread of him is like unto him who
eats swine's flesh." And the hatred was returned.
The Samaritans did their best to annoy the Jews,
confusing their moon-signals, even defiling, it is
said, their temple courts with dead men's bones,
and plotting to murder them as they passed on
their way to the feasts. To avoid the " Cuthite
strip," as the Talmud called it, the Galileans
took a roundabout route to Jerusalem, and would

[1] 2 Kings xvii. 24.

often on their return, with hatred inflamed by
excitement, attack the Samaritans and think
they did Jehovah service by spilling their blood.

The interest awakened by Judæa centres in
Jerusalem, city of the " Great King," the home
of the priesthood and rival parties, the head-
quarters of Rabbinism and all else that, wilfully
shutting out light from the world around, made
Jewish life unlovely as the Judæan landscape,
and stunted as the desert shrubs. But any
account of this and of its renowned temple
will more fitly follow in connection with the
public life of Jesus; here it is of greater
moment to learn what was the general feeling
among the Jews on the loss of their independence.

The conquests of the Romans, by which they
had gained mastery over the world from the
Atlantic to the Euphrates, and from the Rhine
and Danube to the deserts of Africa, were not
unmixed with good, for the advance of races
was quickened in many ways by their being
brought under one powerful rule.

But the matchless skill of the iron-handed victors in fusing their subject peoples one with another was sorely tested in dealing with so unique a race as the Jews. For their traditions and religion, deep-rooted in the past, were, as we have seen, fed by this one idea, that Jehovah had chosen them and set them apart from the rest of mankind; that he was their only King, and the fulfilling of his laws their sole duty; therefore that no foreign power had title to rule over them or impose its laws on them, still less to gather taxes from the land, the produce of which was tithed for the support of the worship of its invisible Owner. Here was a people who would rather die than fight on a sabbath or than eat food which they regarded as unclean; who shrank from the touch of Gentiles, would not buy of them or let houses or fields to them, and permitted no man to be a priest whose mother had been captive among them, and thus cast doubt on the pure descent of her children.

Added to the dislike which every nation feels towards its conquerors, it was to the Jew a

desecration that the land which Jehovah had
given his fathers, a land whose praises the
rabbis never tired of chanting—the centre of the
earth [1]—whose very air made men wise and
immortal, should be trodden by the Gentiles;
an impious thing that he should be called upon
to pay divine honours to the Roman Emperor,
whose soldiers planted their standards beside the
temple, and, most horrible, had peered into its
innermost shrine, since which awful day, so said
the rabbis, flowers had lost their perfume and
fruits their flavour!

The bitter feeling was deepened when there
was set over them a man of the race of Edom
(or "sons of Esau"), a friend, too, of the
Cutheans. Herod "the Great" was brave,
able, and cultured; his reign was one of outward splendour; the country had peace under
him; he cleared the hills of robber-gangs,
made the highways secure, and left proof of
his enterprise and taste in many great public

---

[1] There is a circle of marble and a short column under the
dome of the Greek church at Jerusalem to mark the spot!

O

works, while to win the favour of the Jews he
replaced the second temple, a mean-looking
building, by a costly and splendid structure, and
in time of distress parted with his gold and silver
plate to buy food and clothing for the people.
But his good deeds were marred by crafty and
cruel ones. He angered the Jews by setting up
an eagle, symbol of the Roman power, whose
creature he was, over the chief gate of the
temple, and by building theatres and places for
public games in the holy city, as well as temples
to his master and shrines to the gods of Greece
in different parts. In his fits of savage rage this
hot-blooded Eastern spared not his nearest and
dearest, and at the close of his life, when, a hated
and dreaded old man, he was stricken with a
loathsome disease, he ordered the murder of
certain nobles, that thus there might not fail
mourning at his death ; but the command was
not obeyed. The Jews sent to Rome to entreat
that none of his house might succeed him, and
that they might live according to their own law
under the governor of Syria. But their prayer

was refused, and after tumult and bloodshed the kingdom was divided among Herod's three sons ; Archelaus being placed over Judæa and Samaria, Herod Antipas over Galilee, and Philip over the country beyond Jordan. Six years after this Archelaus was banished on account of his many crimes, and his territory added to the province of Syria, thus coming under the direct rule of a Roman governor, whose seat was at Cæsarea.

The darker the night the brighter flashed the hope of the Jews in the advent of a Messiah. How steadfast it was is illustrated in the touching parable from the Talmud of a man who, having betrothed himself to a beautiful maiden, went away. The girl waited and waited, but he did not return, and her friends and rivals mocked her, saying, " He will never come." Then, weeping, yet not despairing, she would go into her room and read over and over again the letters in which he had promised to be ever faithful, and was comforted. At last he came back, and asking her how she had kept her trust without faltering, she showed him his letters. So Israel,

in exile and in bondage, was mocked by the
nations ; but she went into her schools and
synagogues and took out the ancient writings in
which Jehovah had spoken through the seers and
prophets, and was cheered.   He would in time
redeem it and say, " How could you alone among
all the mocking nations be faithful ? "   And she
would point to the sacred books and answer,
" Had I not your promise there ? "

The book of Daniel and like writings which
it had inspired were eagerly studied ; and while
it is not easy to gather from the tangled visions of
" seers " the actual form in which it was believed
the deliverer would come, it suffices to say here
that the feeling abroad was that he might appear
at any time to " restore the kingdom to Israel,"
and, as the ancient foes had been overthrown,
overthrow this last and terrible fourth beast,
" exceeding dreadful "[1] . . . " that had power
over the world with great fearfulness,"[2] the
empire of Rome.   This hope and the flying
rumours of violations of the law by Romans and

[1] Dan. vii. 19.   [2] 2 Esdras xi. 40.

Greeks kept all classes at fever heat, arousing a more extreme section, known as "Zealots," to fruitless revolts in which, altogether, many thousands were slain. And, indeed, so widespread was the expectation, that writers outside Palestine, who gave small heed to its concerns, speak of the "ancient and firm faith of a people who take their origin from Judæa, that they would become the masters of the whole world,"[1] while the general state of the empire, then one of profound peace, yet of many unhealed wounds, afforded that resting-time in which men may pause to think of the future and give heed to the course which events threaten to take.

Now the Romans, who had many great and fine qualities, were not the people to calmly brook the scorn and hatred of a conquered race, and we cannot wonder that they regarded its notions about its chosen place and destiny as crazy nonsense, to be treated with contempt unless it threatened mischief, when it was to be

[1] Tacitus, *Hist.* v. 13.

crushed by force. The wits in Rome, whither
Jewish slaves had been brought, made merry
over their belief in an imageless god, their
refusal to eat pork, or to work on the sabbath,
repeated shameless fables about them, and
accounted for their holding aloof from the
Gentiles as arising from a terrible oath to hate
all men. Even sober writers, taking no pains
to acquaint themselves with the beliefs and
history of the Jews, did injustice to the sterling
virtues of that mistaken but remarkable race,
the famous Tacitus speaking of them as not inclined to religion because they disdained the
Roman gods, as, in after time, the early Christians were for a like reason called "Atheists,"
(from the Greek *a*, without, and *theos*, God).

The maddening irritation aroused among the
Jews through the taxes imposed by Rome was
increased by the merciless way in which they
were collected. To prevent loss or fraud the
central power sold the revenues of a province
for a fixed sum of money, and the buyers made
as much as they could out of the bargain by

extorting the utmost from the unhappy people, stripping them bare, and goading them again and again to become bandits or rebels.

Such, in brief outline, were the relations between the Jews and their masters at the time when Jesus was born at Nazareth, a mountain village of Galilee. His name, a Greek form of the Hebrew "Joshua" or "Jeshua," meaning "deliverer" or "preserver," was not an uncommon one among the Jews. In the works of their great historian, Josephus, we read of fourteen men, more or less noted, who had borne it; and in the most ancient copies of the lives of Jesus it occurred as a first name of Bar-Abbas [1] ("son of Abbas"), a celebrated rebel of his time; but it was afterwards left out because it was thought a dishonour to Jesus of Nazareth that his name should be worn by a man deemed unworthy.

The exact year when Jesus was born is uncertain. Following an old practice among nations in reckoning time from some striking event in their history—as, for example, the Romans from the

[1] See p. 350.

building of their city, the Greeks from the revival of their public games, the Mohammadans from the flight of their prophet from Mecca— Christians reckon time from the birth of Jesus, the date of which was fixed by a monk named Dionysius, who lived about thirteen hundred years ago. But he was wrong in his figures, because it is certain that Jesus was born before the death of Herod the Great, which took place seven hundred and fifty years after the foundation of Rome, or four years before the Christian era begins.

Therefore, all that can be said with sureness is that Jesus was born somewhere near the Roman year 750 A.U.C.,[1] in the reign of Cæsar Augustus.

It is worth while learning how the 25th of December was fixed on as his birthday, because it is an example of one of the many proofs which history supplies of the mingling of pagan rites and customs with the Christian religion.

In the Roman calendar that day was the day

----

[1] *Ab urbe conditâ,* " from the founding of the city."

of the winter "solstice;" that is, when the sun, reaching its apparent furthest point from the equator, seems to "stand still," and then to turn back wheel-like in its path through the heavens. When, with the entrance of the Oriental religions, the worship of Mithra, one of the Vedic sun-gods, spread from the East into Rome, this day became dedicated to him as the "birthday of the unconquered sun," and was ushered in with feasting. For men rejoiced when the turning-point of the year was reached, and when nature, awaking from her winter sleep, doffed her sombre dress and put on the fresh green robe of spring-time, decked with early flowers, in witness of renewed life. These combined to make the season celebrated, and at last, during the fourth century of our era, the Roman Christians gave to the birthday of Mithra a fuller and richer meaning in fixing upon it as the birthday of him in whom they believed as "the light of the world." It was a happy and beautiful thought on which they loved to dwell; and when their missionaries went forth to convert the tribes of

Northern Europe they found it easy to impart such glad observance of the season, it being the merry "yule" time among those rude sun-worshippers. And in the blazing logs and ornamented trees and hanging sprigs of mistletoe— a sacred plant among them—there linger the customs of our forefathers, as in each rite and ceremony as well as in certain doctrines of the Christian religion there are the traces of Egyptian and still older influences.

Nazareth was an obscure place until the birth of Jesus made it famous, for it is not named in the Old Testament, neither in the Talmud, nor by Josephus. It lies on the slopes of steep and lofty hills which rise from the plains of Galilee ; its houses, built of limestone quarried from the rocks on which they stand, bowered in vines, palms, and olive trees, make a bright picture, to which the richness of the surrounding country adds its charms—"a handful of pearls in a goblet of emeralds." From the breezy hilltops which overlook the town a view exceeding fair is commanded of green plains and fruitful valleys, wooded heights, and, beyond these, westward, the purple sea ; northward, snow-capped Hermon ; while all the land around is dotted with places famed in Jewish history and dear to all pious hearts.

Changes come about so slowly in the East that to the traveller in Palestine who knows the Bible well, the past stands before him, not only in the manners and customs of the people, but in the very phrases that fall from their lips ; and as he climbs the steep and winding path that leads him to the streets of Nazareth it is not difficult to picture the scenes amidst which Jesus played in his boyhood and toiled in his manhood. He was one of a large family of boys and girls, whose parents, Joseph and Mary, belonged to the working class, the father being a carpenter. Their home was, doubtless, like the homes of such humble folk at this day—a plain stone building, lighted solely by the doorway, its only furniture a painted chest or seat built along the wall, a stool on which the food

is put and around which the household sit on
crossed knees or on mats, while a few water jars
complete the scanty contents. Such a home
among us would denote extreme poverty; not
so in Eastern villages, where that hard fight for
a crust which the toilers in crowded places have
to wage, and that foolish and unresting craving
after show and costly trifles to which so many
are slaves, are alike unknown, and where scarce
a want is felt when once food and clothing, both
costing but little, are supplied.

Among the chief buildings of Nazareth are
a mosque, for the larger number of the people
are Mohammadans, and a Roman Catholic
monastery, which, it is pretended, stands on the
site of Joseph's house, and in which is shown
the "grotto" where, according to legend, an
angel appeared to Mary to foretell the birth
of Jesus. But the Greek church has a "grotto"
which is also claimed as the genuine scene of
that event! Among the true relics, however, in
the ancient town is a well called the "fountain
of the Virgin," to which the women of Nazareth

brought their water-jars to be filled, and around
which they gossiped in the time of Jesus, as do
the women there to this day.

When the slender materials from which our
knowledge about him is derived are stripped
of their legends, there is scarcely anything left
with which to form a picture of his boyhood.
He has suffered the common fate of men of
mark in the myths which have gathered round
him, and his lot was cast in a time when every
wonder-tale found ready believers. The fewer
the facts, the greater was the space to be filled
with legend ; and whoever towered above his
fellows was sure to be credited with superhuman
powers, while the followers of such an one saw
in these the means of adding to his fame. Thus
it is that a number of "apocryphal gospels" arose
which have been wisely cast aside as worthless,
yet which possess interest as showing what
childish tales about him found a hearing in
early Christian times. These tell how he tamed
lions and panthers in Egypt, where the idols fell

prostrate at his coming; how a dumb bride who kissed him forthwith spoke and heard; how a girl and a prince were healed of leprosy by the water in which he had been washed; how a bandage from his body, made into a little shirt and worn by a child, saved it from burning in a blazing oven, and from drowning in a well; how the smell of his clothes raised a dead boy to life; how, when playing with other boys who were moulding clay beasts and birds, he made his images walk and leap; how he turned some of his playmates, when hiding from him, into goats; and how, entering a dyer's shop, he threw all the pieces of cloth into a vat of indigo, and then relieved the man's distress by bringing each piece dyed the exact colour he wanted.[1] In contrast to this drivel we have the following and only story of his boyhood in the New Testament, the general features of which have an air of truth.

Every year crowds of Jewish pilgrims journeyed

---

[1] See *Apocryphal Gospels*, translated by B. H. Cowper, *passim*.

from all parts to Jerusalem in obedience to
the law to keep the great feasts. Among those
who went from Nazareth to observe the Passover
were Joseph and Mary, taking Jesus with them,
who, having reached his twelfth year, was on the
eve of becoming a "son of the law;" for at the
age of thirteen a youth was required to practise
all its commandments.[1]   On their return home-
ward, his parents seem to have travelled some
distance before they found that he was not
with the caravan, and, after seeking for him
in vain, they went back to Jerusalem in sore
distress.   They scoured the city without success,
and, as a forlorn hope, made their way to the
temple, where, to their joy, they found him
among the scholars, sitting round the teachers
of the law in the "hall of hewn stones."   He
was not only listening, intently to their debate over knotty matters, but taking part in
it, giving such clear answers, and asking such
puzzling questions in return, that "all who
heard him were astonished at his understand-

---

[1] *P. Aboth*, p. 111, addenda.

ing." Such cases of ripeness of knowledge
in early boyhood are by no means rare in the
East, where both body and mind develop much
quicker than with us. According to the "apocryphal gospels" he strikes the teachers and
elders speechless, solves all questions in the law,
makes clear the meaning of the prophets, and
teaches astronomers and others the leading
truths of their sciences, so that they fall worshipping at his feet; but, in the "gospel according to Luke," the story is more soberly
concluded by his mother asking—

"Son, why hast thou thus dealt with us? behold thy father and I have sought thee sorrow-
ing. And he said, How is it that ye sought me?
wist ye not that I must be about my Father's
business? And they understood not the saying
which he spake unto them. And he went
down with them, and came to Nazareth, and
was subject unto them: but his mother kept
all these sayings in her heart. And Jesus increased in wisdom and stature, and in favour
with God and man." [1]

[1] Luke ii. 48–52.

These few closing words, with their faithful touch of his mother treasuring the sayings of her bright boy, comprise all that we are told about Jesus from his twelfth year till he had long passed manhood, for his name was obscure until he flashed into fame as a teacher, and the facts of his earlier life were unknown or matters of slight concern to his disciples. It was not till some time after his death that enquiry was set afoot about his origin, and then it was that the few facts at hand were made to yield to legends of his birth at Bethlehem, and of the wonders that attended it, by which it was vainly sought to prove that the foretellings of old concerning a Messiah were fulfilled in him.[1] Therefore the only means we have of knowing aught concerning his boyhood and training is in learning what we can about the education given to Jewish youths in Galilee in his time, adding to this all that may be gathered from current histories as to the circumstances surrounding him and shaping his character.

[1] See pp. 107-114.

P

Both law and custom among the Jews made the instruction of their children a sacred duty. Among no other people has the family bond been so strong, and next to the command to honour Jehovah stood the command to honour father and mother. These saw in their children the gifts of God, and the childless wife was a reproach among her people and a sorrow to herself, since none knew from whom the Messiah might be born. The Old Testament gives us charming pictures of the influence of the mother in the training of her children, and the Talmud, despite many slighting remarks upon woman, says, " He is best taught who has first learned from his mother ; " but the duty of instructing the child in the law was laid chiefly on the father. " Blessed," said the rabbis, " is the son who has studied with his father, and blessed is the father who has taught his son ; " while Josephus boasts that " our honour and the highest end of life is the education of our children and the observance of the law."

" The world is saved by the breath of schoolchildren" is one of the most beautiful sayings of the rabbis; but although schools were founded in Palestine some eighty years before the birth of Jesus, they were confined to the larger towns, the schoolmaster in smaller places like Nazareth being the "reader" in the synagogue.

The poorest home was probably not without some roll or portion of the sacred books, and in every act of family life the precepts of the "law" were set before the children; but more complete knowledge of the scriptures, combining as they did history and religion in one, was gained in the synagogue, where, as laid down by the rabbis, a boy would attend as early as his fifth or sixth year, and hear them read and explained. Judging from the after career of Jesus, the "law" had small charm for him, compared with the music of the psalms, and the brilliant visions of the prophets to which he was to give so lofty a meaning, while many of his discourses show that he was familiar with the book of Daniel and similar writings which then fed and fired the imagination, as well as with some of the more beautiful sayings of the rabbis.

Beyond these and learning to read and write in his Aramaic mother-tongue, the book-knowledge of Jesus did not go; the rabbis said since it was written of the law, "Thou shalt study it day and night," any other study could be carried on only when it was neither day nor night—that is, never. A curse was pronounced against the Jew who taught his children Greek, nor could he hope for eternal life who read the books of other nations, or taught the Gentiles to read the law. So the schooling of Jesus was of a scanty kind; he shared the common superstitions of the humble peasants among whom he lived, and grew up ignorant of the general state of the world, and of such progress as the more advanced nations had made in science.

But he was not therefore badly educated, for nature and human life were his chief teachers. It was a gainful thing for the work which he was to do in the world, without which, indeed, it would not have been done, that his lot was cast amidst the fair beauty and open surroundings of despised Galilee instead of amidst the barred-in life of gloomy Judæa, that thus he could readily pass into the larger life of mankind, to whose struggles after unity he was to render such splendid service. The lack of book-knowledge, in itself a cramping thing, left more room for storing within all that was brought by eye and ear; the wealth of parable and illustration drawn from the beautiful hills and bowery dales of Nazareth, and from the busy lives of men passing along the great highways at its feet, or following their calling, show how keen he was to observe, how, " look where he might, he saw in all things some new knowledge, some revelation concerning the will of the Father in heaven.'

Such were the conditions amidst which Jesus grew up, but when we have learned all that we can about these, there will remain in him, as in the life of every great man, much that fails us to explain. If we knew *all* we should know him, whereas we have but a shred of history about him from his birth till at least his thirtieth year; one somewhat doubtful story of his journey as a boy to Jerusalem, nothing more! Yet we must not say that to the extent to which we cannot understand him he is superhuman, a demigod above the reach of knowledge, for that would be to fall into the error by which man once sought to explain whatever was outside the limits of the knowledge of his time, and furthermore make all effort to be like Jesus beyond our power and fruitful of despair. It would be thought unbecoming if I were to detail in a book of this kind how science makes clear the whilom secret of the transmission of character from parents to offspring, so that every man is a son not only of his own time, but of all time that has gone before him, and how it accounts for the uprising, often amidst commonplace surroundings, of some wondrous genius as the result of subtle, slow-working causes which at last receive the quickening touch producing such an one.

Abler and more scientific books than this must be read for the understanding of a matter so important in its bearing on our conduct, and so potent in ridding the mind of the old notion concerning the great ones of our race, that "the gods have come down in the likeness of men."[1]

No mention is made of Joseph after the story of the finding of Jesus in the temple, and we may fairly conclude, apart from a statement in the "apocryphal" history about him that he died when Jesus was nineteen years old,[2] that Mary was widowed somewhat early, and that the care of maintaining the household fell upon the sons. These, in accordance with Jewish custom, had been taught some handicraft, probably their father's, and it would appear that for some years Jesus, whether the eldest among them or not we cannot say, worked as a carpenter, and waited as a pious Jew for the kingdom of God. The event which called him from Nazareth, and

[1] Acts xiv. 11.
[2] *Apoch. Gospels*, pp. 111, 112. Cowper's ed.

but for which his life of toil and quiet thought
might never have been disturbed, was the preaching of John the Baptist. News had reached
Galilee of the appearance of a man altogether
unlike the teachers of the day, and who seemed
rather as one of the old prophets, the like of
whom had not been heard for full four hundred
years. Crowds were flocking to this man—no
smooth-tongued preacher, but one whose words
were as of fire, that, like Elijah's, " burned as
a torch." He was clad in the prophet's dress
of camel skin, fastened with a leather girdle, and
had come from the wilderness near the Dead
Sea, where he had lived on such food as that
barren place yielded—honey from the wild
flowers, and locusts dried in the sun, the fare of
the poorest in the East—while his soul had fed
itself with thoughts of God's presence and swift-
avenging power, and been quickened into action
by the story of Israel's past. Between him and
the prophets, wide as was the gap in time, there
was deep fellow-feeling, and he found in their
unheeded words the truth to which his soul re-

sponded and which he must perforce proclaim to his people.

When and where he was born, or who were his parents, we know not; but he was probably a native of Judæa, the unlovely land that nursed the loveless religion of priests and rabbis. Against their irksome and insipid rules his richer nature revolted, and broke forth in this stern message to men to change their lives, and thus make themselves worthy of freedom : " Repent : the kingdom of heaven is at hand."

All classes gathered from Jerusalem and other parts to hear him. A motley crowd of half-curious and half-earnest folk they were; Pharisees and scribes, soldiers from Roman garrisons, tax-collectors, shame-stricken women, and other outcasts from the commonwealth of Israel.

The place itself added to the striking features of the scene. Not far from where the preacher stood declaring that "the axe is laid to the root of the trees, and every tree that bears not good fruit God will hew down and cast into the fire," was the plain where, according to the legend

that still had weird power upon the people, the
wicked cities had been destroyed by fire from
heaven. So powerful and heart-hitting were the
words of counsel and reproach, that many confessed their sins and were baptized in the Jordan,
as a symbol of the cleansing of their souls from
guilt ; and, although when the novelty had worn
off some went back to live their old lives, a
society of faithful disciples was formed of which
we find traces long after the death of John.

Among the hearers drawn by the fame of the
preacher from Galilee was Jesus, then in the
prime of manhood. He found in John a spirit
which beat akin to his own ; in his words life-
bringers, satisfying yearnings that in Galilee
could not be uttered, or if uttered, not understood by his fellows there ; and, in token of his
acceptance of John's demands and of his desire
to give himself to God, was baptized by him.
The fair repute which he had borne in Nazareth,
and which no slanders and libels of his foes
years after his death could tarnish, is proof of his
devout and holy life ; yet the burning words of

John made him feel that he fell short of the ideal he had striven to reach. For it is not the self-contented but the pure who dare not thank God that they are "not as other men are."

After his baptism Jesus joined himself to John, and prepared himself after the manner of men committed to great things by withdrawing to some part of the wild desert in the neighbourhood of the Dead Sea, where he fasted "forty" days and "forty" nights, so says the story.[1] There he underwent a terrible struggle. Doubts perplexed him as to his fitness, as to his sufficing goodness for the work of "preaching the kingdom," as to the rightness of the step which cut him adrift from home and kindred and sent him on a path beset with peril. In the end the weariness of body induced by hunger and sleeplessness so affected and overturned his brain, that the demons with which popular ignorance peopled such lonesome spots seemed to have actual shape, and in the supreme moment of agony and struggle between the better and the

[1] Matt. iv. 2.

worse, Satan, the archfiend, who was commonly believed in at that time, appeared to stand before him and beguile him from his purpose by bribes and taunts which Jesus repelled with words from the Jewish scriptures. The battle with the "tempter" over, there fell on the soul of Jesus a great calm, and the repose that followed was sweetened with visions of ministering angels.

So in the old Persian scriptures [1] the evil spirit Drukhsh comes forth to frustrate the holy aims of Zarathusthra, and is routed by sacred words, and in the temptation of Gautama the Buddha [2] the author of evil, Mâra, has, after many attempts to entice him, to retire defeated, when guardian angels attend the victor with words of comfort and scatter flowers and pour perfumes over him. At the base of these legends, as of those about the "saints" of the early and middle ages, where half-starved monks and nuns see the devil in all sorts of forms,

---

[1] *Vendidâd*, fargard xix, cf. Haug, p. 252.

[2] Beal's *Romantic History of Buddha*, pp. 199, et seq.

ghastly and alluring, as also of the traditions of savage races, there is the fact of their origin solely in unhealthy action of the mind induced by weakness or weariness, and, to an intense degree, by fastings. As Dr. Tylor says, " Bread and meat would have robbed the saint of many an angel's visit ; the opening of the larder must many a time have closed the gates of heaven to his gaze." [1]

On leaving the desert news reached Jesus that his dear friend and counsellor had been cast into prison by Herod Antipas. According to the account in the " gospel according to Luke," John's offence was that he had dared to reprove the king for his unlawful marriage with his brother's wife, while Josephus tells us Herod feared that the great influence which John had over the people might put it into his power to raise a rebellion.[2] For he went about preaching the advent of the " kingdom of heaven," and whatever he and his followers may have meant by that phrase, to the Romans it savoured of

[1] *Prim. Culture*, ii. 376.   [2] *Antiq.* xviii. 5, 2.

treason—setting up another rule.   Herod knew
that John shared the hopes then uppermost in
the minds of his race, shared therefore their
bitter hatred of the power that drained them of
their young men for soldiers, and of their goods
for taxes.   So he silenced the bold man who had
wandered into his territory, fearful that he might
excite a rebellion, the slightest success of which
imperilled Herod's favour with the emperor.

No doubts crossed the mind of Jesus on hearing this cheerless news as to the course which he
should take.   It was to carry on John's work, if
not in exactly the same way, for they were
men of unlike temperament, with the same
unflagging zeal ; and breaking new ground he
returned to Galilee, fixing his preaching-centre
at the little town of Capernaum, situate on the
busy shores of the lovely Lake of Tiberias, " the
eye of Galilee," and dwelling as a guest in the
house of two brothers, Simon Peter and Andrew,
who gained their living by fishing, and whose
friendship he may have made in earlier days.

II.

Sources of Knowledge about Jesus.

BEFORE attempting any sketch of the public life of Jesus it is needful to say somewhat concerning the materials from which it is drawn, and thus justify the uncertainty with which one must speak about all that attaches to him. These materials are found mainly in the "gospels" with which the New Testament begins, for although certain "epistles" or letters in that collection were written earlier, they supply no account of the life of Jesus. Their author, the apostle Paul, who did not know him, was addressing people supposed to be acquainted with the traditions then current, and moreover his main object was to set forth the relation in which he believed Jesus, as ascended into heaven, from whence he was expected to return, stood towards his disciples. Outside the New Testament the references are very scanty. Josephus, who was born two years after the

death of Jesus, makes mention of him in two
places in his celebrated history, but the longer
passage[1] has been altered by a Christian hand,
so as to make it appear that Josephus regarded
Jesus as more than a man. In the Talmud he is
spoken of with contempt and stupid rancour,
while among the few passages in pagan writers
the most precious is that of Tacitus,[2] who alludes
to the death of Jesus under the Roman governor,
Pontius Pilate, in a way that shows what little
stir that event created at the time. Indeed, he,
like other observing men of his day, did not
realize what a tremendous power the Christian
religion was to become in the world. To them
it was only an offshoot of Judaism, and the
remarks even of noble-minded men like Epic-
tetus and Marcus Aurelius are pitched in the
same tone of contempt in which they spoke of
the Jewish religion. The pagan faiths were
decaying, and they knew it, yet failed to see in
the Christian religion that which most surely
answered to the aims and emotions of men, and

[1] *Antiq.* xviii. 3, 8.   [2] *Annals,* xv. 44.

to that feeling of world-wide brotherhood which the loftier minds were expressing. We must not blame them that they could not read aright "the signs of the times," for such insight is given to few, and to the many the noisiest force is the strongest.

Of the four gospels, those "according to" Matthew, Mark, and Luke, although written from different standpoints, are on the whole in fair agreement concerning what they narrate, and are for that reason called the "synoptics," from a Greek word, meaning "seeing together;" but the fourth and latest, that "according to" John, is so clearly the work of a man full of the views of a certain school about Jesus, and more intent on setting these forth than on writing a narrative about him, that although it is of exceeding beauty it is of small value for our purpose.

Jesus wrote nothing himself, and these lives of him are based solely upon traditions which were preserved in the memories of his disciples, and handed down by word of mouth. They believed so fully in his speedy return to them after his death that all motive for writing down his sayings was taken away, and they were suffered to float in unfixed form for some years, until the circle of the earlier disciples growing smaller, and the hope of his coming back fainter, danger arose lest the treasured words should be lost, and so little " sayings of the Lord " were made by one and another, and passed current among the believers, receiving additions from time to time. From these and oral traditions " in the air " were compiled the memoirs out of which grew the gospels, the earliest trace of which in their present form is in the latter half of the second century.[1]

From this we see that any record of a man so remarkable as Jesus of Nazareth has been left to chance alone. No disciple attended him to note down the warm words as they fell, and guard every utterance with jealous care ; no one took up the pen directly after his death to tell the beautiful and moving story, and we are left

[1] Note E.

to grope our way among confused and meagre records, gleaning from them how a peasant of Galilee who had lived in an obscure village for full thirty years, appeared as a preacher of the "kingdom of God," was attended by crowds of eager listeners, of whom but a few remained faithful, and, changing his views regarding himself, attacked priestcraft in its stronghold at Jerusalem, and was there put to death as a mover of sedition.

Coming to us in the way I have outlined, it is no matter for wonder that the records sadly lack arrangement, and that we cannot set down, except in very rough and uncertain fashion, the *order of events* in the life of Jesus. According to the " synoptics," his ministry lasted about a year, beginning in Galilee, where it was carried on till he went to Jerusalem and there met his death. According to the fourth gospel, it began at Jerusalem, and was varied by journeys into Galilee, and even through Samaria, lasting in all about three years. A like difficulty meets us in striving to arrange the *order of the sayings* of

Jesus, because in the gospels discourses given at various times are lumped together, as, for example, in the unsurpassed " Sermon on the Mount," which, by the way, Luke says was preached upon a plain ; and the only method of picking out the earlier sayings from the later is by first acquainting ourselves with the earlier and later views of Jesus concerning his mission, and thus fixing the probable occasions which called forth his utterances.

No less a difficulty faces us when we ask what warrant we have that the gospels record his *exact words*, for they were addressed to unlearned men mostly drawn by Jesus from his own rank in society, and sharing the gross notions of their class, who could not understand his meaning, and so the words as they passed into their minds conveyed quite another sense than that in which he who was so much " over the heads " of his hearers used them. And then the records, the work of men who wrote from hearsay, differ from one another in reporting the same matters, so that we cannot say

which is the correct version, and must lament
that both he and his hearers, and the writers of
the gospels as well, could not foresee what
opposing views about him would arise in after
years, what value would be attached to his words,
causing these to be quarrelled and fought over
and died for by unnumbered men and women.
The marvel is, even making full allowance for
the greater power of the human memory in
bygone times to faithfully report traditions word
for word, and for the striking and best-remem-
bered form, as parable and pithy saying, in which
so much of his teaching was cast, that what has
survived of all he said impresses us as truly
embodying its spirit;[1] vivid indeed must have
been the image of the teacher; vivid the manner
and matter of his teaching, which, filtered
through many minds and many tongues, touches

---

[1] "The tradition of followers suffices to insert any number of
marvels, and may have inserted all the miracles which he is
reputed to have wrought; but who among his disciples, or
among their proselytes, was capable of inventing the sayings
ascribed to Jesus, or of imagining the life and character revealed
in the gospels?"—J. S. Mill, *Essay on Theism*, p. 253.

us through the simple and stately language of
our English Bible.

Added to the drawbacks which have been
named, there are the legends and miracles with
which the four lives of Jesus are suffused, and
which, in showing us that the prevailing belief
in these things was shared by the writers of the
gospels, make us careful what we accept from
them. Of this, however, more anon; here my
sole object is to show that there are no ancient
writings to which greater importance has been
given, and of which so little can be known,
although from them men are from time to time
constructing lives of Jesus as minute and wordy
as if every detail about him, with undisputed
vouchers of its truth, were in their hands. Now,
the foregoing outline of the nature and value of
the sources of knowledge on this subject will not
be without service if it saves you from reading
the countless books in which scholars have dis-
cussed the age and authorship of the gospels—
an irksome task, which few will perform and from
which none can profit. It will also suffice to

show that a *life* of Jesus, in the usual sense of that word, is *impossible;* that all we can hope for, as we read the obscure phrases and varying statements of these ancient gospels, is to gather some idea of the secret of the enduring power of a man whose influence for good in this world cannot well be overrated. And in this life of ours, which finds so much serious work ready to hand, it is some gain to learn that among the self-appointed and result-less tasks over which men have spent years, are all attempts to construct lives of Jesus from the gospels, and systems of doctrine from his sayings, whereby the beauty and fitness of these may elude us, and the life that is in them escape.

III.

The Public Ministry of Jesus.

JESUS, perhaps attracted by the loveliness of the district and its numerous population, among whom were many welcoming faces, made, as

already stated, his head-quarters at Capernaum,
and thence travelled from town to town in
the neighbourhood, seizing on every chance that
offered itself, whether in the house where he
tarried as a guest, or by the wayside, or in the
market-place, or in the fishing-boat rocking by
the lake shore, or on the hillside and plain, to
proclaim his message. Whenever he could he
made choice of the synagogues, which were open
not only on Saturdays, when the most important
service was held, but also on Mondays and
Thursdays to suit the country folk, who brought
their produce to market, and laid their disputed
cases before the local Sanhedrin which existed
in every town. Success rapidly attended his
mission. Many gathered round him, following
him with more or less stedfastness over the
little tract of country where he laboured, and
forming the kernel of a society, as of brethren
and sisters, from whom he chose fellow-helpers,
twelve in number—perhaps in imitation of the
"twelve" tribes of ancient Israel—and to whom
he gave minute directions as to the mode of

carrying on the work.[1] The simple needs of Jesus, who was never married, and of his co-labourers, were easily and willingly supplied. We read that "many ministered unto him of their substance."[2] Rarely do we find them meeting with churlish treatment, for such was the charm of the Master's manner, such the winsomeness of his message, that he made friends wherever he went. Apart from this, kindness to wayfarers is the rule in the East. Open places, or "khans," for the lodgment of travellers were provided along high-roads, and both the oral and written law of the Jews enjoined kindness to strangers. In Jerusalem each man was expected to throw open his house to pilgrims; and the rabbis not only said, "Let the needy be thy household," but, "Let thy house be a meeting-place for the wise, and drink their words with thirstiness,"[3] thus making the reception of sages and teachers an honour to the host.

At an early part of his ministry, the loving

---

[1] Cf. Matthew x. *passim.*   [2] Luke viii. 3.
[3] *P. Aboth,* i. 4.

heart of Jesus went out towards his kindred and friends that they might hear " the good news of the kingdom of God." So " he came to Nazareth where he had been brought up, and as his custom was, he went into the synagogue on the sabbath day and stood up for to read."

In his time there was no small town in Palestine, or in any place abroad where Jews had settled, without its synagogue, for the most part plain, square-shaped buildings, but slightly decorated, for art had no home among the race to whom the commandment against graven images had been given.[1] These places, which, as we saw at p. 134, had their origin about the time of the exile, (although according to the wild talk of the rabbis, they, in common with many other things, date from the age of the patriarchs,) were the centres of Jewish life " for teaching every virtue which the human and the divine enjoins." There were separate seats for men and women, the scribes and elders sitting on the " chief seats,"[2] a pulpit for the " reader," and

[1] Wisdom of Solomon xv. 4, 5, 17.　　　[2] Matt. xxiii. 6.

in a niche in the wall facing Jerusalem, whither
the Jew turned his face in prayer, the chest in
which the rolls of the "law" were kept. The
sabbath service was very long; first many
prayers, often "vain repetitions," as Jesus called
them, which were offered standing, for the custom
of kneeling was unknown to the Jews; then a
portion of the "law," followed by a reading from
one of the "prophets." After this a scribe or
other adult Jew who so willed, for there was no
fixed order of clergy, gave an address explaining
what had been read or expressing his own ideas
upon it, " bringing forth from his treasure things
new and old,"[1] in which addresses was the germ
of sermons in Christian assemblies. Of course
it happened that the more learned and fluent
came forward to do this, and so the duty fell
into the hands of a class honoured for it with the
title of " Rabbi," or " Master ; " but the privilege
remained with every grown-up Jew, and the
rabbis were more often than not men who
toiled as handworkers for their bread.

[1] Matt. xiii. 52.

On the Saturday morning when Jesus entered
the synagogue of his native town, where he had
worshipped as a boy, and perchance acted as an
expounder when a man, the news of his arrival had
spread, and old friends and neighbours came in
to hear him. The lesson from the "law" being
over, he stood up to read, and the "hazzan," or
minister, "delivered unto him the roll of the
prophet Isaiah. And when he had opened the
book he found the place where it was written,
The spirit of the Lord is upon me, because he
hath anointed me to preach glad tidings to the
poor; he hath sent me to heal the broken-
hearted, to preach deliverance to the captives
and recovering of sight to the blind, to set at
liberty them that are bruised, to preach the
acceptable year of the Lord. And he closed the
book and he gave it again to the minister, and
sat down "[1] (as was the custom of the rabbis
when teaching) to expound the passage. Beginning by saying to them, "This day is this

---

[1] Luke iv. 17-20. Quoted, like most of the Old Testament
passages given in the New, from the Greek version or Septuagint.

scripture fulfilled in your ears," he proceeded
with the ready utterance which practice had given
him to speak words so exceeding sweet and
gracious that the Nazarenes wondered, and put
one to another the question, as if half doubting
when they asked it, " Is not this Joseph's son ?"
according to other accounts, asking, " Whence
hath this man this wisdom ? Is not this the
carpenter's son ? Is not his mother called Mary ?
and his brethren, James and Joses and Simon
and Judas ? and his sisters, are they not all with
us ? Whence then hath this man all these
things ? And they were offended in him." [1]

He had grown up in their midst ; some of
them had played with him as a boy ; he had received no better education than had been given
to them, and now the commonplace dullards
stood agape when it appeared what loftier spirit
than their own had dwelt among them unheeded. The cause of their anger is not clear,
but it would doubtless arise through the wider
scope which he gave to the words of Isaiah ; their

---

[1] Matt. xiii. 54-56; Mark vi. 2, 3.

narrowness evoked reproof from him ; he retorted
by telling them that " no prophet is accepted in
his own country, or in his own house ; " and then
some of the angrier among his hearers, so it is
said, sought to kill him by throwing him from
a steep rock, but he escaped down the mountain path, and returned to Capernaum.

How slender was the tie between Jesus and his
relations, caring as he did so little for the mere
bond of nature where no kinship of spirit was
present, is shown in the following incident, which
perhaps belongs to a later period in his ministry.
One day, when a crowd had gathered round the
house at Capernaum where he was preaching,
some one pushed through to tell him that his
mother and brethren wanted to speak to him.
According to one account, they had given it as
their belief that he was mad,[1] and now perchance
sought to restrain him or take him back with
them.   Whatever may have been their motive,
he harshly resented the interruption, asking,
" Who are my mother and my brothers ? "   Then

[1] Mark iii. 21.

looking upon his disciples, he said, "Behold my mother and my brethren! For whosoever shall do the will of God, the same is my brother and sister and mother."[1] On another occasion, when a woman in the crowd, moved by his winsome teaching, "lifted up her voice and said unto him, Blessed the womb that bare thee and breasts which thou didst suck, he answered," with what reproof, if the after idolatry of his mother had been known to him, let them ponder who practise it, "Nay rather, blessed they that hear the word of God and keep it."[2]

IV.

His Mode of Teaching.

CONCERNING the method of his discourses, one of the "fathers," as the early Christian writers are called, thus tersely describes it :—"His speeches were short and convincing, for he was not a sophist, but his word was the power of God."

[1] Mark iii. 31-35.   [2] Luke xi. 27, 28.

Like the sages and rabbis, he delighted in the use of pithy, telling sentences, which often sparkled with a fresh, kindly humour, and sank into the memory when more wordy discourses might have passed by unheeded. As, for example, in such sayings as these :—

"No one puts a new patch upon an old garment, for that which is put in to fill it up taketh from the garment and the rent is made worse."

"Neither do men put new wine into old skins, else the skins burst and the wine runs out. But they put new wine into new skins and both are preserved."

"They that are healthy need not a doctor, but they that are sick."

"First pluck the beam out of thine own eye, and then thou shalt see clearly to cast the mote out of thy brother's eye."

"Which of you by anxious thought can add to his life-time one cubit?"

"Some men strain out a gnat and swallow a camel."

"Do men gather grapes off thorns and figs off thistles? So men, like trees, are known by their fruits."

"If ye keep not that which is small, who will give you that which is great?"[1]

"The lamp of the body is the eye ; if thine eye be sound, thy whole body will be full of light."

---

[1] Westcott's *Study of the Gospels*, p. 426, where a list of the traditional sayings of Jesus is given.

Sometimes he spoke in enigmas, as when he said :

" Let the dead bury their dead."
" A camel shall go through the eye of a needle before a rich man shall enter the kingdom of God."
" He who saveth his life shall lose it."

But following an art dear to the story-telling East, earliest home of our fables and folk-lore, he freely made use of the "parable," *placing beside*, as that word means, the truth he taught some "illustration" from the life of men and the world around to *throw light* upon it, and make it clear or awaken attention, as in the story of the sage who one sultry afternoon, when expounding a subtle question of the law and seeing his listeners becoming drowsy, suddenly burst out, "There was once a woman in Egypt who brought forth at one birth six hundred thousand men." At this his hearers roused themselves, and then the teacher calmly went on to tell them that her name was Jochebed, and that she was the mother of Moses, who was worth as much as all that number of armed men

R

said to have gone up from Egypt under him, and
having thus secured their attention went on with
his subject.[1]

Of this art of teaching by parable and striking
illustration Jesus was a master, not only winning
men by the vividness and simpleness of his
language, but by the homeliness of the sources
from whence his sketches are taken. Not often
does he draw from the stores of Jewish history,
never from the stars, perhaps because he shared
the mystic awe with which his race looked on
them, for in the Hebrew tongue the same word
serves for "angel" and for "star." But intro-
ducing his story after the manner of the rabbis

---

[1] Which reminds us of the story about Demosthenes, to whose
warnings against Philip of Macedon the Athenians wearied of
listening. One day, when his hearers turned their backs on
him, he cried out, "A man hired an ass of another man." At
this the audience stopped to hear the tale, and Demosthenes
went on, "At noonday he lay down' in the shadow of the beast
to rest, when the owner passing by saw him sleeping, and
shaking him roughly, said, You hired the ass, not his shadow."
Demosthenes, seeing with what rapt attention the people were
listening, paused and said, "O Athenians! when I tell you of
your country's danger, you turn away, but you crowd about me
when I narrate a silly story."

by asking, "To what is the matter like?" he
depicts men at their daily toil in vineyard, field,
and town, and on the lake; their barterings,
their merriments, mournings, and devotions; the
children playing in the market-place; the debtors
haled to prison; the wounded and robbed
travellers by the highways; the lame and blind
by the roadside; the lepers and the insane
among the whitewashed tombs; in all, as in the
illustrations borrowed from nature, the overcast
or unflecked sky, the cornfields, the flowers in
their unsought beauty, the birds in their toilless
freedom, showing his observing skill.

V.

His Religion.

TURNING from the manner to the matter of his
discourses let us try to gather from them what
was the religion of Jesus; in other words, what
were his ideas about God and man.

Of God he speaks again and again as a father

with whom he lived in close fellowship ever
strengthened by prayer, towards whom his love
went forth without stint, and into whose hands
he committed himself in trust that never
wavered. To speculate or argue about the
nature of that Being was altogether foreign to
his mind ; he, the clearsouled and unquestioning,
had ripened in obedience and love in sunny
Galilee, undreaming of the bewildering guesses
of philosophers, untroubled by the perplexing
thoughts born of larger views of the universe. We
shall seek in vain among the sayings of Jesus for
any additions to human *knowledge*, for any light
on the darkling mysteries that quicken wonder
and deepen reverence where not dulled and
blunted by fables and half-truths ; his work was
to add without measure to the sum of human *goodness*. He uses the terms about God found in the
sacred writings of his people, coins no novel ones,
but gives to the ancient words all the force of a
new truth which he had worked out for himself,
tested and tried by his own heart's experience.
And since man in the poverty of thought images

to his mind the power that is beyond all thought
under some symbol borrowed from that which
stands to him for what is highest and best, it is
not easy to find a more beautiful figure under
which to conceive of the Almighty than as a
parent. Fatherhood implies sonship, and Jesus
in thinking of God as a father, felt himself to be
a son. Nor he alone. Believing this of himself,
there could not fail to go forth from him those
lofty ideas about the relation of men to God
which were the source and secret of his power.
For how could he look with other than reverence
upon, or think meanly of, the meanest made in
the image of God, or fail to be drawn the more
pityingly to the poor, the forlorn and the outcast,
whose relation as children of the " Father in
heaven " no act of their own, no veto of their
fellows, no difference of rank or place in time, or
even of race, since to this the teaching of Jesus
tended, could cancel.

Citing the proofs of God's care with which
the world abounded, Jesus invited his hearers to
trust this heavenly Father, to ask him for what

they needed, assured that nothing which is for their good will be withheld, to leave all fretful care to the " Gentiles," and for themselves take no undue thought about food or clothing, but seek " the kingdom of God," and aim after likeness to him, ever striving to know and do his will. Since religion is no matter of outward signs, they are to repent, that is, change the inner man, to cleanse and guard the heart as that from whence are the " issues of life." The law and the prophets are all summed up in love of God and love of man, and the proof of the first is in the practice of the second ; in the self-forgetting and self-yielding of man for man is the doctrine of the cross.

Every great religion has insisted on the duty which man owes his fellow-man. The Hindu says, " Good people show mercy unto all beings, considering how like they are to themselves. The good show pity even to worthless beings, as the moon withholds not its light from the hovel." Gautama the Buddha said, " Forgive insults, reward not evil for evil. Remember that all virtues spring from charity. Address ye your words to caste and to outcast, for salvation is within their reach." Confucius said, " What I do not wish men to do to me I also wish not to do to them." Rabbi Hillel, when a man came to him and asked him to teach him the whole law while he stood on one leg, calmly replied, " Good, my son, what is unpleasing to thee do not to thy friend. This is the whole law; the rest is only its application." But Jesus, passing beyond this, counselled active charity, " All things whatsoever ye would that men should do to you do ye even so to them."

In other words, the good of one makes for the good of the whole, and the harm which men do arises from their forgetting or not knowing their true place as parts of the whole with which they should strive to work in unison. They are to be active in good deeds, and this not vauntingly; to forgive injuries; to judge righteous judgment, as Rabbi Hillel said, " Judge not thy friend until thou standest in his place; " not to love only those who love them, but their enemies also;

to do good and lend, hoping for nothing again,
save to be the "children of the Highest,"[1] towards
whom their desires are to go forth in the spirit
of this prayer which Jesus taught his disciples:—

"Our Father, who art in heaven, hallowed be thy
name. Thy kingdom come ; Thy will be done in earth,
as it is in heaven. Give us this day our daily bread.
Forgive us our trespasses, as we forgive those who tres-
pass against us. And lead us not into temptation ; but
deliver us from the evil one."

When we remember how the free play of the
human mind has been stifled for centuries since
his day by the notion of its powerlessness to dis-
cern, unaided, the true from the false—notions
born of the old belief in the "fall" of man—it is
very important to note how Jesus, heedless of
such a fiction about his fellow-creatures, addresses
them as able to judge for themselves concerning
the truth or the error of his teaching, and
counsels them to trust and use the powers of
reason and insight which were given them from

---

[1] "Be not as slaves that minister to the lord with a view
to receive recompense, and let the fear of heaven be upon you."
—*P. Aboth*, i. 3.

God. "Why even of yourselves judge ye not what is right?" he asks; that is, do not accept the thing as true because I say it, or because, as is the manner of the scribes, the "thorah" enjoins it or the rabbis require it, but test it, first as approving itself to your better nature, and then by applying it to daily life.

As one dwells on these facts at the core of the teaching of Jesus—the unity and possible goodness of man as the sufficing motives to work for his salvation—one thinks how his great heart, albeit he was no man of science, would have gladdened at all the proofs which are forthcoming in our time in support of a truth which was to him as an inspiration. For science is ever bringing from the treasury of nature witness to the oneness of things seemingly unlike, phases of one force under many forms, showing that their myriad differences are not in kind but in degree, being the resultants of subtle changes in the same compounds which elude the keenest search.[1] It is not to be doubted that all the

[1] "We are, as matters now stand, about as far from a know-

races of men are one in the mode of their
beginning and advance, slow or quick as this
may have been, from lower to higher stages
of culture and belief; that man stands not apart
from creatures beneath him, but is the topmost
branch of the great tree of life, whose roots,
deep down in the past, have formed and fed
alike the humblest and the noblest; as imaged
in the Iggdrasil of our Norse fathers, which,
watered by the Norns, bound together the upper
and the under worlds. Science has further shown
us that the unlikenesses between men themselves
as grouped into races, or as separate one from
another, which we note in their customs and
beliefs as in their faces and skins, arise solely
from the varied life brought about by the
different countries which they inhabit, and that
each is what he is in virtue of past and present
causes. From these facts, while we do not
cease to praise or to blame the motives and

ledge (by vision) of the ultimate structure of organic bodies,
as we should be of a newspaper seen with the naked eye at a
distance of one-third of a mile."—H. C. Sorby, *Microscop.
Jour.* March, 1876, p. 115.

actions of others, we learn lessons of charity, uncover the sources of pity, and are moved to effort to remove the causes which thwart the advance of man and divide him from his fellows.

Now let us see what Jesus appears to have meant by the "kingdom of heaven," which, echoing the message of the Baptist, he announced was "at hand," first saying somewhat more in detail about the Messianic hopes in his time. So vague and unfixed were these, each man shaping them either in gross or refined form, according to the bent and habit of his mind, that they cannot be clearly stated, but one feature was common to all—the advent of Messiah as an earthly deliverer. For to the people at large, whose pride was wounded and whose longing for freedom was fanned by their subject state, no other view was possible. Speaking roundly, it was widely held that between the age that then was and the age that was to come there lay the judgment of the nations, to be ushered in by awful portents. Poring

over the books of Daniel, Enoch, and kindred
writings, and taking the figures of speech of the
old prophets for facts, the Jews had framed a
weird picture of the woes that would usher in
the last days—the light of heaven quenched;
hail, brimstone, and fiery swords falling from the
sky; the "all-producing earth shaken by the
immortal hand;" lofty peaks broken, mountains
crumbling, and misty ravines filled with the dead
foes of God, their blood streaming in torrents
along the plains, their souls cast "into a deep
place, full of fire, flaming, and full of pillars
of fire." At the coming of the judge of all, the
pious who had died nobly would arise to enjoy
the fruit of their self-sacrifice and the chosen
yet alive would be caught up into the sky, where
amidst the vanishing of the worn-out heaven
and earth a new Jerusalem should appear, and
there the temple of God, in which saints and
angels would praise him, would be placed. Then
would the world's empires be shattered and the
world-wide reign of the Messiah begin. Jerusalem, the seat of his throne, would be built

with houses three miles high, as it is written,
" It shall be lifted up,"[1] and guarded with gates
of pearl and precious stones. No sick or maimed
would be found there, men would live centuries ;
the land would yield ready-spun wool ; in every
cluster of grapes, which could scarce be drawn
by a yoke of oxen, there would be thirty jars
of wine ; the stalks of corn would be as thick
as trees, and white flour blown from their ears
by the wind of God.

Such were some of the fantastic forms in
which the poor dreamers after happiness in
Palestine nigh two thousand years ago, yearning
for " what is not," shaped that belief in the
replacement of the old by a newer and better
which is common to " a creature made of Time
living in this place of Hope." As we read
the books of the New Testament, chiefly the
book of Revelation, in the light of these tinsel
visions, we discover from what sources the
early Christian writers drew those ideas of a
final judgment, a glittering heaven and a

[1] Zech. xiv. 10.

burning hell, which are the staple belief of the unthinking and the vulgar, and the instruments wherewith preachers often seek to attract or frighten people into being good. This, however, by the way, for I have quoted thus much to show that if there was any subject upon which the disciples of Jesus were likely to misunderstand him and give a twist to his words, it was this subject of the Messianic hope. Happily we have with the records of his sayings the blundering comments of these unlettered men upon them, by which they exhibit themselves as sharing the popular belief, and it is in the contrast between the two sets of ideas that those of Jesus stand out so clearly. From boyhood he had been familiar with the hopes that burned in the hearts of his race and with the stories of revolts, such as that of Judas of Galilee against a counting of the people for the purpose of taxing them, which happened when Jesus was about ten years old. And he saw that these had all failed ; that if they had succeeded, the state of the nation would be little changed thereby, because, steeped in the study of the nobler prophets, whose rare insight into the secret of human blessedness he shared, he had other ideas than the rabbis and the zealots as to "the things which belonged to Israel's peace."

With loftier meaning and in fairer form than the rugged prisoner of Herod Antipas, he taught that the kingdom of heaven, which would be upon earth, the scene of man's aims and strivings, was not to be heralded by falling stars and trickling swords. Men would not point to this and that portent and omen, saying, "Lo, here! lo, there!" because the kingdom "which shall never be destroyed" was to be a kingdom of the spirit, of noiseless growth like the wheat plant from the seed, of silent working like yeast in meal; it was to be the reign of goodness, that is, of God, in the heart of man, and whether Cæsar or a king of David's line reigned in Jerusalem mattered not to it, "for the kingdom is within you." It was neither in upsetting old laws nor in framing new ones ; neither in washing hands and dishes nor in leaving them unwashed, for in this there was naught to test or verify, save that the thing unclean could be cleansed; it was to be in a change of the inner self; the heart, as the source of good or evil, made pure, that the stream of thoughts and acts might flow clear. That is what Jesus meant by his message, "Repent, for the kingdom of heaven is at hand"—that while men remained uncleansed from selfishness and sin, all fights for freedom, all laws to make them good and purge society of evil, were vain; "cleanse first that which is within the cup and platter that the outside of them may be clean also."

Insisting on rightness of conduct induced by goodness of heart, he utters these sayings, which, if not among the earliest, are as the core of his teaching, and unfold the secret of his power to touch men's feelings as no strings of dry maxims and forbidding laws could touch them.

"Blessed are the poor in spirit: for theirs is the kingdom of heaven.

"Blessed are they that mourn: for they shall be comforted.

"Blessed are the meek : for they shall inherit the earth.

" Blessed are they that hunger and thirst after righteousness : for they shall be filled.

" Blessed are the merciful : for they shall obtain mercy.

" Blessed are the pure in heart : for they shall see God.

" Blessed are the peacemakers : for they shall be called
the children of God.

" Blessed are they who are persecuted for righteousness'
sake : for theirs is the kingdom of heaven." [1]

*   *   *   *   *   *

" Not every one that saith unto me, Lord, Lord, shall
enter into the kingdom of heaven ; but he that doeth the
will of my Father who is in heaven." [2]

And he ceased not to lay stress on this
subdual of man's will to the will of God, drawing
them not by argument, to which there is always
another side, but by demand upon their effort,
setting forth that entrance to the kingdom of
heaven is not by passing an examination in
theology, or by study of the law, or by master-
ing all tradition, any more than one becomes an
engineer by learning how Watt discovered the
power of steam, but by faithful and glad dis-
charge of the duties that lie nearest us. A
man's religion should be that of which he is
most sure, and this comes only by testing it, for

---

[1] Matt. v. 1-10.   [2] Ibid. vii. 21.

says a Hindu book, " He who is practical is the truly learned ; a well-devised medicine does not by its name restore the sick." [1] And in one of his most forceful addresses Jesus compares the man who hears his word and does it, to one who builds a house upon a rock, and he who hears his word and does it not, to a foolish man who builds upon the sand, for when "the rain descended and the floods came and the winds blew and beat upon that house, it fell, and great was the fall of it."

Highest in the scale of duty Jesus placed the casting out of self-love, the yielding of one's self for others' needs. Not that we are to be careless about ourselves and thus engender selfishness in those who profit thereby, but careful only in so far as we best fit ourselves for service ; ruled always by a desire for the welfare of all, in carrying out which we may sometimes do for others and ourselves what is best at the cost of what is most pleasant. Happily, nature in all its beauty, thought for our kin, the love they

[1] *Hitopadesa*, (tr. Johnson), p. 26.

beget and which makes effort blessed, the love of country and pride in its history, the stirrings of some noble and worthy cause, events both sad and sunny, the sight of suffering moving to pity, all take us out of ourselves into the world about us, and have taught men in utter self-abandonment to fling life away for the advancement of what they have felt to be the good and the true. These are they who have "through much tribulation" entered the kingdom; made "perfect as the Father in heaven is perfect," and among the greatest of these was Jesus.

While such is the general drift of his "gospel" ("gods-spell" or *good tidings*) injustice would be done it if the foregoing remarks left in the mind the notion that he built up any system of theology or delivered any creeds, or that it is possible to draw such from his teaching.

That which he did was to diffuse a common spirit of sweet charity and selflessness among men regarded as a brotherhood, because the offspring of one Father; and to pull his sayings apart in search for this were as vain as to scatter

the petals of a flower that we might *see* the
scent.　For the highest truth is that which
cannot be defined, or prisoned in any form of
words, and the secret of the enduring influence
of Jesus is in this, that he enounced principles
of world-wide application, leaving men free to
connect them with any outward forms if they
so willed, yet ever reminding them that "the
letter killeth and the spirit giveth life." Upon
these men have not quarrelled; no questions are
raised as to the duty and blessedness of being
pitiful and loving and helping; the dividers
of mankind which have roused deathless hates,
and stained the fair earth with blood, are the
things which are either beyond proof or the false-
ness of which is now clear.　Happily, the importance once given to them is lessening; the
impure air needful to their life and growth is
dispersing, and as they wither, men sort and
explain them as the extinct and the curious are
arranged and labelled in museums.　But the
spirit of Jesus will abide; under its inspiration
men will reach their oneness, even were his
name to become forgotten.

VI.

Jesus and the Parties of his Time.

IT is now needful to look at the attitude of Jesus towards the great parties into which the Jews were, to their hurt, divided, first acquainting ourselves with the standpoint of each.

The two principal among these were the Sadducees and Pharisees. The former, who were few in number, belonged to the wealthier and priestly classes, and courted the favour of the ruling powers in aiding them to control the masses, by whom they were hated. They obeyed the written law and the oral law, as framed by the "great synagogue," neither adding to these nor taking from them, holding that what was not taught in them might be rejected. They had no belief in angels, and because the law promised earthly blessings in the form of long life to the faithful, they held that the soul dies with the body, and that "on earth lies the aim for man; his resurrection being in the children he leaves behind him "—a doctrine so barren of comfort to the suffering and the poor, that Josephus tells us they "were able to persuade none but the rich."

The Pharisees, or "separated," as that word means, sprang from the body of the people, by whom they were as greatly, and on the whole as deservedly, loved as the Sadducees were detested. Their zeal for the "law" was untiring; they were liberal in their reading of it, accepting the constant additions to the traditions made by the scribes or "repeaters," who were the leaders of the party. The stern and severe language which in the latter part of his ministry Jesus uses in addressing them, has caused great injustice to be done to their piety and earnest charity, because it is overlooked that his attacks were made upon the unworthy among them, who did their devout acts to be "seen of men," and against whom the Talmud speaks still more severely. It divides the party into seven classes, of whom one only is worthy. These are the "heavy-footed," who exhausted by

fasting dragged wearily along; the "bleeding,"
who knocked their heads against walls to avoid
looking at women; the "mortar Pharisees,"
who bent themselves like the handle of a mortar
as they walked; the "hump-backed," who hung
their heads; the "do-alls," ever on the watch
to fulfil some trifling law; the "painted," whose
pious manners could be seen from a distance.
The true Pharisee is he "who does the will of
his Father who is in heaven, because he loves
him." Following the example of Ezra and
Nehemiah, they opposed all union between other
races and the Jews,[1] marking themselves off from
their own countrymen in dress, manner, and
mode of speech, and denying to some of them
any part in a life to come.

Of course there was deep hatred between
Sadducee and Pharisee, the one representing the
priestly power of the temple, the other the widespread influence of the scribes and rabbis

---

[1] "Thou madest the world for our sakes; as for the other
people which also come of Adam, thou hast said that they are
nothing."—2 Esdras vi. 55, 56.

through the synagogues and schools; the one
upholding the letter of the law, the other
explaining it in accord with new times; the
one content with things as they were, the other
dwelling on the hope of a Messiah to change
everything.

The scribes were mainly divided into two
parties, the one more unyielding than the other
in disputes as to the latitude of the law. The
most eminent rival leaders were Shammai, a
man of narrow mind and hasty temper, and
Hillel, a Babylonian Jew, who travelled to
Jerusalem to study the law, working as a wood-
cutter for his living. Half his scanty wage went
to pay his school fees, and once having earned
nothing, and the door-keeper refusing to let him
in without fee, he climbed in the darkness to
the window-sill of the school to listen, where he
was well-nigh frozen to death. The next morning
was a sabbath, and when one of the rabbis,
wondering why the window was so darkened,
went out to look, he found it blocked by the poor
scholar. So they brought him down and saved

him, saying, " It is truly worth while to break the sabbath on his account."

He gained immense knowledge, and at last, in the reign of Herod the Great, was chosen leader of the school and president of the Sanhedrin. He was one of the meekest and kindest of men ; " be gentle as Hillel " became a proverb, and stories abound of the vain attempts to ruffle his patience. Some think that Jesus, who, according to certain accounts, was about ten years old when Hillel died, owed much to his teaching, and we know that the sayings of the rabbis were repeated in country synagogues ; but this matters little. Jesus, like every other man, was a son of his time, but unlike most men, he left it immensely his debtor.

The New Testament speaks only of Pharisees and Sadducees, but there was a third religious order called the Essenes, which is described by Josephus.

These people, about whom little that is certain is known, had withdrawn themselves from the bustle and din of life and settled in groups in

the wilderness near the Dead Sea, where they
lived in obedience to the law, making it their
daily study and keeping the sabbath strictly.
Each worked for the whole; their goods were
held in common according to their maxim,
"Mine is thine and thine is mine." Their life,
divided into seasons of work, thought, and prayer,
is one that has had its charms for quiet-loving
and distracted souls of many creeds and ages,
but it has too often withdrawn the useful from
work near at hand to vain search after happiness
and other selfish aims.

Jesus was beneath the notice of the courtly
Sadducees; the Essenes were scarcely known to
him; with the smaller parties, as the Zealots and
Herodians, he had no sympathy, and his intercourse from first to last was mainly with the
Pharisees. There was at starting much to draw
the two together; in the belief in one Almighty
Being, in the duty of man to keep his commandments and show charity, in the love of righteousness and the longing for the kingdom of God,
and in accepting the current beliefs and super-

stitions, he and they had very much in common. The Pharisees were interested in him, asked him to their houses, and listened to him with respect until he seemed to slight or hold in light regard things on which they set high store.

It was in the very essence of the teaching of Jesus that it should reach beyond the narrow circle of the pious to the outcasts, just as although his mission was at first confined to the Jews it could not fail to extend to the Gentiles, and the first cause of offence to the Pharisees was his conduct towards "sinners" and "publicans." By the former term is meant in the gospels not only those who had fallen into sin, losing sense of shame and self-respect, but persons who had been put out of the synagogues by the leaders for offences against the law. The "publicans" were Jews who acted as agents of Romans who "farmed" the taxes, that is, as already explained, paid a given sum into the Imperial treasury and bought the right to collect the revenue, making what profit they could. Such a system led to overcharges and cruel extortions, and the Jews who accepted this office were bitterly hated, cut off from the rights and privileges of their nation, and ranked among the heathen.

Jesus, who said that he came not to call the righteous but sinners to repentance, invited these classes to come near him, ate and drank with them, spoke kindly and hopefully to them. His faith in the love and mercy of God and the worth of men and women, enabled him, unhampered by any doctrines about their "fall" and inherent badness, to deal with them as he found them ; with their joys and sorrows ; the unrest under the hollow laugh ; and towards these " lost sheep of the house of Israel" his great heart went forth in godlike compassion. For him the featureless commonplace people, whose pulseless, listless lives were unstirred by passion for either good or evil, or by pity for the erring, had no charm ; but he was drawn to those whom the strict law of the Jews had made outcasts, for in them he saw power misused, and his care was to give it right direction, not "breaking the bruised reed."

In loving the sinners, he did not the less hate sin,[1] and in his gracious presence they felt themselves before one who had deep insight into the heart of man, deep hope for it too, and they fell before him, telling him all the truth. The Pharisees had treated them as shut out from the mercy of God and the pity of their fellows, and they had sunk into reckless despair; Jesus had told them that a new and better life was within their reach, and they put forth "lame hands of faith" to grasp it. So the proud and self-elect were shocked; they murmured or complained outright, and brought as a charge against Jesus that which is the grandest tribute to his life-work, that he was "a friend of publicans and sinners."

One day when "all the publicans and sinners drew near for to hear him," he silenced the grumbling of the Pharisees by asking them whether if any man among them had an hundred

---

[1] "Rabbi Meyer once gave vent to his anger against an evil-doer, when his wife gently reproved him by pointing out that David prayed, Let sin cease from the earth, not sinners." — *Berakoth,* 10: *De Sola Mendes,* p. 41.

sheep and lost one, he would not leave the
ninety-nine in the wilderness and seek for that
which had strayed, bringing it home rejoicing
more over it than over those that went not
astray? "Likewise," he added, "joy shall be in
heaven over one sinner that repenteth more than
over ninety and nine just persons who need no
repentance." Then he put into this most
touching parable the quenchless love of God
for the repentant sinner.

A certain man had two sons, the younger of
whom came to him and asked for his share of
the property, receiving which, he left home and
settled in a distant land, where he spent all that
he had in riotous living. To add to the misery
which then followed, a famine arose, and at last
he became servant to a citizen of that country,
who sent him into his fields to feed pigs, the
most degrading work that a Jew could under-
take. So hungry was he that he "would fain
have filled his belly with the husks that the
swine did eat, but no man gave unto him."
Then he bethought himself of home and home

faces, of the hired servants of his father who had bread enough and to spare while he was starving. And he resolved to return, confess his sins to his father and his unworthiness to be called a son, and ask to be made as a hired servant. As he neared the old home, the father, whose thoughts had gone out into the wilderness and the far country concerning him, saw him in the distance, and instead of awaiting him with angry look and folded arms, "had compassion and ran and fell on his neck and kissed him." And the son asked his forgiveness and a place among the labourers; but the father bade them " bring forth the best robe and put it on him ; and put a ring on his hand and shoes on his feet, and kill the fatted calf: for this my son was dead and is alive again ; he was lost and is found." As the feast, enlivened by music and dancing, was going on, the elder son, who had been in the fields, drew near, and wondered what the lights and sounds of mirth and singing meant. When he heard the cause, he was angry and refused to go in, until his father came out and entreated him.

But he complained that he who had never grieved his father had never been given even a kid to make a feast for his friends, whereas directly his scapegrace brother returned, ragged and penniless, a fatted calf had been killed for him. And then the father, reminding him that all was his as the heir, urged his joy at the missing lad's return as excuse for the feasting. "It was meet that we should make merry and be glad: for this thy brother was dead and is alive again, and was lost and is found." [1]

Another parable, in which he reproachfully and more openly sketches the Pharisee, is that describing how two men went up to the temple to pray: one a Pharisee, the other a publican. The Pharisee stood and prayed thus with himself: "O God, I thank thee that I am not like other men, extortioners, unjust, adulterers, or even as this publican. I fast twice in the week; I give tithes of all my income." The publican, standing at the entrance to the temple court, would not lift his eyes to heaven, but smiting his breast in penitence, cried, "God be merciful to

[1] Luke xv.

me a sinner!" "I tell you," added Jesus, "this man went down to his house justified in the sight of God more than the Pharisee."[1]

The attitude of Jesus towards "sinners" is made clear by the following story :—

One day a pious Pharisee named Simon asked Jesus to dine with him. Soon after the meal had begun, there came in through the door, left open for guests in accordance with Eastern custom, a woman of bad life, who hearing that Jesus was there had stolen in. She brought in her hand an alabaster box of ointment, and drawing near to the place where, after the manner of the country, he reclined, leaning on his arm while his body rested on a cushion, the feet being thrown backwards, she bowed her head weeping, and as she reverently kissed his feet, bathed them with her tears. Then recovering from her grief she wiped his feet with her long flowing hair, and poured over them the oil so refreshing to the skin in hot climates. When Simon saw all this he was surprised and

[1] Luke xviii. 10-13.

shocked, and said to himself, or in undertone,
" This man, if he were a prophet, would have
known who and what manner of woman this
is who toucheth him ! "

Jesus, who read Simon's feelings in his face,
said, " Simon, I have somewhat to say to you,"
and receiving assent, told this story. " There was
a creditor who had two debtors, one of whom
owed him five hundred pence (or denarii, nearly
twenty pounds of our money), and the other
fifty (nearly two pounds). And when they had
nothing wherewith to pay, he frankly forgave
them both. Tell me, therefore, which of them
will love him most ? " Simon answered and said,
" I suppose that he to whom he forgave most."
And Jesus said, " Thou hast judged correctly." Then he turned to the woman and
said, " Seest thou this woman ? I entered thine
house, but thou gavest me no water wherewith
to wash my feet after putting off my sandals :
but she hath washed them with her tears, and
wiped them with the hairs of her head. Thou
gavest me no kiss : but this woman since the

time I came in hath not ceased to kiss my feet. My head with oil thou didst not anoint : but this woman hath anointed my feet with ointment." And all for her great love ; "wherefore I tell thee, her sins, which are many, are forgiven, for she loved much, but to whom little is forgiven, the same loveth little. And he said unto her, Thy sins are forgiven." And the guests murmured among themselves, asking who he could be that forgave sins ; but Jesus, heeding them not, said to the woman, "Thy faith hath saved thee : go in peace."[1]

But it was in the eyes of the Pharisees a still greater crime that Jesus should slight the law, which was to them the supreme and complete rule of life and source of knowledge, concerning which, as showing how all-embracing in his day it was regarded, Josephus says, "The giver of the law has left nothing in suspense ; beginning from the earliest infancy and the details of family life of every one, he left nothing even of the very smallest consequence to the disposal

[1] Luke vii. 36–50.

of those for whom he gave laws," [1] and the care
of the scribes had been that nothing should
remain undetermined and so come to be treated
as a matter on which people might use their
own judgment. The exclusion of these men
from public affairs, and from the books of other
nations, left them the more free to spend time
over the " thorah," to haggle over its meaning,
find hidden secrets in its numbers and the forms
of its letters, and multiply inane triflings which
emptied their work of its nobler aim of searching
for the moral facts in writings held as sacred.
But such danger always attends the centring
of the mind on a single subject, giving it an
undue importance, and losing its true measure
of relation to other things. It is an old proverb
which bids us beware of the man of one book. [2]

Upon two matters, cleansings and the sabbath,
rules had been greatly increased by the time of
Jesus, and it was his attitude towards these that
brought him into sharp collision with their
defenders.

[1] *c. Apion,* ii. 18. [2] Cave ab homine unius libri.

The great body of Jewish rites and ceremonies is of kindred origin to that of other races. The laws dividing food into clean and unclean are the outcome not merely of dislike to certain animals, but of that nature-worship under which creatures below man were objects of reverence and awe; and out of the feeling of defilement after touching a corpse, shedding blood, etc., has arisen the widespread practice of dipping or sprinkling persons and things by water, or the passing them over fire, to purify them. The Egyptians had very strict laws concerning uncleanness; the life of a Brahman is one long ceremony of washings; and from the Persians, whose religion had much in common with the ancient Hindu, the Jews appear to have added to their laws as to "purifications." The sixth section of the Mishna or text of the Talmud, containing one hundred and twenty-six chapters, is devoted thereto, and of these four chapters to the washing of hands alone![1] We saw that

---

[1] Of the precepts on this matter the following is a sample : "The hands become legally unclean or legally clean, up to the

John was surnamed the Baptist, as plunging his disciples into the Jordan, in symbol of the washing of the soul from sin ;[1] the apostles in like manner immersed their converts, as do certain Christians to this day. The use of "holy water" has its rise in lower culture ; and the sprinkling of babies, without which some Christian sects actually hold they will go to hell, has its counterpart among savage races, who in naming the newly-born wash or otherwise purify it.

Jesus, be it remembered, was a Jew by birth and training, although "son of man" by thought

wrist. 'How?' 'If one poured the first ablution up to the wrist and the second above the wrist, and the water ran back into the hand?' 'It is clean.' 'If one poured the first and second ablutions above the wrist and the water ran back into the hand?' 'It is unclean.' 'If one poured the first over one hand, and afterwards the second on both hands?' 'They are unclean.' 'If one poured the first over both hands, and afterwards the second over one hand?' 'His hand is clean,'" etc. —Barclay's *Talmud,* p. 326.

[1] In ancient Peru, an Inca, after confession of guilt, bathed in a stream and uttered these words : "O thou river, receive the sins I have this day confessed unto the Sun, carry them down to the sea, and let them never more appear ; " and in like manner the Hindu prays, "Take away, O waters, whatsoever is wicked in me."—Tylor's *Prim. Cult.* ii. 396.

and feeling, and when he began his mission he had no idea of becoming the founder of a new religion, of upsetting the law whose precepts he had been taught to obey, or of attacking the priests and scribes. But his views regarding the nature of the kingdom of God could not fail to make him push mere law and precept on one side when they stood in the way of its advance. Law was to him no rigid thing, but given, as he said, for " the hardness of men's hearts," and they who carried out the spirit, of which the early code was the imperfect expression, were more faithful " sons of the law " than they who, obeying the letter, paid tithe of herbs, mint, anise, and cummin, and left the weightier matters of judgment and mercy undone. Moreover, law as such is for slaves and subjects, and therefore in its essence is opposed to love, by which it is supplanted in those whom the truth has made free. The interest awakened in the towns and villages of Galilee by the prophet of Nazareth had caused the rulers of the Pharisees at Jerusalem to send some of their number to observe him, and

in their scrutiny of his acts they would specially
note his disregard of certain laws. His out-
spoken attitude is clearly shown on the occasion
when the Pharisees, who held that " to eat bread
with unwashen hands was a crime deserving
punishment in this world and the next," and
whom the Sadducees jeeringly said would " clean
the face of the sun if they could," asked him,
" Why walk not thy disciples according to the
tradition of the elders, but eat the loaf with unwashen hands ? " to which he replied:

"Well hath Isaiah prophesied of you hypocrites,
This people honoureth me with their lips, but their heart
is far from me. Howbeit in vain do they worship me,
teaching for doctrines the commandments of men. For
laying aside the commandments of God, ye hold the
tradition of men, as the washing of pots and cups : and
many other such like things ye do. . . . For Moses said,
Honour thy father and thy mother ; and, Whoso curseth
father or mother, let him die the death ; but ye say, If a
man shall say to his father or mother. It is Corban," (that
is, offered in vow to Jehovah, by which a duty was often
evaded) " he is released from his duty as a son, and ye
suffer him no more to do aught for his father or his
mother, making the word of God of none effect through
your tradition which ye have delivered : and many such
like things do ye. And when he had called all the people

unto him, he said unto them, Hearken unto me every one
and understand, there is nothing from without a man that
entering into him can defile him, but the things which
come out of him, those are they that defile the man."[1]

Mercy was more than sacrifice ; prayer was in
vain unless it came from the heart ; the command
not to kill meant also that men were to subdue
the anger which leads to murder ; the oath to
heaven was needless where the truth was spoken ;
thus did Jesus, in the spirit of the old sage, bid
his hearers " keep their heart with all diligence,
for out of it are the issues of life."

Regarding the sabbath, which we saw had its
rise in ancient moon-worship, but which, in the
belief of the Jews, was first proclaimed from
Sinai, the rabbis had indeed " made a hedge
about it " of " line upon line and precept upon
precept," although they kept their own shoulders
free from the burdens which they laid upon
others. They prescribed the kind of oil with
which lamps were to be trimmed, what knots
might be tied, how far a man might walk, what

[1] Mark vii. 6–15.

he might carry. He must not bear the weight
of a dried fig, but he might carry a locust's egg
to cure ear-ache, or a fox's tooth to cure sleeplessness, or the nail of a crucified man for ague ;
he must not wear sandals with nails in them ;
and whether a cripple might go out on his
wooden leg was a matter upon which the rabbis
were not agreed. It was forbidden to set a
broken bone ; also to walk on the grass, because
that was a kind of threshing ; a tailor must not
go out with his needle, nor a scribe with his pen
near dusk on the eve of the sabbath. It was believed that the day was kept " in heaven and hell,
and that even the tortured souls in Gehenna had
rest." [1] Pious streams were known which only
flowed on the seventh day, and yet more pious
ones which then stopped, resuming their course
on the first day.[2]

Jesus did not deny the sacredness of the
sabbath, or dispute the wisdom of a law designed to secure rest to toilworn man and beast,.

---

[1] Hausrath's *New Test. Times*, vol. i. p. 101.
[2] Josephus, *Wars of the Jews*, vii. 5, 1.

but he loathed and scorned the plea that made it an excuse for refusing to do works of mercy and satisfy natural wants. In a sentence which is the essence of his views, he said, "The sabbath was made for man, not man for the sabbath," and made therefore for man's good, man's service of his kind, for which all time and place is sacred, since the thing which it is wrong to do on that day it is wrong to do on any other day. Among the questions in dispute among the rabbis was the course to be taken when a sheep fell into a water-tank on the sabbath—should it be drawn out or given food and left there till the day was past ? and it was with this that Jesus, when he and his disciples were charged with sabbath breaking, in quiet humour foiled his accusers by asking, " Which of you is there whose son or ox shall fall into a pit, and he will not straightway draw him up on the sabbath day ? "[1] And they could not answer him these things.

[1] In the seventeenth century " Alexander Carnie was delaitit " before the Presbytery of Strathbogie "for brak of sabbath in bearing ane sheep upon his back from the pasture to his own house. The said Alexander compeirit and declarit that it was of necessitie, for saving of the beast's lyfe in tyme of storme. Was rebukit for the same and admonished not to do the lyke."

I cannot pass in silence over the way in which his teaching on this matter has been perverted, to the grievous harm of many, and the filling of their hours with weariness. From the time of the apostles to beyond the fourth century, the first day of the week, which was observed as the day when Jesus was said to have risen from the dead, was not confounded with the Jewish sabbath, which it was held to have superseded, and the name of each day was kept distinct. Although the two days became by degrees more blended, it was not till long after the fourth century, when the Christian Church laid claim, like the rabbis, to power "to bind and to loose" the beliefs and actions of men, that the written and oral laws dealing with the sabbath were made to apply to the Sunday, and to be binding upon Christians. The extreme point was reached about three hundred years ago, in the days of the Puritans, who, repelled and shocked by the riotings throughout England on Sundays, rushed in the height of their power to excess of another sort, and enforced such a host of absurd and vexing rules for "keeping holy the sabbath day," that in obeying these men forgot or had scarcely time to be merciful one to another. To wash a dish, or cook a dinner, or take a long walk, or ring more than one bell to call people to church, were accounted as great sins as murder ; and the Pilgrim Fathers, when they settled in America, with the same misled zeal forbade bed-making, room-sweeping, and other needful cleansings, and, if the account is to be trusted,[1] enacted that "no woman shall kiss her child on the 'sabbath' day" or on "fasting days." It is well for us who live in freer and more joyous times to learn from what we are delivered, for although the influence of these men abides among us still, it is slowly yielding to common sense, and by-and-by the Christian Sunday will cease to be confounded with the Jewish sabbath, and to remain, as in so many households yet, a frown upon the children's ringing laughter, and a lock upon their story-books.

[1] From a code said to have been drawn up by Governor Eaton for New Haven Colony in 1656, and embodied in the *Blue Laws of Connecticut*, the genuineness of which is doubted.

VII.

Miracles.

The stir made by Jesus during his preaching tour had not only reached the ears of Jerusalem rabbis, but those of John the Baptist, still lingering in his prison at Machærus, and from him came two disciples to inquire into the truth of what he had heard, and to ask if the Messiah had appeared. "Art thou," they said, "the coming one, or must we look for another?" And he answered and said unto them, "Go and tell John what ye saw and heard, that blind receive sight, lame walk, lepers are cleansed, deaf hear, dead are raised, the poor have the gospel preached to them, and blessed is he whosoever shall not be offended in me."[1]

I cite this interview not to dwell upon the contrast which it led Jesus to draw between himself and the man from whom he had received the

[1] Matt. xi. 1-5.

impetus for his work, but because it seems likely that such a question, coming from one to whom Jesus must have given heed, set him pondering on the nature and aim of his ministry, and because the figures of speech in which, after his manner, his reply was couched, suggest my returning to the subject of the miracles said to have been wrought by him, the record of which fills so large a space in the four gospels. There is the more reason for reference to them because it is a main object of this sketch of his life to show that the value of his teaching is quite independent of any belief in him as a miracle-worker, and of aught else wonderful that is recorded concerning him.

In his day, as in ages before and since, belief in miracles was universal, and as the doubts which writers outside Palestine may have cast on them had not troubled the minds of the masses in their own countries, we are sure that they had not reached the more secluded Jews. It is not possible for us, who, in filling our minds with facts from science books, are in danger

of dulling our sense of the wonder and beauty
of this fair, order-abiding universe, to put ourselves in the place of the ancients and compre-
hend their notions about it. But it is easy
to see that those notions would be their
measure of the causes to which they referred
startling events, or events whose causes were
outside the limits of their knowledge, and to
understand how they, and people after them
during the many centuries when science stood
still, remained content in the easy explanations
of their forefathers, so that the last thing of
which they thought was to seek a natural cause
for the uncommon. For example, we have
seen how the influence of Persia had fostered
Jewish belief in demons. This was rampant
in Galilee, as it is among Syrian peasants to
this day, and it was held that the bodies
of those creatures being mortal, but their souls
immortal, they wandered in search of new
bodies wherein to dwell, taking up their abode
in men (or failing these, in brutes), and all
the ills the cause of which was not clear were

laid upon them. If a man fell down in a fit, or shook with ague, or talked wildly, or even sneezed, it was the work of one or more demons within him, and hence arose the arts of using charms to prevent their entrance, and of exorcising or casting them out from the "possessed," by methods known to a select class. This explanation satisfied men; it seemed to account for the facts, and no further enquiry was deemed needful. In the absence of any science of medicine in that day, the oddest remedies, as kissing a mule upon the nose for a cold, eating the flesh of mice for lung disease and of frogs for toothache, were in vogue, and the mind and body were regarded as quite apart from each other.

We now know that the disease spoken of as "possession" was madness of a more or less severe type, which prevailed largely among the Jews, being fostered by the state of excitement in which they lived, as in Europe cases have occurred of the spread of disorders of the mind among masses of the people ruled by a common

U

delusion.[1] The people thus afflicted were allowed
to roam at large ; no one dared to interfere with
them save the exorcist, whose power, acting on
the sufferer's imagination, often effected a cure ;
for such nervous diseases which medicine fails
to reach will sometimes yield to the influence of
a stronger will and, where belief in the virtue
of these prevails, to the exercise of magic arts.
Now the exquisite feeling of Jesus for every
form of suffering, joined to the look and tone of
authority which marked him, would make him
very skilful in using his gentleness and strength
with soothing yet unmistakable power to bring
the " possessed " to his " right mind." His success in such cases, and in other disorders where
comforting words would be as balm, gained him
high repute as an exorcist, and, joined to the
current belief that the Messiah would signify his
presence by signs and wonders, would largely
account for the reports which, after the manner
of such, grow more wonderful as they spread,
and were in the long years after his death mag-

---

[1] Cf. Carpenter's *Mental Physiology*, pp. 312–315.

nified into tales of the marvels which he wrought,
even to raising the dead. There are many
instances on record in modern times of the
power of the imagination in curing disorders,
and as showing that the foregoing is no far-
fetched explanation, I may cite the following
story, which is given as related by the famous
chemist, Sir Humphry Davy.[1]

A man suffering from paralysis came to him
one day to be treated by electricity. On sitting
down, Davy placed a small glass thermometer-
bulb under his tongue to take the temperature
before beginning. The patient thought this was
the instrument for curing him, and said he felt
it run through all his system. Davy was curious
to see what lasting influence the imagination
only would exert, and without undeceiving the
man sent him away and told him to come daily
and have the operation repeated. He did so,
and each time the thermometer was placed as
before in his mouth with the same effect, and
after a short time the man was cured.

---

[1] See also an article on the " Influence of the Mind on the
Body," *Cornhill Magazine*, August, 1879.

But we are not called upon to account for the source of each and all the miracles related in the Bible as worked not only by Jesus, but by prophets before him and apostles after him, or of those said to have been performed by saints in virtue of power transmitted to them. It suffices that the causes giving rise to belief in these fictions are made clear in acquainting ourselves with those crude notions of past time about the universe which rendered any idea of the unbroken rule of law impossible. As knowledge of the supreme and unchecked sweep of the order of nature advances, belief in miracle dies out, for when the law of a thing is found, we refuse to look for a cause beyond nature, while so long as any department of the universe remains unexplored and unexplained, there the belief is found lingering. For example, in our own time, until weather changes were shown to be within the realm of law, men, in their craving for a cause, looked upon "plagues of rain" and severe droughts as the direct act of an Almighty Being, as the marks of his anger against a people's sin ; indeed, prayers are still offered by some persons for their removal! An amusing illustration is given in Boswell's Life of Dr. Johnson [1] of the confusion which the igno- rant make between cause and effect in the case of the islanders of St. Kilda, who invented all sorts of superstitions to account for their being seized with colds in the head whenever a ship arrived, until it occurred to a "Rev. Mr. Chris- tian of Docking" to find the cause in the fact that a vessel could enter the harbour only when a strong north-east wind was blowing! And in another part of Scotland the servants on a farm suffered every spring from fever and ague, which were viewed as the judgment of God upon their sins, until with proper drainage of the land the disorder disappeared.

Forgetting that other remarkable men besides Jesus, and that evil spirits likewise, have been credited with superhuman power, miracles were once regarded as proving that Jesus was a divine person, indeed, the deity himself, and

[1] Croker's edit. (1860), p. 191.

that the Christian religion was revealed from
heaven; but the number of thoughtful and devout
persons who feel that belief in them is not only
now impossible, but rather a vexation and a
hindrance to the advancement of religion, is
increasing.

1. To believe that Jesus performed miracles
does not make his teaching more beautiful and
more true; the duties he enjoins, the love he
would diffuse as the ground of these duties
abide, whether he did or did not make the blind
to see and bring the dead to life. Such belief,
moreover, must ever remain outside us as facts
or fictions do; they cannot help us to follow the
example of Jesus, and to test for ourselves the
truth of what he says.

2. Belief in miracle is a drag on the progress
of mankind, because it makes them shrink from
interfering with or appearing to thwart the hand
of God. Arguing that the evil is permitted by
him and sent to warn or to punish them, it is
thought impious to remove it. Whereas, as
man learns that the ills he has thus regarded

as heaven-sent are curable and to be prevented, being the result of neglect and ignorance,
he sets to work with a will to banish them by
obeying the law for breach of which he and his
have suffered and smarted so keenly and so
long.

3. It is a false and shallow notion that the
surrender of belief in miracle involves the
lessening or loss of our sense of the wonderful.
There may be those in whom this sense is dead
or sleeping, but a fearless following of the
evidence before them by the truly wise, while
it leaves behind the legends and pseudo-
mysteries which men in the "times of their
ignorance" invented, will bring them to the
threshold of those abiding mysteries of the
universe the continued revelation of whose
unbroken order becomes the inspiration of their
own.

VIII.

Jesus asserts his Messiahship.

RETURNING to the relations between Jesus and
the Pharisees, now becoming so strained, we find
these men basely accusing him of casting out
demons by the aid of Beelzebul, the "prince of
the demons;" to which he retorted with an overwhelming argument; "Every kingdom or city or
house divided against itself cannot stand; and if
I through Satan, whose agents work misery upon
men, perform deeds of mercy, how can Satan's
kingdom stand? But if I cast out demons by
the Spirit of God, then is the kingdom of God
already come unto you."[1]   By such a charge
they had blasphemed God; they were in danger,
he told them, of losing forgiveness both in this
world and in the next.[2]   Baffled and bitter, they
sought to confound him before the people by
asking him for a "sign" whereby he might prove
himself a true prophet and thus command claim

[1] Matt. xii. 24, 28.   [2] Matt. v. 31.

to a hearing; but he reproached them that they, who could read weather-signs and portents of events in the face of the sky, failed to read the future in the outlook of the times, and said that no other sign would come than that of Jonah, whose preaching, in causing the repentance of the heathen Ninevites, was a type of the acceptance by the Gentiles of the teaching of Jesus which the Jews rejected.

But these test-questions, these charges and murmurings, were the rumblings of a coming storm. The excitement aroused a few months before in the early stages of the ministry of Jesus had died away; the rustics of Galilee who, with ears tickled by the music of words about the "kingdom," had flocked round him and made his progress from place to place as a triumph, fell away when the kingdom they looked for came not, and their attitude became listless or hostile. They were "like unto little children sitting in the markets, who call to the others and say, We piped unto you, and ye

danced not ; we sang a dirge and ye lamented
not."[1] And, indeed, this is not surprising,
because, failing their acceptance and practice
of his message to change their lives, there was
nothing left but to fall into their old courses.
Jesus was no sensation preacher, who could
stoop to artifice and show to sustain interest ;
he proclaimed the truth and left the good seed
of the kingdom to the care of God, not unaware,
as shown in his parable of the different fate of
the seeds scattered broadcast by the sower, of its
reception by various hearers. But the disap-
pointment was keen, and gave a sternness to his
words ; the feeling of desertion breaks forth in
the pathetic repining, "foxes have holes, and
birds of the air have nests, but the Son of man
hath not where to lay his head," while in the
closing days of his ministry in Galilee he
mingles upbraidings against its towns with warnings of Israel's rejection and of the admission of
the Gentiles, towards whom his all-embracing,
saddened heart was turning :

[1] Matt. xi. 16, 17.

"Woe unto thee, Chorazin! woe unto thee, Bethsaida! for if the mighty works which were done in you had been done in Tyre and Sidon, they would have repented long ago in sackcloth and ashes. But I say unto you, It will be more tolerable for Tyre and Sidon in the day of judgment than for you. And thou, Capernaum, shalt thou be exalted to heaven? Thou shalt be thrust down to hades; for if the mighty works which were done in thee had been done in Sodom, it would have remained until this day." [1]

On another occasion he said that many would come from east and west and sit down at table with Abraham, Isaac, and Jacob in the kingdom of heaven, while the sons of the kingdom would go forth into the outer darkness.

So the day that had risen with such fair promise on the first gentle preachings by the lake of Tiberias was overcast, and on the gracious soul of Jesus there fell a deep, lonely sorrow. To add to the gloom, news reached him that John the Baptist had at last been put to death by Herod Antipas, an event in which, although the mission of Jesus was free from such colour of rebellion as may have tinged John's, he could not but read his own possible fate.

[1] Matt. xi. 21-23.

For the Pharisees, who were not grieved at the
murder of John, were not likely to protect him
if Herod laid hands upon him, and the people
swerved to the lead of their rulers, so that the
outlook betokened a danger which Jesus, who
had yet much work before him that he would
fain do, avoided by withdrawing with a faithful
few to beyond the borders of Galilee, where,
away from cavillers and the fickle crowd, he
might commune in quiet with his Father and
ponder over his course for the future.

Much uncertainty hangs over his movements
at this period; but whatever they may have
been, he at last reached the neighbourhood of
Cæsarea-Philippi, the most northerly town in
Jewish territory. In the delightful spot where
Herod the Great had raised a "beautiful temple
of the whitest stone" to Augustus, Herod Philip
had newly built the place which he called after
his Roman master and himself, and it was near
this that Jesus one day put a question to the
disciples which revealed what course his ideas
regarding his mission and himself were taking

within his own mind. He asked them, "Who
do men say that I am?" or, according to
another account, applying to himself a favourite
title borrowed from the book of Daniel, not
as claiming divine nature, but call to human
service, "Who do men say that the Son of
man is?" They replied that some, the re-
morseful Antipas among them, said he was
John the Baptist, who, in their belief, had
risen from the dead; others, that he was the
prophet Elijah, whom Malachi had said would
be sent "before the coming of the great and
dreadful day of Jehovah;" others, Jeremiah,
or some other prophet. Making no comment
on this, he then asked them, "But who say ye
that I am?" when Simon answered him, "Thou
art the Messiah," and Jesus, approving, said,
"Blessed art thou, Simon, son of Jona, for flesh
and blood revealed it not to thee, but my
Father who is in heaven." That no excitement
hindering and, perchance, frustrating his purpose
might arise by public announcement of this,
"he charged them that they should tell no man
of him."

By what steps he had arrived at a belief in his own Messiahship we cannot know; maybe, like many large results to which men come, the progress was too slow and subtle for Jesus himself to trace, and we may only guess, with the rough outline of his career before us, that the growth of this idea was due to many causes, among which the following seem likely.

The withdrawal of the feather-headed people had thrown him the more within himself and the more upon his God, his trust in whom, and sense of oneness with whose will, never failed;[1] opposition to his teaching had made him the more sift it, only to convince him that no higher was needful or possible to men; the sense of power over the wills and disorders, whether in mind or body, of his fellows was deepened by his ministry of success with the despised and outcast; in the likeness of Israel's "suffering

---

[1] Perchance, too, he shared the belief of the Jews in divine intimation through the *Bath Kol* (or *daughter of a voice*), by which, so they said, the Holy spoke to them under the second temple, when the Urim and Thummim were lost and the line of the prophets closed.

servant" drawn by the prophet whose words were oftenest on his lips—one "despised and rejected; a man of sorrows, and acquainted with grief"—he traced his own career; and last, but by no means least, the question from the Baptist, "Art thou the coming one?" had seemed to bring its own answer with it, and to resolve, once for all, the hesitation into conviction.

Whatever views men held concerning the Messiah, they were in agreement that he would appear in Jerusalem, and thither Jesus had resolved to repair, making his appeal to the nation in the person of the chief priests and elders, and of the crowds who would be gathered there during festival time. In disclosing this intention to his disciples, he did not shrink from telling them what forebodings filled him that an enterprise so bold as attacking the stronghold of priests and rabbis might cost him his life. So mournful a prediction stunned them. That he, in whom they with uplifted hearts had declared their belief as the "anointed

of the Lord," should be maltreated and killed
seemed impossible. They "understood not this
saying, and were afraid to ask him," until
Simon, foremost spokesman, said, "Be it far
from thee, Lord: this shall not be unto thee."
To Jesus, through whose mind flashed the
memory of his terrible struggle in the desert,
Simon seemed, as it were, another tempter, and
he rebuked him, calling him Satan and a
stumbling-block, seeking the things desired by
men, and not those in accord with the will
of God.[1] Of course the secret of their misunderstanding was in this—that, while he was
intent upon the work to which he was called,
not by descent of blood (for he was at pains
when in Jerusalem to argue that the Messiah
was no son of David[2]), but by fitness and doing
of the will of God, and not quailing before the
sacrifice this might demand, they, vain dreamers,
were speculating how he would distribute the
high places among them in the kingdom which
they thought he was about to set up, and

[1] Matt. xvi. 21-28.   [2] Mark xii. 35-37.

wrangling with one another who should be the greatest! He, perceiving the thoughts of their greedy hearts, "called the twelve, and said unto them, If any man desires to be first, he shall be last of all and servant of all." And he took a little child and set him in the midst of them, and when he lifted him in his arms he said, "Whosoever will receive one of these little children in my name, receives me: and whosoever receives me, receives not me but him that sent me." Enforcing the law of self-denial as the foundation of faithful service, he said—

"Whosoever desires to follow after me, let him deny himself and take up his cross and follow me. For whosoever desires to save his life will lose it ; and whosoever shall lose his life, for my sake and the gospel's, will save it. For what does it profit a man to gain the whole world and lose his life? For what must a man give in exchange for his life? For whosoever shall be ashamed of me and of my words in this adulterous and sinful generation, of him shall also the Son of man be ashamed when he comes in the glory of his Father with the holy angels. . . . Verily, I say unto you that there are some of those standing here who will not taste of death till they see the kingdom of God already come with power." [1]

----

[1] Mark viii. 34-38 ; ix. 1.

X

We need not stay to surmise what course
Jesus would have taken had all Jerusalem
welcomed him as the Messiah, and falsified the
sad presentiments of danger and death drawn
from the temper of the Pharisees in Galilee, for
he must have speculated on the bare chance
of success ; enough that he would not have
made its plaudits the war cry for an earthly
throne, and thus given the lie to his sublime
teaching concerning the kingdom of God. Yet
he would have been something more than
human never to have wondered and pondered
over the future which lay beyond suffering and
the grave, and here in the unravelling of his
talks upon this matter we have a well-nigh impossible task. For they have come down to
us so wound about with the crude notions of
his misconceiving hearers, and the weird ideas
current about the end of the world in the first
century, that we can with no sureness say which
are his words and which are not. Speaking
broadly, he must have been in accord with the
belief of the Jews in the return of the souls of

the righteous to earth, for in dying without living
again, what would become of the kingdom of
God, of which earth, not some remote place
above the clouds, home of Jehovah and the
angels, was to be the purified seat? Banishing
as foreign to the mind of Jesus his reported
sayings about the signs ushering in the last day,
and about his judgment of the nations, all
"of the earth, earthy," there are too many
passages left in the "synoptics" to allow us
to ignore the fact that he instilled into his
disciples his belief that he would return to
them; that though he might lay down his life
he would take it again. When this might be
was known to the Father only, in whose hands
were "times and seasons;" enough for them in
view of such uncertainty, to make it their care
to note the signs of the age, and their duty,
like faithful servants, to watch with loins girt
about and lamps burning as men who wait
for their lord.

Vague as our knowledge of the precise ideas
of Jesus on this matter must remain, the belief

in his "second advent," as it is termed, was most
vivid and all-absorbing among his followers.[1]
The earlier epistles of the New Testament teem
with proofs that the event of which they felt
most sure, which no twisting of words can
explain as referring to a later time, and concerning which they and all who came after them
were utterly mistaken, was the speedy return
of the Master whose loss they so keenly mourned.
The belief was at fever-heat in the minds of
Paul and other writers, and was harmful to the
extent that it absorbed attention upon a shadowy

---

[1] The belief in the second coming of Jesus to reign with the
saints for a thousand years upon the earth, from which evil
should then be banished, known as the Millennium (Lat. *mille*,
a thousand, and *annus*, a year), passed into the Christian religion,
and survives in more or less vigour among many to this day.
The subject attracted men, burning with desire to peer into the
future, yet forgetful that "the Spirit which is holy is reserved
and deals in laws," to search the writings which seemed to hide
the precious secret ; and ever and anon the minds of people have
been panic-stricken and progress checked by announcements
from prophecy-mongers that the world would come to an end
at such and such a time, and stating the year when Jesus would
appear. The delusion will die out only when the "immense
misunderstanding of the Bible" is corrected, and the teaching
of science about the earth's past and future accepted by Second-
Adventists.

future to the neglect of improvement of the present. For the early Christians, regarding the earth as soon to vanish away, gave their sole concern to, and set their affections upon, an unseen world which was enduring ; feeling that the present state of things might cease at any moment, they bestowed small care upon its passing wants and held lightly even the ties of home and kindred which might be snapped suddenly. The loss of property could be suffered without repining, and wrong pass unredressed by those to whom Jesus, "judge of quick and dead," would open the kingdom "prepared from the foundation of the world." Art and learning were vain compared to the knowledge "making wise unto salvation," and the heavens were watched, not for the glory of the sunlight and the stars, but that the chosen might catch the first glimpse of their coming Lord, whom they would be caught up in the air to meet, and so be ever with him.[1] Out of this illusion there grew a terrible misconception by Christians of

---

[1] 1 Thess. iv. 13-18 ; v. 1, 2 ; etc., etc.

their relation to the earth and human kind, which still too largely separates reason and feeling, and sustains false divisions in our life. God's beautiful world, whose flowers and children's faces were so dear to Jesus, was called a "waste, howling wilderness," through which we are doomed to pass to a heavenly Canaan; the love of it and interest in its affairs were said to ill comport with setting the heart on things above, and to arouse the jealousy of God; life upon it was to be endured only as a preparing for eternal life elsewhere. All this is not only false, but wicked. The earth is no place of exile, but our fatherland, calling forth our reverence and our best service. Here, or nowhere, is our sphere of duty, where a zest and sacredness is given to work in aiding to clear away all that hinders the advance of man in everything that is of good report, and in the slaying of selfishness—the root of all that chokes the growth of charity. And to play well our part in this great struggle, doing nought to retard the issue, is a nobler task than to pine for a land of

dreamless ease, where no spur is given to effort,
and to pass our days fretfully wondering what
is to become of our poor selves, each one of
which is in the hands of God. 'Tis the—

"'Glory of virtue to fight, to struggle, to right the wrong—
She desires no isles of the blest, no quiet seats of the just,
To rest in a golden grove, or to bask in a summer sky ;
Give her the wages of going on and not to die." [1]

IX.

Jesus in Jerusalem.

On returning to Galilee, Jesus made a short
stay at Capernaum, but did not resume his
public teaching there. The news of his intended
visit to Jerusalem spread, however, in the neighbourhood, and when he set out on that most
eventful journey, a goodly number, among whom
were a few faithful women, followed him. Moreover, the season for keeping the Passover was
drawing nigh, and many were wending their
way to the city for that purpose. At various

[1] Tennyson's *Wages.*

parts of the route he met with the Pharisees, who attacked him with catch-questions, and otherwise sought to draw him into debate, but we may turn from these to incidents of wider interest; stories of enduring fragrance. One day as he tarried in a house, some parents brought their children that they might receive, after Jewish custom, a rabbi's blessing, when the disciples, perhaps filled with overweening sense of their master's importance and therefore of their own, pushed them aside. "But when Jesus saw this he was much displeased, and said unto them, Suffer the little children to come unto me, forbid them not; for of such is the kingdom of God. Verily I say unto you, whosoever will not receive the kingdom of God as a little child, he shall not enter therein. And he took them up in his arms and blessed, putting his hands on them." [1]

Another time one came to him and said:

"Teacher, what good thing shall I do that I may have everlasting life? And Jesus said unto him, Why askest

[1] Matt. xix. 13, 14.

thou me concerning the good? One is the good." (Or as another account has it, "Why callest thou me good? none is good but one, God.") "But if thou desirest to enter into life, keep the commandments. Which? says he. And Jesus said, Thou shalt not kill, Thou shalt not commit adultery, Thou shalt not steal, Thou shalt not bear false witness, Honour the father and the mother, and, Thou shalt love thy neighbour as thyself. The young man says unto him, All these I kept: what lack I yet? Jesus said unto him, If thou desirest to be perfect, go sell thy goods and give to the poor, and thou shalt have treasure in heaven; and come follow me. But when the young man heard he went away sorry; for he had great possessions. And Jesus said unto his disciples, Verily I say unto you that a rich man will hardly enter into the kingdom of heaven. It is easier for a camel to enter through the eye of a needle than for a rich man into the kingdom of heaven. And when they heard they were exceedingly astonished, saying, Who then can be saved? But Jesus looked upon and said unto them, With men this is impossible; but with God all things are possible."[1]

Jesus and his companions had passed by way of Peræa, on the east of the Jordan, which river they recrossed at the ford of Bethabara, near the plain where grew "the palm trees by the water, the rose plants which are in Jericho." This place, celebrated in Jewish history as the first to yield

[1] Matt. xix. 16–26.

to the attack of the "sons of Israel" on the
invasion of Canaan, was an important town and
centre of traffic in balsam, which was not only of
great value both as a perfume and a medicine,
but a source of much revenue to the Romans.
It is now a village of black tents and mud
huts. As it was needful to rest here before
climbing the steep and rugged gorge which led
to Jerusalem, Jesus chose to become the guest
of a Jew named Zaccheus, chief of the tax-
collectors there. He was a little man, and being
unable to see over the heads of the crowd that
surged around Jesus, "ran on before" and climbed
a sycomore tree, to catch a glimpse of him. As
Jesus passed near the tree he saw Zaccheus, and
bade him come down that he might receive
him into his house.

"And he made haste and came down and received
him joyfully. And when they saw it they all murmured,
saying, He is gone in to lodge with a sinner. And
Zaccheus stood and said unto the Lord, Behold, Lord,
the half of my goods I give to the poor ; and if I took
aught from any one by false accusation, I pay fourfold.
And Jesus said unto him, This day is salvation come to
this house, inasmuch as he also is a son of Abraham, for

the Son of man came to seek and to save that which was lost." [1]

On the next day Jesus ascended the dreary path that led to the mountain village of Bethany, which was about two miles from Jerusalem, and there he abode in the house of friends to whom he was already known, or whose acquaintance, in the free manners of the East, he then made, and for whom he conceived an abiding love, which caused him often to return among them after the bickerings and vexations of his public encounters in Jerusalem.

The first view of that place is featureless and unpleasing from every other side than the approach from Bethany over the Mount of Olives, from the summit of which is seen at a glance the great valleys which cut it off from the surrounding tableland. The city itself spread before them, with its walls and turrets, its palaces and groups of houses—for Eastern cities have no well-planned streets; above all, the temple, whose golden-plated and spiked roof shone as a

[1] Luke xix. 7-10.

dazzling crown from Mount Moriah, the valley
between which and the opposite hill of Zion,
whereon towered Herod's palace, was spanned by
a bridge. The site of many of its noted buildings
is matter of great doubt, for the city, which has
borne the brunt of a score sieges, and been twice
razed to the ground, is choked with mounds of
rubbish many feet in depth, on which the present
Jerusalem is built.

The square-shaped platform of rock on which
the temple stood had been levelled at great cost
and enlarged by Herod. The outermost and
largest enclosure was the Court of the Gentiles,
upon which he had lavished taste and expense.
It was paved with stones of various colours, double
and treble rows of marble pillars ran round it,
forming aisles or halls from which many noble
gates led to the city and outskirts, that facing
the Mount of Olives being called Solomon's
porch. The colonnades round this court were
places of public resort ; there the rabbis taught,
and there Jesus addressed the people. There,
too, a busy traffic, with its deafening noises, the

shouting of men and the lowing of cattle, was carried on by traders in sheep, oxen, lambs, and kids, or, for those who were too poor to offer these, in doves, for the sacrifices; by sellers of oil, incense, and other needful things for the temple, and by money-dealers who exchanged the current foreign coin for the sacred shekel, in which alone the temple-tax could be paid.

In an angle of this Court of the Gentiles there was a raised terrace on which were notices in Greek and Latin, forbidding any but Jews to pass nearer under pain of death. Within this second enclosure was the Court of Women, approached by the Beautiful Gate, and containing the treasury, into which the temple-gifts were dropped by rich and poor; also the Court of Priests, with the laver and a huge altar of unhewn stones, and, in cloisters round the walls, places for stores and other purposes, and a synagogue where the Sanhedrin met. Twelve steps above these, in "the pupil of the eye," stood the temple itself, as says the Talmud, "The world is the eye, the ocean is the white

of the eye; the pupil is Jerusalem, and the
image in the pupil is the sanctuary." The
erection of sacred buildings to face the east
is a relic of sun worship, and another proof of
the survival of pagan customs among both Jews
and Christians; so looked the temple, to which
allusion is thus made in the Talmud :—

" Our fathers who were in this place
Turned their backs upon the temple
And their faces towards the east
And worshipped the sun eastward ;
But we unto Jehovah,
To Jehovah are our eyes."

It was a flat-roofed building of white marble,
and divided, like the "tabernacle" and the
temples before it, into two parts separated by a
curtain : the Holy, wherein stood the golden
candlestick, table, and altar; and the Holy of
Holies, imageless, bereft of cherubim and ark,
since the terrible destruction under Nebuchadnezzar.

Jerusalem was a city of priests ; Josephus
reckoned their number at twenty thousand,

besides whom were the Levites. It was the head-quarters of the rabbis; of the Pharisees sweeping by with their phylacteries and deep-fringed garments; while jostling these were white-robed Essenes, Roman soldiers, gay courtiers—a motley crowd, swelled at festival seasons by so many pilgrims that the city could not contain them, wherefore they pitched their tents and green booths outside its walls, or found lodging in the surrounding villages.

Our interest now-a-days in the numerous and unceasing rites and services of the Jewish temple is solely in their relation to the customs and modes of worship of men in bygone ages, the tracing of which is beyond the purpose of this book. Here I allude to them only to point out how the interest of every one in and about Jerusalem was bound up in maintaining them; for the crowd of priests and Levites, who spent years in learning their duties, were supported by the temple-tax and free-will offerings, while the influx of pilgrims from time to time, and the supply of numberless things, as cattle, salt,

wood, oil, etc., for the temple service, was an
unfailing source of gain to the inhabitants. How
daring and well-nigh hopeless then was the task
of any man, the effect of whose teaching was to
show the needlessness of all this outward and
costly service ; for if religion was not in this,
but in self-denying service of man for men, and
the acceptable worship of God one of the spirit,
the priests were not wanted, the temple flame
might be put out, the daily sacrifice might be
stayed, its whirling smoke no longer darken the
air, and the mob of chaffering, cheating trades-
men turn their hands to honest work.

As Jesus neared the city, the excitement of
his followers became intense ; they resolved to
make his entry one of triumph, and, either with
or without his consent, procured an ass on which
he should ride through the gates. Their unsought tribute was not unwelcome to him, for,
like all reformers, his hope of success lay among
the masses ; so mounting the ass (an animal
ridden by persons of note in the East, and, in

contrast to the horse, which was used only in war, an emblem of peace), he rode amidst the plaudits and hosannas of the crowd.

"Many spread their garments in the way and others branches, having cut them out of the fields. And those going before and those following cried :
'Hosanna !
Bless him that comes in the name of the Lord !
Bless the coming kingdom of our father David !
Hosanna in the highest !'"[1]

Familiar as the people of Jerusalem were with the shouts and singing of pilgrim-bands as they approached the sacred, dazzling shrine, the entry of Jesus and his followers set them agape and asking what it all meant ; "all the city was moved saying, 'Who is this?' and the multitude said, 'This is the prophet Jesus, from Nazareth in Galilee.'"

Passing through the Sheep-gate, the procession stopped not till the temple courts were reached, and there Jesus dismounted and mingled with the crowd. If he had come yearly from Nazareth to keep the feasts, the scene was not strange

[1] Matt. xxi. 8, 9.

Y

to him, but whether he had or not, he entered
upon it now in a very different mood and
character—a *sceptic*, as he would now be called,
one who had by *thinking* cut himself adrift
from the religion of his people—yet all aglow
with reverence and pious zeal. The trafficking
at the very foot of the " Holy of Holies"
shocked him, its noisy clatter grated on his ear
and so irritated him that without ado he pushed
his way helter-skelter among the traders and
money-changers,overturned their stalls and tables,
and with a whip, perhaps made from small cords
lying scattered on the pavement, drove them
out, saying, " Is it not written, My house shall
be called an house of prayer for all the nations ?
but ye have made it a den of robbers!" So
daring an act, successful in the suddenness of its
surprise and in the support doubtless accorded
it by many Jews, shocked, like Jesus, at the
noise and barter in the holy place, was an attack
upon the temple-system itself, and could not fail
to direct towards its author the attention and
displeasure of priests and Pharisees.

The memory of bickerings and debates between these men and Jesus, and the cruelties, even unto death, which he suffered at their hands, were uppermost in the minds of his disciples, and scarce a word is given to the matter of his addresses in the temple courts. That these were in keeping with his unwavering conviction that the kingdom of which he believed himself the "anointed" herald was a kingdom of the spirit there can be no doubt, but the subject is dismissed in the bare record that "in the day time he was teaching in the temple, but at night he went out and lodged at the mount that is called the Mount of Olives. And all the people were coming early in the morning to him in the temple to hear him." [1]

Soon after his attack upon the traders, the rulers of the Sanhedrin came forward to ask by what authority he acted, and who gave it him. With ready skill he said to them, " I also will ask you one question, which if ye tell me, I also will tell you by what authority I do these things.

[1] Luke xxi. 37, 38.

The baptism of John, whence was it? from
heaven or from men?" Now Jesus had described John to his disciples and the multitude
as the Elias who had come before him, the
Messiah, and if, therefore, the chief priests and
elders had replied that the baptism of John was
from heaven, he would have claimed to be
the "coming one" whom John had preached,
while on the other hand, if they said that the
baptism of John was from earth, the multitude,
who believed that he was a prophet, would have
been enraged against them. So they simply
said, " We know not," and Jesus answered them,
" Neither shall I tell you by what authority I do
these things," following up his reply by a parable
warning them of the fate of the Jews : " A man
had two children : he came to the first and said,
Child, go work to-day in the vineyard. But he
answered and said, I will not ; afterwards he
repented and went. And he came to the other
and spake in the same manner. And he answered and said, Yea, sir, and went not. Which
of the two did the will of the father? They

say the first. Jesus says unto them, Verily I say unto you, the publicans and harlots go before you into the kingdom of God. For John came unto you in the way of righteousness and ye believed him not, but the publicans and harlots believed him; and when ye saw it, ye repented not afterwards so as to believe him."[1]

Although Jesus, at the outset of his work in Jerusalem, thus attacked the classes whose support he felt he could never command, they did not resent the onslaught by acts of violence. Once or twice the hot-headed among them would, in accordance with Jewish law, have stoned him, had they not feared the multitude, among whom he at first secured no mean following, and who revered him as a prophet ; but the weapons they mostly used were cunning and craft. How well he parried these is shown on an occasion when, in tones of flattery, they sought his opinion on the vexed question of paying taxes to the foreigner. "Rabbi," said they, "we know that

[1] Matt. xxi. 23-32.

thou art true and teachest the way of God in truth and carest for no one : for thou regardest not the person of men. Tell us, therefore, what thinkest thou, is it lawful to give tribute to Cæsar or not ?" Jesus saw through their designs. Had he said " no," he would at once have been seized as a rebel ; had he said " yes," he would have forfeited the support of the people. " Why tempt ye me, ye hypocrites ?" he said ; " shew me the tribute money." And they brought unto him a denarius [1] (a Roman coin bearing the name and head of the emperor, and representing the tribute money, about sevenpence threefarthings, payable by each Jew to him.) And Jesus says unto them, " Whose is this image and super-scription ?" They say, " Cæsar's." Then says he unto them, " Render therefore unto Cæsar the things which are Cæsar's, and unto God the things that are God's." And when they heard, they marvelled, and left him and went away. [2]

One day, some remarks that he had made

---

[1] This word is still preserved in our £ *s. d.*
[2] Matt. xxii. 16–22.

on the resurrection had attracted the notice of
the Sadducees, rarely his hearers, and they sought
to confute him by citing the case of a woman
who had had seven husbands, asking him whose
wife she would be in the resurrection. Jesus
replied that their denial of this doctrine rested on
a misreading of the scriptures and an underrating
of almighty power. "For when they shall rise
from the dead they neither marry nor are given
in marriage, but are as angels in heaven." And
as proving that the dead are raised, "Did ye not
read in the book of Moses in the bush passage,
how God spake unto him, saying, ' I am the God
of Abraham, and the God of Isaac, and the God
of Jacob ?' He is not the God of dead, but of
living. Ye do greatly err." That is, if God
called himself the God of the patriarchs hundreds
of years after they were dead, it must be inferred
that they are not dead for ever, but will return
from the land of shades and walk the earth in
their bodies,[1] and moreover includes the larger
fact of His close and abiding relation with

[1] Matt. xxii. 23–32.

living men.   This reasoning seems to have
silenced the Sadducees, who were, however, in
the right, for the facts of science confirm their
belief that dead bodies decay, and, mingling with
the common dust of the globe of whose particles
they consist, become one with it to nourish suc-
ceeding forms of life born of the all-quickening
earth, the "stuff" of which, as we may call it,
being neither added to nor lessened, is thus
used over and over again.

The record turns from these stories of his
triumph in debate with Pharisee and Sadducee
to exhibit him as exalting the commandment
of love to God and one's neighbour, than which
"there is none greater," conveying a reproof
they do well to take to heart who maintain the
needfulness of believing doctrines which no
words of his sanction, and which, were he among
us now, he would condemn and oppose, as
making "the word of God of none effect."

"And one of the scribes came, and having
heard them reasoning together, perceiving that
he answered them well, asked him, Which is the

first commandment of all? Jesus answered,
The first is, Hear, O Israel; the Lord our God
is one Lord; and thou shalt love the Lord thy
God from all thy heart, and from all thy soul,
and from all thy mind, and from all thy strength.
The second is this, Thou shalt love thy neighbour
as thyself. There is none other commandment
greater than these. And the scribe said unto
him, Well, master, thou saidst of a truth that
there is one, and there is none other but he:
and to love him from all the heart, and from all
the understanding, and from all the strength,
and to love his neighbour as himself, is more
than all the whole burnt-offerings and the
sacrifices. And when Jesus saw him that he
answered intelligently, he said unto him, Thou
art not far from the kingdom of God. And no
one durst question him any more." [1]

---

[1] Mark xii. 28-34.

X.

His Arrest, Trial, and Crucifixion.

So the days passed in teaching the multitude, in warning them against lip service in religion, and in sharp debate with those against whose example Jesus cautioned his listeners,[1] and who, as they one after another advanced with their questions, retired foiled and silenced. But they retired to plot how best they might silence him, and, to accomplish this, Pharisee and Sadducee laid aside their common quarrel.

As the records tell us, when the day was over, Jesus passed to some retreat from the "strife of tongues" and the reach of the factions which, under cover of the darkness, might have harmed him, spending the night either among the fig and olive groves of Olivet or at Bethany, where, in the society of the two sisters, Martha and Mary, and their brother Lazarus, he forgot his troubles. He was no bravado, courting a death

[1] Matt. xxiii. 3.

which none in the flush and flower of life may
think of without a shudder. Life was his, not
to throw wildly away, yet not to cling to when
its work was done.

And it was nearly done. The quick and large
increase of faithful disciples, which could alone
foil and disarm the priests and scribes, had not
come, the zeal aroused by his entry had died
away, the story of his mission in Galilee repeated
itself in Judæa, and the bitter sorrow of dis-
appointment breaks out in such words as these:
"O Jerusalem, Jerusalem, that killest the prophets and stonest them who have been sent
unto her, how often did I desire to gather thy
children as a hen gathers her chickens under the
wings, and ye desired not!" And in these too,
when the thought of the impending doom of the
city, where religion was a traffic, drew tears from
him as he looked upon it from the slopes of
Olivet: "If thou hadst known, even thou, at
least in this thy day, the things which belong
unto thy peace! but now they are hid from
thine eyes." [1]

[1] Luke xix. 42.

It is most doubtful whether Jesus had any
intercourse with either Samaritans or Gentiles
during his brief public life; but the rejection of
his mission by his own people had caused him
to look to the heathen as the supplanters of
Israel, and in the parable of the "good Samaritan" he portrays the hated Cuthean as showing
kindness to a robbed and wounded Jew which
was denied him by both priest and Levite.
As a Jew, believing that to Jews the "gospel
of the kingdom" must be *first* proclaimed,
he had confined his teaching to them, and
in sending out his disciples he instructed
them to act likewise; but he shared the larger
belief of the nobler prophets of old, that the
Gentiles would be brought into the one fold.
Moreover, it was impossible that the fatherhood
of God and the brotherhood of man which Jesus
proclaimed could be narrowed to one zone or
people—a religion, the essence of which was
love of God, manifest by love of man, was
destined to be world-wide and all-embracing,
and its preacher, in eating with outcasts and

doing deeds of mercy on the sabbath, had already broken down the "middle wall of partition," . . . "creating the two into himself."

In such parables as that of the "two sons," already quoted, and of the "marriage of the king's son,"[1] where the chosen guests frame all kind of excuses to avoid coming to the feast, so that the wrathful king at last sends his servants to gather in from the highways and call to the feast whoever they might find, he proclaims the admission of the Gentiles; while in that of the "wicked husbandmen" he hints at the fate of those who had slain the prophets, and would lay hands on the Messiah. "Therefore say I unto you, the kingdom of God will be taken from you and given to a nation bringing forth the fruits thereof. And when the chief priests and Pharisees heard his parables, they knew that he spoke of them."[2]

In plainer words than parables, he whose sweetness and gentleness had given place to bitterness at the sight of hypocrisy and

[1] Matt. xxii. 1–14.   [2] Matt. xxi. 33–43.

swagger, poured forth invective upon those "who did all their works to be seen by men : for they make broad their phylacteries, and enlarge the fringes, and love the chief place at feasts and the chief seats in the synagogues, and the salutations in the markets, and to be called by men, Rabbi." . . .

"But woe unto you, scribes and Pharisees, hypocrites![1] for ye shut the kingdom of heaven before men : for ye neither go in, nor suffer those that are entered to go in.

"Woe unto you scribes and Pharisees, hypocrites! for ye compass sea and land to make one proselyte, and when he becomes such, ye make him a son of hell twofold more than yourselves. . . .

"Woe unto you, scribes and Pharisees, hypocrites! for ye pay tithe of the mint and the anise and the cummin, and have left the weightier matters of the law, the judgment, the mercy, and the faith : these ought ye to have done, and not leave those undone. Blind guides, who strain out the gnat and swallow the camel. . . .

"Woe unto you, scribes and Pharisees, hypocrites! for ye are like unto whited sepulchres, which indeed appear beautiful outwardly, but within are full of dead bones and every uncleanness. So also ye appear outwardly righteous unto men, but within ye are full of hypocrisy and iniquity.

"Woe unto you, scribes and Pharisees, hypocrites! for

---

[1] Literally *actors*, as the Greek *hypokritai* means.

ye build the sepulchres of the prophets, and garnish the tombs of the righteous, and say, If we had been in the days of our fathers, we would not have been their partners in the blood of the prophets. Wherefore ye witness against yourselves, that ye are sons of them who killed the prophets. Fill ye up then the measure of your fathers. Serpents, brood of vipers, how can ye escape the judgment of hell?"[1]

These biting and terrible words burnt as hot iron into the souls of those whom he thus described, but they could scarcely afford an excuse for using violence, and, mayhap, were but the retort to strong words from his opponents. But when, mingling his dislike of all connected with the temple with his dreams of a purer faith whose temple should be co-extensive with the earth, he said, in figure of speech that so fitly expressed his meaning, "I will destroy this temple that is made with hands, and within three days I will build another made without hands," he gave his foes, ever on the alert to trip him, the pretext they wanted, and these words of "heresy" and "blasphemy," as they were deemed, formed the chief count in the charge against him, and were flung scoffingly in his teeth as he hung a-dying.

[1] Matt. xxiii. *passim.*

The seizure of Jesus appears to have been determined upon at a meeting of the Sanhedrin held on the Tuesday evening before the passover (the celebration of which began on the Thursday evening, the fourteenth of the Jewish month Nisan, the time of the first full moon in spring), at the house of the high-priest Caiaphas. But "lest there was an uproar among the people" at the festival time through any attempt to arrest him in public, and so the feeling, wrought to high excitement at that season, flame out in tumult, perhaps rebellion, despite all that the Sanhedrin might do, they decided to postpone action till after the passover, when the pilgrims had dispersed, and then to lay hold of Jesus quietly. But the carrying out of their designs against him was hastened by aid from a quarter whence they least expected it.

It is easy for us, in the quiet of our lives, touched, as we cannot fail to be, by the tale of the patience of Jesus under suffering and of the horrible death he died, to blame these men for the course which they took, and to wonder how the Jews could turn deaf ear to so lovable and earnest a prophet. But the account which has been given of their ideas concerning a Messiah show how utterly he failed to answer to these, giving no proof in miracle or sign of a divine mission, and content to teach, argue, reprove, and denounce, like the holy men of old, whose spirit he shared with added measure. We should, indeed, in the light of these facts, wonder if they, limited in their notions and puffed up with vain hopes, had seen in him other than a Jew of extreme, perverted, mystical, and unworkable ideas, who, angered at their refusal to welcome him, a man of Galilean manners and brogue, but claiming hearing as their Messiah, at last violently attacked the religion whose laws about sabbaths and cleansings he had broken, and insulted their sacred shrine. The law which they regarded as divine was clear as to their duty concerning such an one; it was written, " Thou shalt stone him with stones, that he die." [1]

[1] Deut. xiii. 10; cf. 1-5, and ch. xviii. 20.

Z

On the evening of Thursday, the fourteenth of Nisan, Jesus and his twelve disciples assembled under the roof of some secret or open follower in Jerusalem to eat the passover together.

At this feast the chief dish in every house was a lamb which had been declared free from blemish by the priests, with whom were left its fat and blood for sacrifice,[1] and which was roasted whole, eaten with bread, bitter herbs and fruits, and washed down with red wine. Prayers and thanksgiving (for the feast in its later meaning was one of rejoicing in memory of Israel's deliverance from the bondage in Egypt) were offered, psalms cxiii.–cxviii. were sung as the wine-cup went round, and the meal closed with strains of praise. But amidst this little company of thirteen in that unknown upper room, joy was not a guest; a heavy gloom weighed on the heart of the Master ; one among the number betrayed signs betokening a mind ill at ease, and the quick eye of Jesus saw these, yet he strove not to impart the gloom to his

[1] See p. 24.

friends, and in the old, sweet manner spoke now to one, now to another. "With longing," he said, "I longed to eat this passover with you before I suffer: for I say unto you, that I will not any more eat it until it be fulfilled in the kingdom of God."[1] Then he did a beautiful and touching thing, the poetry of which has been well-nigh stifled out by the tedious and harmful debates to which it has given rise among Christian sects, but which we may easily see suggested itself at the time to a mind like that of Jesus, so rich in its store of symbols and its boundless wealth of illustration. Offering the usual blessing, he took a cake of bread, broke it into fragments, and as he gave a piece to each the act seemed to prefigure a swift-coming fate, for he said, "Eat; this is my body which is broken for you." Then he filled the cup with wine, and after thanksgiving, drank of it and passed it round, saying, "This is my blood of the covenant, shed for many."[2] "Verily I say unto you, I will not drink of the fruit of the

---

[1] Luke xxii. 15.   [2] Luke xxii. 19.

vine, until that day when I drink it new in the kingdom of God." [1]

It was their last act together, and abode in the memories of the disciples as the sacred words of the dead. When, after their faithless desertion of him in the moment of peril, they rallied together and talked over what he had said, the unleavened bread and the red wine had fuller meaning for them, and that simple fare became a solemn rite. To this day wherever men and women, and young folk too, gather together to repeat it in remembrance of the sacrifice of a noble life for the truth, they do well so long as it becomes no other to them than an example to follow and is not lowered into a rite in which virtue is believed to dwell. For, shocking to say, millions of Christian people to this day are taught that Jesus by a miracle changed the bread and the wine into his own body and blood! and that in some occult way

[1] Mark xiv. 25. The enjoyment of the world to come is figuratively spoken of in Rabbinic writings as the *banquet.* Cf. *P. Aboth,* p. 74 (notes on iii. 25).

priests have power from him to change the wafer and wine used during the "mass," as the service connected with this rite is called among Roman Catholics, so that the very body and blood of Christ take their place, and as a matter of course the rite is invested with an awful importance and made a powerful instrument in the hands of the clergy. In former times it was used as an "ordeal," or one of the many tests of the guilt or innocence of accused persons, it being held that when taken by the guilty, divine punishment quickly followed the impious act, but that no harm resulted where the accused was innocent.

Near midnight, when the supper was ended, Jesus and the twelve left the city, passed through the valley of Kidron to the foot of the Mount of Olives, and as they journeyed one of the number slunk away under cover of the darkness. This was Judas of Kerioth (called Judas Iscariot in the gospels), bound on his errand to carry out a bargain he had made, perhaps the day before, with the Sanhedrin to show the temple guard the place where Jesus might be surprised and seized.

What led this man to so shameful a deed it is not possible to say, for, greedy of nature as he seems to have been, the sum for which he is said to have bargained to do it, thirty silver shekels, or barely four pounds in English money, was too paltry; enough that he had sought the chief priests and that they had gladly accepted his offer to betray the Master, and so hasten an event, which they had intended deferring until after the feast.

Meanwhile Jesus went on his way with the eleven till they reached a grove or garden near Olivet, called Gethsemane, or the "oil-press," which may indicate that it was a not unfit resting-place at an hour when it might be too late to reach Bethany, on the route to which it lay. There Jesus, from whose eyes looming trouble at the stealthy act of Judas had driven sleep, bidding the other disciples remain while he retired to pray, took Peter, James, and John, " and began to be sorrowful and cast down. Then says he unto

them, My soul is exceeding sorrowful, even unto
death ; abide here and watch with me. And he
went forward a little and fell on the ground, and
prayed that, if it were possible, the hour might
pass from him, and said, Abba, Father, all
things are possible unto Thee; take away this
cup from me ; nevertheless, not what I will, but
what Thou wilt."

For Jesus, completely submissive, as this
prayer denotes, and fearless withal, was in the
prime of manhood, and quailed as men brave
and tender as he have quailed before and
since, at the thought of taking "from death's
hand the cup that we all must take," and leaving
dear earth, scene of toils and joys and friendly
faces ; the more painfully so as he felt that
he would die misunderstood by those whom he
yearned to save. Returning to the three, " he
found them sleeping, for their eyes were weary,"
when suddenly the flame of burning torches
amidst the trees dazzled their eyes, and a band
of armed men, belonging to the temple guard
and therefore under the control of the priests,

appeared, headed by Judas. That they might
know which was Jesus, the traitor went up and
kissed him as signal, whereupon hands were laid
on him. One of the disciples who had a sword
strove to defend him, and in the scuffle wounded
one of the high-priest's men, but Jesus, bidding
him sheath his sword, surrendered without resistance, quietly saying to his captors, " Ye come out,
as against a robber, with swords and staves to take
me ; I was daily with you in the temple teaching,
and ye did not lay hold of me ! " His disciples,
craven-hearted, and careful only to save their
lives, "forsook him and fled," and Jesus, deserted
by the eleven and betrayed by the twelfth, was a
lonely prisoner in the hands of his enemies.

They lost no time, but marched him in the
dead of night to the palace of Caiaphas,
where such members of the Sanhedrin as could
be found were assembled, and with them witnesses able, falsely or otherwise, to depose to
certain " blasphemous " words uttered by Jesus.
In the absence of his disciples (for Peter, who
had slunk into the courtyard in the darkness

to learn how things were going on, was accused by a servant girl of being a follower of the Nazarene, and had slipped away after denying all knowledge of Jesus), we have no trustworthy account of the proceedings within the council-chamber, and moreover, our knowledge is scanty concerning the mode of conducting trials by the Sanhedrin. But the course taken seems to have been that of summoning the witnesses to give evidence in support of the charge against Jesus as a false prophet and "corrupter" of religion, and after hearing several whose testimony "agreed not together," two came forward to declare that they had heard him say, "I will destroy this temple made with hands, and in three days I will raise up another made without hands," which was of course not taken as a figure of speech, but as signifying impious intent.

Caiaphas then stood up in the midst and asked Jesus if he had any answer to make to the charge; "but he held his peace," for what could words avail where, as he felt sure, the

judges had resolved beforehand upon their ver-
dict ? Their minds were made up ; let them do
their worst. Die ? he could die but once, and
in such a dying was secured the life of the
truth to which he had witnessed ; acquittal
could be had only at the cost of denying all
that in life he accounted dear. But Caiaphas, anxious that Jesus should by some word
of his own justify the intended sentence, said
solemnly, " I adjure thee by the living God,
that thou tell us whether thou art the Messiah,
the Son of God." Then Jesus broke silence,
answering him, " Thou hast said it," and there-
upon the high priest—in sign of horror at an
admission which to him was blasphemy—" rent
his clothes," saying, " He blasphemed ; what
further need have we of witnesses ? behold, now
ye heard the blasphemy. What think ye ?"
They answered and said, " He is guilty of
death." [1]

Thus was a short and hurried trial, in which
only the bare forms of justice were respected,

[1] Matt. xxvi. 59–66.

ended against the unbefriended Jesus in the darkness of that passover night, and the members of the Sanhedrin, cold and weary, after agreeing to meet early in the morning and complete what in haste had been left unsettled, dispersed to their homes. Jesus was placed in the charge of mocking and insulting guards.

At dawn of day the Sanhedrin reassembled, chiefly to discuss how best to present the charge against him before the Roman governor, and thus ensure his not escaping the meshes of the Imperial law, for they had no power to carry out the sentence which they had pronounced. They artfully and unjustly decided to ensure his conviction by charging him with sedition, on the ground that his claim to the Messiahship involved a claim to kingship over the Jews, therefore casting off the rule of Rome. So he was marched to the "prætorium," the famous palace of Herod, a gloomy building without, but all gaiety and luxury within, and now occupied by the Roman procurator, Pontius Pilate, who, according to his duty, had come from his favourite seat, Cæsarea, with a body of soldiers to maintain order and suppress any tumults that might arise among the excited Jews during the great feast.

The proceedings took place in an open court before the palace, called in the Hebrew "Gab-batha," or "the pavement," where stood the chair of state, from which judgment was delivered in the hearing of the people, and where Pilate now seated himself to listen to the Sanhedrin and note their prisoner.

The part played by him in this sad business is not easy to discover, for according to the gospels he was unwilling to deal with the case as hastily and severely as the Jewish rulers urged. To him Jesus appeared a harmless enthusiast, whose head had been somewhat turned by the flattery of rustics, and who had got into trouble with the heads of his nation over matters for which Pilate had small regard, rather contempt. As he surveyed the poor Galilean, he may have smiled at the thought of such an one claiming a kingship and heading a rebellion, the more so because if he were a Messiah commending himself to the Jews they would not have made that claim an indictment against him. The Romans were tolerant of all religions, one god more or less in their Pantheon mattered little, and they allowed the Jews, as these passover feasts and temple-services show, freedom in their worship, so long as it was not made a pretext or an engine for revolt ; indeed the emperor himself did honour to their religion and assigned a share of the taxes to be applied towards maintaining its splendour in Jerusalem.

At the same time Pilate ran the risk of losing place and favour if he winked at any movement which threatened mischief, and after hearing the charge of sedition against Jesus, he asked him if he was " king of the Jews ; " but it would appear that " he answered him not even a word, so that the governor marvelled greatly." [1]

Puzzled and withal vexed at what seemed to him " much ado about nothing," he was inclined to inflict a light punishment and let Jesus go,

[1] Matt. xxvi. 14.

catching at a practice common at passover time, of setting free some prisoner chosen by the Jews. But the chief priest and elders, fearful that their victim might after all escape them, moved the multitude to clamour with them for the release of one Jesus Bar-Abbas, who appears to have been in favour with them as the hero of some tumult, perhaps against the Romans.

Pilate, having thus committed himself, was compelled to yield, and then asking the crowd, "What then will ye that I should do with him whom ye call the king of the Jews?" was answered by shouts of "Crucify him," thus demanding that he should be put to the most degrading death that the Romans inflicted, the death of the vilest criminals. And the cry rose louder and louder from the surging crowd, so that Pilate, glad at last to be quit of the affair, and having at heart a pagan's contempt for human life, "gave sentence that it should be as they asked."[1]

So Jesus was delivered to the soldiers to be

[1] Luke xxiii. 24.

stripped and scourged with leathern thongs tipped with bone or metal, according to the brutal custom adopted towards the condemned, and to this terrible pain succeeded mocking tortures; a reed being thrust into his hand as sceptre, prickly twigs wound into a crown and forced upon his head, and an old scarlet cloak thrown over him, while the unpitying ruffians saluted him in jeering homage as "king of the Jews."

The sentence—and well it was so rather than such agony should be endured by him who had never harmed a creature of God, but made life sunnier for the desolate and outcast—was carried out as soon as things could be made ready, and in a short time Jesus was led through Jerusalem to a hill called, perhaps from its bald rounded top, Golgotha,[1] that is "a skull," situate outside the city gates, but the exact site of which is unknown. Before this crownless king of men there went a herald proclaiming his offence, while the

---

[1] *Calvaria,* from *calva,* "bald-scalp," is the Latin form of this word.

prisoner himself struggled under the weight of a beam of the cross on which he was to die, but his strength failing by the way, the soldiers laid hold of a man named Simon, coming cityward, " and him they compelled to bear his cross."

That upon which Jesus suffered was probably ┼ shaped (the common Roman form known as the *crux immissa*). To this the body, stripped of clothes, which were divided among the soldiers, was nailed and bound, nails being driven through the hands and feet, which latter, for the cross was not so high as commonly depicted, nearly touched the ground, and over the culprit's head a board was affixed, stating the crime for which he suffered. Thus, crucified between two thieves who were sentenced to a like death, and guarded by sentries, Jesus hung, exposed not only to the sun's burning glare on that Friday morning, and suffering the cruellest anguish in thirst[1] and ebbing blood and strained limbs, but the object

---

[1] He is said to have sipped and rejected the drink, frankincense in wine, which the compassion of the ladies of Jerusalem provided for the condemned to stupefy them.

of the raillery and taunts of the brutal crowd that then, as now, gloated over spectacles of human agony. Over his head was affixed a mocking notice written in Latin, Greek, and Aramaic, " The King of the Jews."

The scene around his cross is thus described in the simple words of the " Gospel according to Mark : "

" And they that passed by reviled him, wagging their heads and saying, Aha, thou that destroyest the temple and buildest it in three days, save thyself by coming down from the cross. In like manner also the chief priests mocking said among themselves with the scribes, He saved others, himself he cannot save ; the Messiah, the King of Israel, let him come down now from the cross, that we may see and believe. And they that were crucified with him reproached him." [1]

The disciples were still in hiding ; of all that

[1] Ch. xv. 29–32. In my quotations from the New Testament throughout this book the translation by Dr. Davidson, based upon the text of Von Tischendorf, has been for the most part adopted.

throng that had welcomed the Master's incoming
to Jerusalem with hosannas and waving branches
only a few faithful women, who had followed
him from Galilee, were " looking on afar off be-
holding these things." Whether Jesus uttered
or not the broken sentences of trust in and submission to his Father and of forgiveness of his
foes, which are recorded in the gospels, no one
can say with sureness, for the common sources
of knowledge altogether fail us here ; enough
that the words are in accord with all we can
learn of a life whose loveliness and faithfulness
were undimmed in death.

The time during which the crucified lingered
depended much on their strength of endurance ;
in the case of Jesus death came in mercy to the
poor worn-out and finely-strung frame after
about six hours of agony ; as the end neared
some kindly bystander moistened the parched
lips with a sponge dipped in the sour drink of
the Roman soldiers ; a few minutes afterwards
Jesus uttered a cry of pain, and then all was
over.

As a rule the Romans denied burial to the crucified, leaving the corpse to rot upon the cross, or be devoured by beasts and birds of prey, but they had relaxed this law in favour of the Jews, whose code required that the body of a man hanged should " not remain all night upon the tree." [1] This there was now special anxiety to obey in view of the nearness of the sabbath, that the day might not be defiled by the repulsive sight on Golgotha. In the case of Jesus, a rich man named Joseph of Arimathea, who is said to have been a member of the Sanhedrin, although not of the number who tried him, and who at least must have had keen sympathy with his teaching, being one that " waited for the kingdom of God," went to Pilate and boldly begged the body, that he might give it more worthy burial than it would have if left to the Jews to inter. On being assured that Jesus was really dead, Pilate, per-chance bribed thereto, assented ; whereupon Joseph had the corpse taken down from the cross, perhaps in sight of the women weeping,

[1] Deut. xxi. 23.

and borne to a tomb which he had hewn for himself in the rocks near at hand, closing the entrance by a great stone to guard the remains from prowling beasts of prey.

The spot where Jesus was thus buried is unknown, but upon the site marked by tradition there stands, filled with sham relics and tricked out with gewgaws, the Church of the Holy Sepulchre, within the walls of which, where all sweet and gentle influences should rule, Armenian, Greek, Latin, and other sects that " profess and call themselves Christians," scowl and wrangle, and are kept from flying at one another's throats only by the presence of Mohammadan soldiers.

In the rapid execution of their plans and the flight of his most trusted friends, the priests and scribes had some warrant for thinking that, beyond the gossip to which the event gave rise,

the last had been heard of Jesus. These pur-
blind men, who had compassed his death as a
blasphemer, failed to see that in yielding himself without effort at defence or escape, he had
willed to die for quite another thing, thereby
exalting the cross into the sublimest symbol of
self-surrender, at whatever cost, to the will of
God, and abiding in larger form than he himself had dreamed, as the holiest and tenderest
influence of all time.

When the immediate excitement was over,
the disciples, of whose whereabouts in the meanwhile we have no knowledge, ventured to show
themselves in Jerusalem, where they stood in
little danger of rough treatment from the rulers,
by whom they were regarded as misguided, but
harmless men. They were careful to manifest
zeal in obeying the law and frequenting the
temple ; indeed, the only feature that marked
them off from other Jews was their belief in
Jesus as the speedy-returning Messiah. Had
the future of his teaching depended on this
"sect of the Nazarenes," as we find them

afterwards scornfully called,[1] it would merely have fostered party feeling amongst the already divided nation. For the disciples worked in the old narrow grooves, resisting, even with persecution unto death, the efforts of larger minds to admit the Gentiles into fellowship without insisting on their compliance with Jewish rites and ceremonies. But in the end the freer view prevailed.

Among those who abetted violent deeds was a man destined to become the chief agent in converting the heathen to what he conceived to be "the faith as it is in Jesus." Of strong and subtle intellect and passionate heart, Paul, after much thought upon the matters which divided the community, joined the liberal side, and applied his fine reasoning powers to the skilful construction of a system designed to show that the old and limited "covenant" from Sinai was annulled by a new and limitless covenant sealed upon the cross. The zeal with which he had "consented unto the death" of heretics like

[1] Acts xxiv. 5.

Stephen was thenceforth poured into mission work. Unresting, despite opposition and peril, in his labours, he began at Damascus, afterwards reaching Antioch, where the Greek name "Christian" was first applied, as a term of reproach, to the converts, and thence travelled through Asia Minor and certain parts of Greece; finally, so runs the tradition, dying a martyr's death at Rome.

To this brief hint concerning the spread of the Christian religion, it must suffice to add that its after history records how the disputes which divided the first disciples increased as time rolled on, riving its converts into countless sects fired by deathless hate ; how corruptions born of lingering Jewish and intruding pagan elements, impaired the vigour which it drew from the inspiration of the beautiful spirit of Jesus ; and how what truth abode within it was foolishly made to stand or fall with notions about man and the universe which are utterly false.

Such matters interest us only as they help to explain the varying fortune which has, in com-

mon with that of other and older faiths, marked
its course ; and, moreover, profit us only as we
learn that its influence for good has lessened in
the degree that it has departed from, or made
" a hedge" of rites and dogmas around, the
simple and sufficing teaching of Jesus.

That love of God, shewn forth in love of man,
which was but a maxim of "repeaters" in his
time, and to which all gave assent of lip, but
few assent of life, was, so to speak, arrested in
him and drew towards him the quenchless affec-
tion of the sinful and the suffering. This, more
than all creeds about him, is the secret of an
influence which, bounded by a few months and
a narrow tract of country, has filled centuries
since from east to west with adoring followers
and, despite their frightful quarrellings and
slaughterings, kept aglow their ardour to serve
and save their fellow-men. And if it moves us
to like service, our life cannot be vain or harmful,
because it will nourish and diffuse the spirit
which, dwelling in high-souled men of other
lands and ages, abode in richest measure in
Jesus of Nazareth.

APPENDIX.

NOTE A.

THE SEMITIC FAMILY.

The various languages included under this term are a group of cognate dialects rather than a family of widely varied branches, and are commonly divided into the Northern, or Aramaic; the Middle, or Hebraic; and the Southern, or Arabic, as shown in the following table, which is copied from Prof. Max Müller's *Lect. on Language*, vol. i., p. 450.

	DEAD LANGUAGE.	LIVING LANGUAGE.
Aramaic	Chaldee (Masora, Talmud, Targum, Biblical Chaldee) Syriac (Peshito, second cent. A.D.) Cuneiform Inscriptions of Babylon and Nineveh	Neo-Syriac
Hebraic	Biblical Hebrew Samaritan (Pentateuch) Carthaginian, Phœnician Inscriptions	Dialects of the Jews
Arabic	Ethiopic or Gees Himyaritic Inscriptions	Dialects of Arabic Amharic (Abyssinia) „ Ehkili or Mahri (S. Arabia).

Chaldee is the name sometimes given to the dialects of Assyria and Babylon, which were adopted by the Jews during the captivity, not only for conversation, but as their literary language. The earliest records of it occur in the books of Ezra and Daniel, and it was probably the language of several of the Apocryphal books, although these have come down to us in Greek alone. Other relics are the Targums, or free translations of the Old Testament, and the Talmuds, while the untranslated sayings in the New Testament, attributed to Jesus, as *Talitha kumi*, *Ephphatha*, *Abba*, *Eloi*, *Eloi*, *lama sabachthani*, are Aramaic, then the vernacular of Palestine.

Syriac, or Western Aramaic, is still spoken in a corrupt form by certain tribes in Mesopotamia, and among the most important specimens of it which are preserved is the Peshito version of the Bible, ascribed to the second century.

The *cuneiform*, like the Egyptian hieroglyph, has its origin in picture-writing, but lost its elaborate form through the desire and need for simplicity necessitated by the softer material on which, as contrasted with the Egyptian, it had to be traced. The signs were more easily indented on mud and clay slabs by sharp and straight strokes made with a triangular stylus (whence our word *style*) and then baked in the sun or by fire. Great ingenuity has been applied to their decipherment, and as the famous Rosetta stone, with its inscription in three languages, the hieroglyphic, demotic (chiefly phonetic), and Greek, supplied the key to the Egyptian picture-writing, so the inscription on the rocks at Behistun in Media, on which Darius Hystaspes relates his enterprises in three cuneiform characters, the Persian, Median, and Assyrian, rendered great service in unravelling the meaning of the queer wedge-shaped strokes which had been pronounced talismanic signs, symbols, and charms, and even as due to the destructive activity of worms!

Hebrew ceased to exist as a spoken tongue some four centuries B.C., but it remained, as it remains to this day, the sacred language of the Jews, and the study of the learned.

The *Samaritan* is an impure dialect of the Hebrew, having a very large admixture of Aramaic words. Its oldest monument is a version of the Pentateuch, of which an admirable account is given in Deutsch's *Lit. Remains*, pp. 404, *et. seq.*

Of the *Phœnician* but few traces survive, only inscriptions on coins and weights, on votive tablets, sacrificial stones, tombstones, and on sarcophagi (Deutsch, p. 155) the inscribed coffin of a king of Sidon being its chief monument.

Of the *Arabic* group, the most ancient relics are the Himyaritic inscriptions, the date of which is unknown. Although the earliest documents are pre-Mohammadan, it was with the rise of Islam that Arabic became one of the richest literatures in the world, and, as the many words still employed in science show, the vehicle of learning, spreading over the civilized parts of Europe, Asia, and Africa.

NOTE B.

THE NAME JEHOVAH.

The peculiar feature of the Semitic languages is that the consonants are everything, and the vowels nothing, " every word consisting, in the first instance, merely of three consonants, which form, so to speak, the soul of the idea to be expressed by that word." And as in ancient times the consonants only were written, the name *Jehovah* appeared as J H V H. Its exact pronunciation is utterly lost, and, as we saw, such veneration gathered round it that when the Jews came to it they substituted some other name, usually *Adonai*. Afterwards, when vowels were added to the Hebrew text, those in *Adonai*, or its phonetic form *Edona*, were inserted between the letters of the sacred name, and thus J H V H was written JeHoVaH.

Although its first appearance in Israelitish history remains obscure, the arguments of Kuenen (*Religion of Israel*, vol. i., pp. 398 *et seq.*) conclusively refute the reasoning of Laud, Goldziher and others who contend that it is post-Mosaic and assign it to the period of the "awakening idea of nationality" among the Israelites, *i.e.* until their settlement in Canaan. Its connection, now generally admitted, with the verb *to be* justifies the interpretation attached to it in Exodus iii. 14, "I am that I am," by which may be understood, "He that is" or, as including the being whose "verb has no tenses;" the "Eternal." Curious correspondences, for no more than these dare we call them, are the *nuk pu nuk*, "I am he who I am," of the Egyptian "Book of the Dead," and the declaration of Ahuramazda to Zarathustra (*Ormuzd Yasht*, Haug. p. 195) "I am who I am, Mazda," while Brugsch states that *ánkh*, the divinity worshipped at Pithom, which city the Israelites enlarged while in bondage, means "he who lives" or "the Living One," and ventures the suggestion that it affords a clue to the meaning attached to the Hebrew Jehovah. The last word has not been spoken on this matter, perhaps it never will be ; but that a semi-barbarous people like the Israelites evolved, while in the polytheistic stage of development, the philosophical ideas of "being," ultimately connected with

Jehovah, is in accordance "neither with psychology nor history." The impulse in this direction seems to me to have come from Egypt through Moses, who, consciously or not, could scarcely remain unaffected by contact with a religion under whose symbols the conception of a Highest appear traceable.

NOTE C.

THE TALMUD.

This huge *mélange* consists of two parts : Mishnah, or text ; and Gemara, or commentary on the text.

The *Mishnah* (from *shanah*, to learn) is divided into the following sedarîm or sections, which are subdivided into treatises and chapters or paragraphs—

1. Zeraim, or *Seeds*, treating of Agriculture, the tithes and gifts due to the priests, Levites, and poor, and the forbidden mixtures in plants, animals, and garments.

2. Moed. or *Feast ;* of sabbaths, festivals and fast days ; the work forbidden, ceremonies and sacrifices ordained ; special chapters being devoted to the principal feasts. as Passover, Tabernacles, etc.

3. Nashim, or *Women ;* treating of marriage and divorce, etc.

4. Nezikin, or *Damages ;* dealing with the civil and criminal law, and concluding with the famous ethical treatise *Pirqe Aboth*, or " Sayings of the Fathers."

5. Kadashim, or *Sacred Things ;* treating of sacrifices, etc., also of the dimensions of the Temple.

6. Teharoth, or *Purifications* (see p. 277).

"The *Mishnah*, being formed into a code, became in its turn what the Scripture had been, a basis of develop-

ment and discussion. It had to be linked to the Bible,
became obscured by speculations, new traditions sprang
up, new methods were invented, casuistry assumed its
sway, and the *Gemara* ensued. A double Gemara ; one,
the expression of the schools in Palestine, called that of
Jerusalem, redacted at Tiberias about 390 A.D., and
written in what may be called East Aramaic ; the other,
redacted at Syra in Babylonia, 365–427 A.D., and couched
in Western Aramaic. . . . The Babylonian Talmud is
about four times as large as that of Jerusalem." (Deutsch's
Literary Remains, Art. "Talmud" pp. 40, 41.)

In further explanation of the reference made at p. 152,
to the necessity for translating the "Thorah" from the
Hebrew into the vernacular, it may be added that these
popular paraphrases, or free renderings, are known as
Targumim, the reader and expounder being called the
meturgeman, a name of which the word *dragoman*, applied
to interpreters in the East, is a corruption.

In addition to the immense body of expositions of the
Jewish scriptures embraced under the general term
Midrashim, there arose a system of fanciful speculations
based upon supposed hidden and mystical meanings in
them, to which the name *Kabbalah* (from *kabal*, to "hand
down") is given.

NOTE D.

THE BOOKS OF THE OLD TESTAMENT.

The Bible (from Greek *biblia*, "little books") is divided
into two parts, called the Old and New "Testaments," or
" covenants," *testamentum* being the Latin equivalent for

the Greek *diatheke*, " covenant." As stated at p. 84, the
idea of a covenant made between Jehovah and their forefathers arose among the Israelites about the time of
David, and the term was in due course applied to the
books in which it was narrated. Christians accepted the
Jewish scriptures in their entirety, and when their own
were placed by the side of them, called the former the
" Old Testament," and the latter the " New," which not
only prevented confusion, but implied a kind of connection,
historical and doctrinal, between the two sets of documents.

Following the arrangement of the Vulgate, or Latin
translation, which was itself copied from the Septuagint,
the Old Testament consists of thirty-nine books, grouped
in accordance with their general features, into historical
(Genesis to Esther), poetical (Job to the Song of
Solomon), and prophetical (Isaiah to Malachi). But
among the Jews a more definite threefold division prevails, viz., the Law, the Prophets, and the Writings [1]
wherein the books are placed in different order, and grouped
into twenty-two,[2] so as to agree with the number of letters
of the Hebrew alphabet. This division corresponds to
the mode [3] in which the whole was gradually collected,
viz., of the Law by the scribe Ezra and his co-workers ; of
the Prophets, under the statesman Nehemiah ; and of the
Writings, during the Maccabean period, when the national
independence quickened literary activity, and the memory
of the destruction which the books narrowly escaped under
Antiochus Epiphanes led to measures for their preservation.

The tradition current among the Jews before the time

[1] Cf. Prologue to *Ecclesiasticus*, where the first notice of this
division occurs.

[2] Josephus, *c. Apion*. i. 8.   [3] See pp. 150, 162, 175.

of Jesus, and accepted by Christians, was to the effect that the original manuscripts of their earlier scriptures were destroyed when the first temple was burnt, and that Ezra, as a "second Moses," made a recension, as it is called, of such copies as could be found, to which was afterwards added the books bearing his name and that of Nehemiah.

This tradition accords with the facts in so far as it gives Ezra credit for the collection of the "Law," but not so as implying that he was inspired by Jehovah to preserve writings said to contain the very words which that god had spoken to Moses. In tracing the sources of history we saw how ancient records became in the course of time invested with a sacred character, and the veneration paid first to the "law," and then by degrees to the "prophets" and the "writings," has its counterpart in the notions of a divine origin which attach themselves to the scriptures of other religions than the Jewish and Christian, which have slowly arisen out of traditions, been fenced round with theories of verbal inspiration, and made the subject of endless commentaries.

The titles of each of the five books comprising the "Law" or "Pentateuch," as it is more often called,[1] indicate the current belief, shared by Christians as well as by Jews, that Moses was their sole author, but no intelligent person who has looked even slightly into the matter can fail to note indications here and there of composite authorship. The many passages which refer to events long after the time of Moses[2] suffice in themselves to show that even if he were the author of the Pentateuch additions have been made to his work; but the most

---

[1] From Greek *pentateuchos* = "five books in one volume."
[2] Gen. xii. 6, xiii. 7, xxxi. 31 ; Lev. xviii. 28 ; Deut. ii. 12 ; etc.

striking proof that it proceeds certainly from two, and probably from several, hands is in the frequent interchange of the names *Elohim* and *Jehovah* for the Deity. For example, in Genesis i. and ii. 1-3, *Elohim* (which is almost always translated " God ") occurs thirty-five times, and *Jehovah* (which is always translated " LORD "[1]) not at all, and in the narrative of the journey of Abraham's servant to Haran (Gen. xxiv.) *Jehovah* occurs nineteen times, and *Elohim* not once.

This feature was noticed very many years ago, but was explained by assuming that Moses had a special reason for the alternate use of these names, and even Astruc, a French doctor, whose work, published in the middle of the last century, gave an impetus to critical study of the Pentateuch which has gone on with increasing vigour to this day, did not deny the common belief, but only suggested, as the title implies,[2] that Moses had certain older documents before him which he worked into the story.

Scholars have been at immense pains to assign the Elohistic and Jehovistic parts of the Pentateuch to their several authors, but the results, as might be expected in dealing with so mixed a document, are speculative, and, indeed, it is not settled which are the older portions, although those of the Elohists are generally so considered, a conclusion from which I venture to dissent. But the broad fact abides of differences in style and aim which are explicable only on the theory of composite authorship.

Apart from the failure which, in view of the above facts, as well as of the lack of order, of needless repetitions,

---

[1] *Adonai* is printed " Lord."

[2] *Conjectures sur les Mémoires originaux, dont il paroit que Moïse s'est servi pour composer le livre de la Génèse (Bruxelles, 1753).*

contradictions,[1] and impossible stories, attends any claim
on behalf of the Pentateuch to historical accuracy and
unity, there is the large admixture of legend which,
hitherto, has been regarded as divine revelation concerning
the creation of the universe, the primitive state of man,
and the origin of sin and death in the world, and which is
now found to stand in intimate connection with cognate
legends in Chaldean records and Persian scriptures, while
the serious matters with which it deals receive an altogether different, and either verified or verifiable, explanation from science.

Numberless books have been written in vain to prove
that the accounts of the creation in the early parts of
Genesis are in agreement with the discoveries of science
concerning the origin and succession of life upon the
earth ; and the six " days " have been made to square with
the vast periods demanded by geology, by contending
that "days " really mean "ages," quite ignoring the fact
that each "day" is said to have had a morning and an
evening. But no ingenuity of reconcilers, fertile as that
has been, can harmonize the statement in Gen. iii., that
agony and death came into the world as the punishment
of man's disobedience, with the evidence which the rocks
beneath us supply of the existence of pain and struggling
and death countless ages before man appeared. And in
the ever-accumulating evidence from all quarters of the
globe, inhabited once or habitable now, of the primitive
condition of man, as one of savagery, the tribes still in
that state representing not the degradation to which
through the "fall" of a remote ancestor they have sunk,

---

[1] Cf. Gen. xxii. 14 with Exod. vi. 3 ; Exod. xx. 17 with Deut.
v. 22 : Numb. xxi. 35 with *ib.* xxxii. 39 ; etc.

but the condition out of which all races above them have emerged, there is no harmony possible with the declaration in Genesis that man was created in pristine purity, and placed amidst luxurious surroundings. The abandonment of the statements in scripture as to the position of the earth in space and its recent creation in time did not involve the surrender or negation of any fundamental dogma, but the admission that death raged in the world before man is fatal to the doctrine that it was the result of his disobedience, and with the denial of his "fall" the whole scheme of redemption as formulated in Christian theology is swept away. But in place of the cheerless theory of divine purpose frustrated at the outset of man's career, and, assumed divine intervention notwithstanding, unaccomplished to this day, science gives us in the revelation of the wondrous advance which, despite local checks, man has accomplished, heart and hope to contribute to the realization of what Jesus and like-minded men have meant by the "kingdom of God."

The Pentateuch remained the sole sacred book of the Jews long after its final redaction, for the primary object of the collection of the "prophets" and the "writings" was their preservation ; and only by slow degrees did they acquire the divine authority which was accorded to the "law." There was doubtless a fairly general agreement of opinion concerning them, but the nature and contents of certain books, *e.g.*, Ecclesiastes, in which the vanity of human life is asserted, and Esther, which is quite devoid of a religious spirit, led to much discussion as to their admission, and it was not until the end of the first century, A.D., that the *canon* was settled. This Greek word, meaning a "straight rod " or " bar "—metaphorically, a " rule " or " model of excellence " was in course of time applied to the books of the Bible as containing the rule of faith or truth ; the " holy library " as Jerome called them.[1]

Some use has been made in the foregoing pages of a number of uncanonical writings comprised under the general term " apocryphal," meaning " hidden," or " secret," given to them as containing hidden things, or as kept secret, or, in a later sense, as spurious. They were formerly inserted between the Old and New Testaments, a position which well indicates the light some of them throw on Jewish history from the period with which the Old Testament concludes, and although they are on the whole inferior to the canonical books, it is a pity that they no longer find a place in our authorized version, and are consequently so little known. They were probably composed during the first and second centuries before Jesus, and are of mixed origin, some being written in Palestine, as the valuable *First Book of Maccabees* and the *Wisdom of Jesus son of Sirach, or Ecclesiasticus;* others in Alexandria, as the *Wisdom of Solomon, Second Book of Maccabees,* and " the rest of the chapters of the " *Book of Esther;* while several bear traces of Persian influence, as *Baruch the Prophet,* the *Book of Tobias* (or *Tobit*), the third and fourth books of *Esdras* (or *Ezra*), and the *Song of the Three Children,* etc. The Church of England speaks of them in her Articles of Religion as " read for example of life and instruction of manners, but yet doth it not apply them to establish any doctrine."

[1] A convenient summary of the history of the Bible canon is given by Mr. Matthew Arnold in *God and the Bible,* pp. 167, *et seq.*

NOTE E.

THE GOSPELS.

The early Christians had no New Testament, and the idea that one day the traditions and stray documents relating to Jesus and certain letters of his apostles would be gathered into a book as a sacred and inspired canon like the Old Testament, never entered their heads.

Confining my remarks to the four gospels, the earliest definite testimony that we have to their existence is from Irenæus, who wrote in the latter part of the second century (about the year 180) to this effect :

" Matthew it was, who among the Hebrews, brought out in their own language (the Aramaic) a written gospel, when Peter and Paul were preaching in Rome, and founding the church. Then, after their departure, Mark, the disciple and interpreter of Peter, he too delivered to us in writing what Peter preached, and Luke, moreover, the follower of Paul, set down in a book the gospel preached by Paul. Then John, the disciple of the Lord, who also lay on his breast, John too published his gospel, living at that time at Ephesus, in Asia."

Irenæus then indulges his fancy in finding mystic meanings in this number of four ; " as there are four zones of the world and four winds, plainly the Church must have four columns and from them must come forth four blasts," etc.

Passing by Justin Martyr, who was born A. D. 89, and lived to the age of seventy-six, and who, although he appears to quote from what he calls " Memoirs of the Apostles," never speaks of the gospels by name, the only testimony prior to Irenæus is that of Papias, bishop of Hierapolis, who flourished in the first half of the second century, and possibly had known the apostle John. His writings are lost, but Eusebius (third century) after calling him "a man of shallow understanding," quotes him as mentioning two gospels, first, that Mark wrote *memorabilia* (acts and words) of the life of Jesus, derived from the apostle Peter, and second, that Matthew wrote a collection of sentences (*logia*) in "the Hebrew tongue," that is, in Aramaic or Syro-Chaldaic, "which each one has translated as he could."

Beyond this slender information concerning the origin of writings on which Christians have for centuries set such store as the "word of God," all is dim with impenetrable mist, rendering futile the ceaseless discussion about the authorship, and as regards the synoptics, the relative order of the gospels, since none doubt that the fourth gospel was the latest.

The writer of the gospel of Matthew clearly intended his work for Jewish converts, and is ever on the alert to show that the foretellings of Hebrew prophets about a Messiah were fulfilled in detail in Jesus, whom he exhibits as preaching the "good news of the kingdom," and as proving his divine mission by miracles.

Mark, the shortest, and probably the earliest, of the four lives, was compiled for the use of Gentile Christians, before whom it sets the leading events in the career of Jesus with much detail and small embellishment.

The author of the third gospel admits at the outset that he proposes to make a recension of the many existing memoirs of Jesus, and this he does in a style of much beauty and vividness.

The fourth gospel, over the authorship of which such

stormy disputes are waged, is altogether unlike the synoptics both in matter and manner. Omitting much which they narrate, as the birth, the baptism, the temptation, the agony in Gethsemane, the discourses " on the mount," those concerning the second advent and earthly kingdom, and the clear precepts which " he who runs may read " in pithy saying or delightful parable ; it gives us prolix harangues full of mystical talk, of self-analysis, and lofty pretensions ; long prayers and wearisome controversies. Instead of a plain and simple story, it is an essay in which Jesus is merely a lay figure into whose mouth is put certain doctrines which had arisen about him through the intermixture of Hebrew and Greek speculation on Egyptian soil.

But the spirit of love that permeates it is the spirit of Jesus, and in such stories as that of his meeting with a woman of Samaria, the essence of his teaching is expressed in the words, " an hour comes and now is when the true worshippers will worship the Father in spirit and truth : for the Father seeketh such to worship him. God is spirit ; and they that worship, must worship in spirit and truth."

John is known to have lived for some years after the death of Jesus, and it may be that the germ of this gospel is in certain well-remembered sayings of the Master which the apostle in his old age, and perhaps with confused additions incident to lapse of time, repeated to men ignorant of current traditions in the other gospels, ignorant too of Jewish customs and places, who steeped what he told them in the thoughts of later times and of a foreign land, blurring for ever the portrait of Jesus of Nazareth.

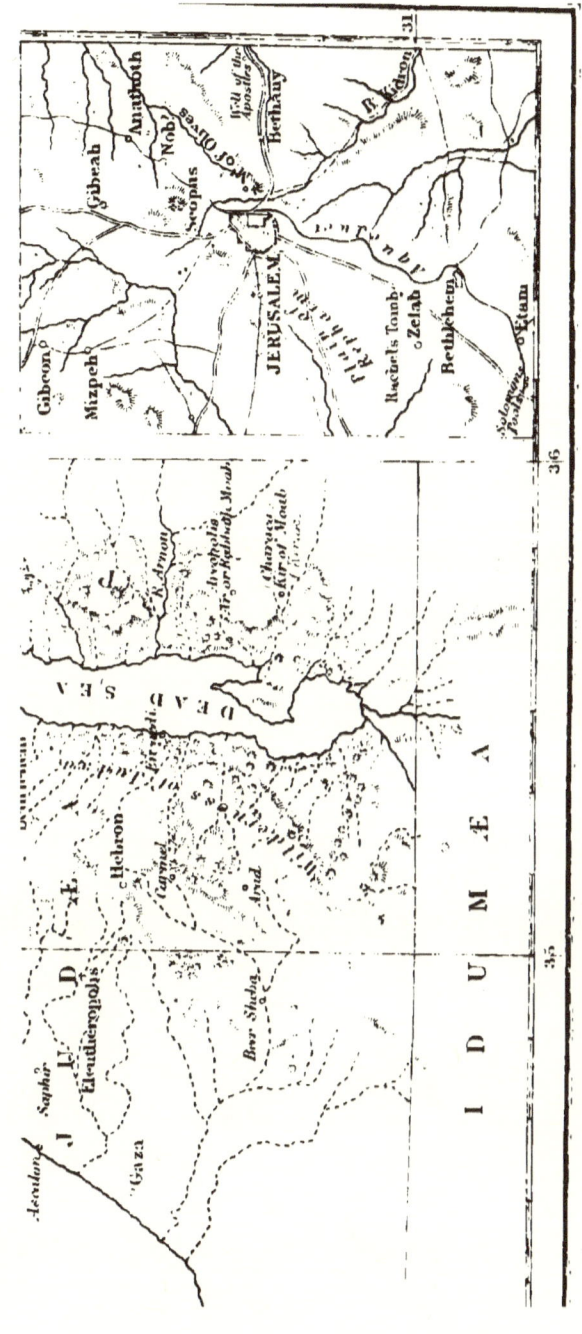

C. KEGAN, PAUL, & CO., 1 PATERNOSTER SQUARE, LONDON.

INDEX.

A

Accadians, 11 ; religion of the, 13

Adonai substituted for Jehovah, 163, 360

Advent, the Second, 308

Ahab, 98

Ahriman, 143

Alexander the Great, 105

Alexandria, 165

Ancestors, myths about, 8

Ancestry of the Jews, 10

Angels, Jewish and Persian belief in, 143

Antiochus Epiphanes, 167, 171

Apocryphal books, 374

Apocryphal gospels, 205

Arabic language, 305

Aramaic, adoption of, by the Jews, 152 ; language, 363, 375, 376 ; words in the gospels, 364

Archelaus, 195

Ark, sacred, 50 ; capture of, by the Philistines, 62 ; brought to Jerusalem, 71 ; placed in the Temple, 90

Arrest of Jesus, 343

Assyria, rise of, 103 ; fall of, 121

Assyrians, origin of the, 16

Astruc on the Pentateuch, 371

B

Baal, 21

Babel, Tower of, 6, 131

Babylon, 130 ; fall of, 139

Babylonians, origin of the, 16 ; rise of the, 121

Baptism, 278 ; of Jesus, 218

Bar-Abbas, 199, 350

Bath-Kol, the, 302

Beelzebul, 290

Behistun inscriptions, 364

Bethany, 315, 330

Bible (and see Old and New Testament), misreading of the, 112

Blasphemy, Jesus accused of, 346

Buddha, story of the, 94 ; legend of temptation of the, 220

Burial of Jesus, 355

C

Cæsar, Jesus and tribute to, 326

Cæsarea Philippi, 300

Caiaphas, 344 ; trial of Jesus before, 344

Canaan (see also Palestine), invasion of, 53, 59 ; described, 54

Canaanites, 53, 60; survival
among peasants, 188
Canon of the Bible, 373
Capernaum, Jews at, 222, 232,
311
Carpenter, Jesus probably a, 215
Chaldæans, 120
Chaldee dialect, 363
Children, Jesus and, 312
Cherubim, 90
."Christ," meaning of, 114
Christians, early notions of,
about a return of Jesus, 309;
origin of name of, 359
Christmas, origin of, 200
Church of the Holy Sepulchre,
356
Cleansings, Jewish law of, 277
Conscience, growth of, 43
Courts of the temple, 316, 317
Covenant, between Jehovah and
Israel, 84, 369; the new, 358
Cross, the, 352
Crucifixion of Jesus, 352
Cuneiform writing, 13, 364
Cutheans (*see also* Samaritans),
190
Cyrus, 135, 137

D

Daniel, book of, 172; influence
of the, 196, 211
Date of birth of Jesus, 200
David, king of Israel, 70; cha-
racter of, 72; poetry of, 74
Davy, Sir Humphrey, story of,
291
Day of judgment, 174, 309
Dead Sea, 55
Death of Jesus, 354
Demons, Jewish belief in, 144,
288

Demosthenes, story of, 242
Disciples, belief of, in Jesus as
Messiah, 301; flight of the,
344
Divining, modes of, 63

E

Eastern hospitality, 233
Eastward position of sacred
buildings, 318
Education of Jesus, 211, 212
Egypt, 27; antiquity and reli-
gion of, 28–30; slavery in, 32
El, 21, 26
El-Shaddai, 22
Elijah, 98, 155
Elohim, 371
Ephraim. *See* Israel, kingdom
of
Epics, 81
Essenes, 265
Exile of the Jews, 129; in-
fluences of the, 133; return
from, 140
Exodus, the, 36
Exorcists, 289
Ezekiel, 150
Ezra, reforms under, 146–150,
370

F

Feasts, Jewish, 151
Foods, clean and unclean, 277
Future life, Egyptian ideas concerning a, 32; Israelite ideas,
51, 145; Persian, 145; Jewish, 173; source of current
ideas about, 174, 253; denial
of a, by the Sadducees, 261

G

Gabbatha, 348
Galileans, character of the, 188
Galilee, 187
Galileo, story of, 39
Gehenna, 174
Gemara, the, 368
Gentiles, Jesus and the, 298, 332; mission of Paul to, 358
Gerizim, rival temple on mount, 161, 168; destruction of temple on, 170
Gethsemane, 342
God, idea of Jesus about, 243
Golgotha, 351
Gospels, the four, 225, 375-377
Greek myth about history, 78; conquest of the Jews, 165: influence among Jews, 165; version of the Old Testament, 166

H

Hades, 51
Hebrew language, disuse of the, 152
Hebrews, the, 4; migrations of, 17
Herod Antipas, 195, 221, 229
Herod the Great, 178; character of, 192
Hezekiah, 116
High-priest, power of the, 164, 170
Hillel, Rabbi, 247; story of, 264; and Jesus, 265
Hinnom, Valley of, 174
History, growth of, 78-83; value of, 86
Holy and Holy of Holies in the temple, 89, 318
Holy water, 278

I

Imagination, power of the, 291
Immanuel, 116
Irenæus, 375
Isaiah, 105
Isaiah, the second, 135; quotations from, 136
Israel, the kingdom of, 97; annals of, 97; fall of, 103
Israel, sons of, 4
Israelites, origin of the, 10; religion, 18, 51; oppression in Egypt, 33; escape therefrom, 35; route taken, 40; invasion of Canaan, 53, 59; disunion, 60; state under "judges," 61; defeated by Philistines, 62; rise of prophets, 64; election of a king, 66; ruled by Saul, 67; David, 70; Solomon, 88; disruption, 96; captivity, 103

J

Jehovah, gross notions about, 23; human sacrifices to, 25; ideas of Moses about, 47; meaning of, in the Pentateuch, 47, 366; ark as the dwelling of, 50, 71; shrine of, at Shiloh, 61; will of, how sought, 64; covenant between, and Israel, 84; temple to, at Jerusalem, 89; surrounded by angels, 143; avoidance of name of, 163; origin of name of, 366
Jeremiah, 120
Jericho, fall of, 59; Jesus at, 314
Jerusalem, capture of, by David, 70; features of, 70, 315; temple at. 89, 316; Jesus in, 314: his feelings towards, 331

Jerusalem, the new, 252

Jesus, birth of, 178, 199; meaning of name, 199; parents and home of, 203; legends about, 205, 208, 219, 290; at Jerusalem, 207; education, 209, 212; slender facts about, 213, 223, 226; occupation, 215; leaves Nazareth to join John the Baptist, 215; baptism of, 218; temptation in desert, 219; public ministry, 222; chooses fellow-helpers, 232; revisits Nazareth, 234; reception there, 236-238; mode of teaching, 239-243; religion of, 244-260; ideas about the "kingdom of heaven," 255; contact with Pharisees, 266; attitude towards publicans and sinners, 267-275; towards the law of cleansings, 255, 280; the sabbath, 282, 283; cures disorders, 290; decline of popularity, 297; visits Cæsarea Philippi, 300; resolves to become the Messiah, 302; visits Jerusalem, 303, 311, 320; expels the dealers from the temple, 322; debates with the rulers, 323-329; feeling towards the Gentiles, 298, 332; denounces the Pharisees, 334; utters fatal words about the temple, 335; eats the passover, 338; retires to Gethsemane, 342; betrayed by Judas, 344; tried before Sanhedrin, 344-346; before Pontius Pilate, 347; sentenced to be crucified, 350; scourged and mocked, 351; death and burial, 354, 355

Jewish history, sources of, 83; special features of, 85; summary of, 179-183

Jewish sabbath, 283

Jewish youth, education of, 210

Jews, forefathers of the, 3; known as such after the exile, 5; legends of the forefathers of the, 10; in exile, 132; return from exile, 140; under Persian rule, 164; under Greek rule, 165; under Roman rule, 192-199

Job, story of, 122-126

John the Baptist, 216; preaching of, 218; message of, from prison to Jesus, 286; death of, 299

John, gospel according to, 225, 376

John Hyrcanus, 170, 177

Jordan, valley of the, 54

Joseph of Arimathea, 355

Joseph, father of Jesus, 203, 215

Josephus, 5, 172, 189, 199, 221, 223, 275

Joshua, 59

Josiah, reforms under, 118; death of, 120

Judah, kingdom of, 97; invasions of, 97, 119, 127; annals of, 104; fall of, 127

Judas Iscariot (or Kerioth), 341; betrays Jesus, 344

Judas Maccabeus, 169, 175; alliance of, with Rome, 177

Judæans, exile of, to Babylon, 129; return of, from Babylon, 140

Judges, rise of the, in Israel, 61

Judgment, day of, 174, 253

Justin Martyr, 375

K

Kalevala, collection of songs of the, 81

Kingdom of heaven, 221; current ideas of, among the Jews, 251–254; ideas of Jesus about, 255

L

Law, finding of the book of the, 118; collection of the, 150; public reading of the, 151; supremacy of the, 153, 164; Jesus and the, 275, 379, 281

Law, oral, rise of the, 153; in nature, 292; of love to God and man, 329

Laws, early notions about origin of, 41; historical sketch of growth of, 42–45

Legend of Bishop Hatto, 6; tower of Babel, 6; deluge, 13; Exodus, 36; giving of law, 40, 153; cities of the plain, 56; Dead Sea, 56; Samson, 62; temptation of Jesus, Buddha, etc., 220

Legends, origin of, 57; about Jesus (*see* Jesus); Old Testament, 135, 372

Lives of Jesus, 223

Lot's wife, legend of, 56

Lots, casting of, 64

Luke, gospel according to, 375, 376

M

Maccabees, books of the, 141; account of the Romans in, 176

Maccabeus, Judas, 169

Man, ideas of Jesus about, 245, 248

Mankind, unity of, 87

Marriage of foreigners by Jews, 147, 161

Mary, mother of Jesus, 203, 238

Mattathias, 169

Matthew, gospel according to, 375, 376

Messiah, belief in a, 110; belief in Jesus as, 114, 300; later views about, 137, 172

Messianic passages from the prophets, 107–109; hopes in time of Jesus, 195, 197, 251–253

Millennium, 308

Miracles, origin of, 57, 292; belief in, 287

Mishnah, the, 397

Mithra, 201

Molech, 21, 24, 174

Moon-worship, 20

Moses, 35; song of, 38; as a law-giver, 40, 49

Myths about names, 6; ancestors, 9; standing stones, 50; Samson, 62; growth of history, 78; Iggdrasil, 350

N

Nabi, 64

Names of places, 6; confusion of savages about, 7

Nazareth, 202; Jesus born at, 199; preaches at, 230

Nazirite, 63

Nebuchadnezzar, 127

Nehemiah, 151; reforms by, 161; sacred books collected under, 162

New Testament, lives of Jesus in the, 223, 375–378
Nile valley, 27
Numbers, use of, in the Bible, 39

O

Old Testament, collection of books of the, 83, 162, 175, 369, 373; sources of the, 83, 119, 134, 150; misreading of the, 112; divisions of the, 369
Oracles, belief in, 63
Oral law, rise of the, 153; importance given to, 154

P

Palestine under Roman rule, 187
Parables of Jesus, 241, 270, 272, 324, 333
Parents, duties of Jewish, 210
Parents of Jesus, 203
Passover eaten by Jesus, 338
Paul, 223, 358
Pentateuch, 150, 151, 370, 373; composite authorship of, 370, 371
Persecution of Jews under Antiochus, 168
Persians, religion of the ancient, 143
Peter denies Jesus, 345
Pharaoh, the, 29
Pharisees, 171, 261, 319; classes of, 263; and Jesus, 266, 296, 334; conspire against, 330
Phœnician art, 89; language, 365
Philip, 195
Philistines, 61, 62

Pilgrim Fathers, 285
Pirqe Aboth, 153
Plagues, legend of, in Egypt, 36
Pompey, 178
Pontius Pilate, 347; trial of Jesus before, 348
Possession by demons, 144, 288; explained, 289
Prætorium, Jesus at the, 347
Prayer of Jesus, 248, 343
Priests, as historians, 85; in Jerusalem, 318
Prodigal son, parable of the, 270
Prophets, rise of the, 65, 102; work of the, 99; specimens of teaching of the, 101; yearnings of, for a Messiah, 107, 110
Proverbs, 92; from the Talmud, 160
Psalms, book of, 74
Publicans, 267; and Jesus, 268
Purifications, 277
Purim, feast of, 145
Puritans, the, and Sunday, 285

R

Rabbis, fancies of the, 193, 234; rise of the, 235
Ramses II., 33
Red (or reed) Sea, 37
Religion, of the Accadians, 13; Israelites, 18; influence of scenery on, 19; of the Egyptians, 30; Persians, 143; influence of Persian, on Jews, 143, 145; of Jesus, 243–260
Resurrection, Persian belief in a, 145; Jewish belief in a, 173; Jesus and the doctrine of a, 327

Revenge, law of, 49, 125
Romans, alliance of Jews with, 177; supremacy of, in Palestine, 178; influence of conquests of, 191; Jewish feeling towards the, 192, 198; contempt of, for Jews, 197; tolerance of, for religions, 349
Rosetta stone, 364
Ruth, story of, 147-149

S

Sabbath, origin of, 12; observance of, 134; rabbinical rules about, 281
Sacred books, origin of, 80
Sacred numbers, 39
Sacrifice, 24
Sadducees, 171, 261; and Jesus, 327
Sages, 91
St. Kilda, story of islanders of, 293
Samaritans, origin of the, 105; disputes of, with the Jews, 142, 162, 190; language of, 365
Samson, legend of, 62
Samuel, 63, 65, 67
Sanhedrin, 176; local, 232; trial of Jesus by, 345
Saoshyas, 143, 145
Satan, 123, 144, 220
Saul, chosen king of Israel, 67; elegy on death of, 68
Savages, notions of, about names, 7
Saviour, the Persian, 143
Sayings of Jesus, specimens of the 240, 241, 256
Schools, of the prophets, 64, 102; in Palestine, 211

Science and the Bible, 372, 373
Scribes, 146, 264, 276
Scythians, 119
Sea, Dead, 55
Second Advent of Jesus, belief in, 308
Seers, 63
Self-denial, insistance of Jesus on, 258, 305, 312
Semitic languages, 363, 365
Semitic race, earliest traces of, 11; migrations of, 16; religion of, 21
Sennacherib, 117
Septuagint, 166, 236, 309
Shammai, 264
Shemitic. *See* Semitic
Sheol, 52, 145, 173
Shiloh, shrine of Jehovah at, 61
Simon and Jesus, story of, 273
Simon the Just, 175
Sinai, 40, 158
Sinners, meaning of term in the gospels, 267; and Jesus, 268
Slavery, origin of, 33
Solomon, 88; temple to Jehovah built by, 89; wisdom of, 92, 93
Son of man, 278, 301
Song of Moses, 38; of the bow, 68; earliest history in, 78; of Solomon, 113
Standing stones, legends about, 56
Star and stone worship, 19
Summary of Jewish history, 179-183
Sunday, confusion of, with the sabbath, 284
Sun-god, Jehovah a, 23
Sun-worship, traces of, in Christian religion, 201, 318
Synagogue, men of the great, 150, 175

2 C

Synagogues, rise of, 134 ; education of Jewish youth in, 211 ; service in, 235
Syriac language, 364
Syro-Chaldaic. *See* Aramaic

T

Tabernacle, 51
Tacitus quoted, 171, 197, 224
Talmud, the, 155 ; stories from, 155–157, 195, 241 ; sayings from, 158–161, 210, 233, 248, 269, 277 ; summary of contents of, 367, 368
Targums, 152, 364, 368
Taxes, Roman mode of collecting, 198, 267
Temple, building of, by Solomon, 89 ; burning of, 128 ; building of a second, after the exile, 141 ; desecration of, 168, 178, 193 ; building of a third, by Herod, 315 ; Jesus in the, 321
Ten Commandments, 46, 48
Ten tribes, fate of the, 103
Thorah, compiling of the, 151 ; veneration for the, 153
Tiberias, lake of, 188, 222

Tradition, history based upon, 79 ; records about Jesus based upon, 226

U

Ur, 12
Urim and Thummim, 64, 302

V

Veda, the, 82

W

"Writings," collection of Jewish, 175

Y

Yahweh.　*See* Jehovah

Z

Zaccheus, 314
Zarathusthra, legend of temptation of, 220
Zealots, the, 197, 266